DISPATCHES

FROM

THE

REPUBLIC

OF

LETTERS

IN MEMORIAM

Doris Westheimer Neustadt
(1897–1991)

Walter Neustadt Jr.
(1919–2010)

"We recognize that the power of the written word is one answer to a broader understanding between the peoples of the world and thence to a more peaceful and cooperative life together in this ever-narrowing universe."

—Walter Neustadt Jr., Address at the 1972 Neustadt Banquet

Royalties from the first edition will be donated to the Walter Jr. and Dolores K. Neustadt Scholarship fund for University of Oklahoma students.

DISPATCHES

FROM THE

REPUBLIC

OF

LETTERS

FIFTY YEARS OF THE
NEUSTADT INTERNATIONAL PRIZE FOR LITERATURE
1970–2020

EDITED AND WITH AN INTRODUCTION BY DANIEL SIMON

PREFACE BY ROBERT CON DAVIS-UNDIANO

PHONEME
MEDIA

DEEP
VELLUM

DALLAS, TEXAS

Phoneme Media, an imprint of Deep Vellum
3000 Commerce St., Dallas, Texas 75226
deepvellum.org · @deepvellum

Deep Vellum is a 501c3 nonprofit literary arts organization
founded in 2013 with the mission to bring
the world into conversation through literature.

FIRST EDITION, 2020

ISBN: 978-1-64605-033-8 (hardcover) | 978-1-64605-034-5 (ebook)

LIBRARY OF CONGRESS CATALOGING IN PUBLICATION DATA

Names: Simon, Daniel, (Professor of English) editor author of introduction.
| Davis, Robert Con, 1948- author of preface.
Title: Dispatches from the republic of letters : fifty years of the Neustadt International Prize for
Literature, 1970-2020 / edited and with an introduction by Daniel Simon ; preface by Robert
Con Davis-Undiano.
Other titles: World literature today.
Description: First edition. | Dallas : Phoneme Media, Deep Vellum Publishing, 2020. | Includes
bibliographical references and index.
Identifiers: LCCN 2020010120 (print) | LCCN 2020010121 (ebook) | ISBN
9781646050338 (hardcover) | ISBN 9781646050345 (ebook)
Subjects: LCSH: Literature, Modern—20th century—History and criticism. | Literature,
Modern—21st century—History and criticism. | Authors—21st century—Biography. |
Authors—20th century—Biography. | Neustadt International Prize for Literature. | Authorship.
Classification: LCC PN771 .D63 2020 (print) | LCC PN771 (ebook) | DDC
807.9—dc23
LC record available at https://lccn.loc.gov/2020010120
LC ebook record available at https://lccn.loc.gov/2020010121

Distributed by Consortium Book Sales & Distribution
Cover design by Jen Rickard Blair
Interior layout by Kirby Gann
Printed in the United States of America

CONTENTS

The Neustadt Prizes and *World Literature Today*

"Norman, Oklahoma, sounded to many a European ear as Persepolis or Samarkand once may have done to Marlowe or to Keats: the name of a remote, half fairy-like city from which the broadest-minded review in the world of letters radiated information, disseminated ideas, and appraised trends of taste."

—Henri Peyre, *Books Abroad*, Autumn 1976

The Neustadt International Prize for Literature

The Neustadt International Prize for Literature is sponsored by *World Literature Today*, the University of Oklahoma's award-winning magazine of international literature and culture, currently in its ninety-fourth year of continuous publication. The prize, conferred every two years, consists of $50,000, a replica of an eagle's feather cast in silver, and an award certificate. An international jury of writers convenes on the University of Oklahoma campus every other year to decide the winner of each prize.

The charter of the award stipulates that the Neustadt Prize be given in recognition of important achievement in poetry, fiction, or drama and that it be conferred solely on the basis of the literary value of the writer's work. The prize may serve to crown a lifetime's accomplishment or to direct attention to an important body of work that is still developing.

Established in 1969 as the Books Abroad International Prize for Literature, then renamed the Books Abroad / Neustadt Prize in 1972 before assuming its present name in 1976, the Neustadt Prize is the first international literary award of its scope to originate in the United States and is one of the very few international prizes for which poets, novelists, and playwrights are equally eligible. Funding for the prize has been ensured in perpetuity by a generous endowment from the Neustadt family of Dallas, Texas; Denver, Colorado; and Watertown, Massachusetts.

The NSK Neustadt Prize for Children's Literature

Since 2003, *World Literature Today* has also sponsored the NSK Neustadt Prize for Children's Literature, awarded every other year to a living writer or author-illustrator with significant achievement in children's or young-adult literature. Made possible through the generosity of Nancy Barcelo, Susan Neustadt Schwartz, and Kathy Neustadt, the NSK Prize celebrates literature that contributes to the quality of children's lives. Candidates for the award are nominated by a jury of writers, illustrators, and scholars, and the jury also selects the winner of each biennial prize. Laureates receive a check for $35,000, a silver medallion, and a certificate at a public ceremony at the University of Oklahoma in odd-numbered years.

www.neustadtprize.org

Laureates of the Neustadt International Prize for Literature
1970–2020

1970	Giuseppe Ungaretti (Italy)
1972	Gabriel García Márquez (Colombia)
1974	Francis Ponge (France)
1976	Elizabeth Bishop (United States)
1978	Czesław Miłosz (Poland / United States)
1980	Josef Škvorecký (Czechoslovakia / Canada)
1982	Octavio Paz (Mexico)
1984	Paavo Haavikko (Finland)
1986	Max Frisch (Switzerland)
1988	Raja Rao (India)
1990	Tomas Tranströmer (Sweden)
1992	João Cabral de Melo Neto (Brazil)
1994	Kamau Brathwaite (Barbados)
1996	Assia Djebar (Algeria)
1998	Nuruddin Farah (Somalia)
2000	David Malouf (Australia)
2002	Álvaro Mutis (Colombia)
2004	Adam Zagajewski (Poland)
2006	Claribel Alegría (Nicaragua / El Salvador)
2008	Patricia Grace (New Zealand)
2010	Duo Duo (China)
2012	Rohinton Mistry (India / Canada)
2014	Mia Couto (Mozambique)
2016	Dubravka Ugrešić (Croatia / The Netherlands)
2018	Edwidge Danticat (Haiti / United States)
2020	Ismail Kadare (Albania / France)

Preface
Robert Con Davis-Undiano

In 1974, when Francis Ponge received the third Neustadt International Prize for Literature, he made comments that have become part of the aura of the prize. He called it "perfectly magnificent," "so original and so unlike any other in the conditions of the deliberations." He was referencing aspects of the prize that traditionally have caught the attention of many, starting with its being housed at the University of Oklahoma, not in Paris, Buenos Aires, Berlin, Tokyo, or another cosmopolitan, literary capital. He celebrated the transparency of the voting process, the unique Neustadt practice of a jury voting *for* rather than *against* nominees. Every fall, for the Neustadt Prize or the NSK Neustadt Prize for Children's Literature, nine of the most important writers in the world join forces as a legislature unto themselves to choose a Neustadt or NSK laureate. Instructed by the Neustadt charters to hold at bay all outside pressures or subtle encouragement to steer the process in a given direction, Neustadt juries famously ignore politics in any form or the political impact of one writer winning over a rival. They focus instead on each writer's literary accomplishments.

Landlocked and far from all world capitals, Norman, Oklahoma, site of the University of Oklahoma, is a small town on the Southern Plains that does not obviously have a cosmopolitan culture that can sponsor the celebration of world literature and internationalism. And yet, against all odds, this is precisely where these amazing prizes originated and launched into fame. That fact has fired the imagination of many writers. The rise and renown of the prizes, as Nobel laureate Czesław Miłosz, the fifth Neustadt Prize winner, notes, are among "those things which should not exist." And why should they not exist? Because these prizes represent rare forces for good pitted against some overwhelmingly strong, negative tendencies in the world connected to commercialism, lassitude, and fashion. The glorious fact of the Neustadt

Prizes, in other words, is welcome and hugely beneficent but not an inevitable development or one that anyone could have predicted. These famous prizes came into existence precisely to push back against what Miłosz calls the "the dark and immutable order of the world," an amazing occurrence, as he allows, that "favors all those who in the game of life bet on improbability."

The wager on improbability is the miracle of the Neustadt Prizes and possibly—as many of the jurors note—of the United States itself. Indigenous peoples and colonial powers originally came to Oklahoma and the Americas searching for new truths and fresh beginnings, and their incessant searching has defined this part of the world in terms of innovation and cultural energy. Dubravka Ugrešić, the twenty-fourth laureate, notes the welcome persistence of this American spirit in the prizes and in Oklahoma itself. "The literary landscape that has greeted me in Norman," she writes,

> has touched me so deeply that I, briefly, forgot the ruling political constellations. I forgot the processes underway in all the nooks and crannies of Europe, I forgot the people who are stubbornly taking us back to some distant century, the people who ban books or burn them, the moral and intellectual censors, the brutal rewriters of history, the latter-day inquisitors; I forgot for a moment the landscapes in which the infamous swastika has been cropping up with increasing frequency—as it does in the opening scenes of Bob Fosse's classic film *Cabaret*—and the rivers of refugees whose number, they say, is even greater than that of the Second World War.

Ugrešić attributes this sense of hope and wonder upon visiting Norman to the unlikely success of the Neustadt Prizes, the wager on literary excellence and celebration. She further credits these prizes as iconic representations of American ideals, the grand experiment dedicated to new beginnings. This understanding that the Neustadt Prizes thrive in an explicitly American context is yet another reason that writers and literati from around the world have been so powerfully captured by the Neustadt tradition.

There is ample evidence that Neustadt laureates, many of the most important writers of the last five decades, commonly see the Neustadt Prize in this vein. Elizabeth Bishop, the fourth laureate, heralds the Neustadt Prize as "a [rarefied] place so far inland" and an icon of possibility and hope far away from traditional literary venues where one must peck "for [mere] subsistence along coastlines of the world." Tomas Tranströmer, number eleven, addresses the difficulty but also the importance of translating poetry today and credits the Neustadt Prize as creating an atmosphere in Norman where translation, with all its risks and imperfections, is simply "what we do here in Oklahoma." Adam Zagajewski, number eighteen, judges the Neustadt Prize, with its traditional tilt toward poetry, as commensurate with "the immense risk involved in writing poetry today . . . perhaps the most daring thing in the world" to do. Mia Couto, number twenty-three, views the Neustadt Prizes as beacons working against "what unites us today, in all countries, on all continents . . . fear," seeing in the prizes a source of hope more powerful than fear.

In effect, these Neustadt laureates are explaining why this prize is regarded among writers at least as second in importance, as the *New York Times* once noted, only to the Nobel Prize itself. Their answer is that the Neustadt Prizes encompass the promise of literature and the model of what America stands for. To this day, the prizes continue to reward and celebrate the best writers anywhere, often the "best" before they are recognized as such anywhere else. It is encouraging that this extraordinary profile of integrity and boldness has been tested repeatedly since the inception of these prizes, and that reputation has survived unblemished to the present day. The fact of these prizes coming into existence in the U.S. heartland, embodying some of the most important of American ideals and continuing to thrive beyond all measure to be a force for good in the world, explains both the audacity and the beauty of this amazing tradition.

Norman, Oklahoma
August 2019

Robert Con Davis-Undiano *is the executive director of* World Literature Today.

Introduction
The Neustadt Prize on the World Stage
Daniel Simon

"UNGARETTI VINCITORE BOOKS ABROAD PRIZE PREGOTI COMUNICARE ANSA"

Telegram from Piero Bigongiari to Romano Bilenchi

February 9, 1970, 11:00 a.m.

In February 1970, with the transmission of a telegram from Norman, Oklahoma, to a correspondent of *La Nazione* newspaper in Florence, Italy ("Ungaretti winner Books Abroad Prize please inform National Associated Press Agency"), news about the winner of a fledgling literary prize made its way into the world. Over the next fifty years, that fledgling's uncertain wings would come to be represented by a magnificent silver eagle feather symbolic of both the flights of literary imagination as well as the writer's traditional quill.

Nothing guaranteed that the initial fledgling would have more durable wings than Icarus, however. The Neustadt International Prize for Literature, which in time came to be known as "the American Nobel," started out as a modest initiative that, in several respects, aimed to remedy what many perceived to be the Nobel Prize in Literature's perennial flaws, a critique still often heard today when the Swedish Academy makes its annual announcement. Formally unveiled as the "Books Abroad International Prize for Literature" by Ivar Ivask at the thirty-sixth congress of PEN International in Menton, France, in September 1969, the spark for this new international prize preceded Ivask's tenure as the longest-serving editor (1967–91) of *Books Abroad* and its successor, *World Literature Today*. A lively discussion surrounding the merits (and demerits) of the Nobel Prize had taken place five years earlier during the annual meeting of the Modern Language Association in New York City in December 1964. At the behest of Robert Vlach, *Books Abroad*'s editor at the time, Herbert Howarth—a British-born translator of Arabic and professor of English from the University of Pennsylvania—convened a panel of scholars to discuss the Nobel's track record at the MLA convention. Those talks formed the core of the subsequent "Nobel Prize Symposium" featured in the Winter 1967 issue of *Books Abroad* that included Howarth's introductory essay, "A Petition to the Swedish Academy," which in turn sowed the seeds of Ivask's 1969 charter. (To read the charter, turn to page 319.) More on that connection in a moment.

Although Ivask didn't realize it when he took over as editor in 1967, *Books Abroad* had almost foundered on the rocks of financial hardship in the mid-1960s. In that same winter of 1964–65 when Vlach and Howarth convened their MLA panel in New York, the very existence of the journal itself was hanging in the balance. During the fall of 1964, Pete Kyle McCarter, the University of Oklahoma's vice president for academic affairs (who would eventually become provost and interim president in 1970–71), apparently called on Vlach to make a case for *Books Abroad*'s continued existence— namely, whether the university could justify funding the journal even as protests over civil rights injustices and the escalating U.S. war in Vietnam increasingly occupied the country's (and the administration's) focus.[1] Vlach responded in an impassioned three-page letter about the indispensability of institutional support, the journal's efforts to expand circulation, the perennial problem of inadequate staffing, and the desirability of paying foreign contributors (two cents a word for articles, three cents a word for book reviews). Vlach challenged McCarter that unless the university could come up with the funding to adequately support the journal, the administration should let it migrate to an institution that would. At the end of the letter, Vlach wrote: "Dr. House's idea is worth a better fate than suicide."[2] Thankfully, the administration ultimately decided that the journal did deserve a better fate.

Dr. House was Roy Temple House, who had served as *Books Abroad*'s founding editor from 1927 to 1949. By the mid-1940s, the journal that House had built during his two-decade tenure achieved such renown that the Nebraska-born scholar was nominated for the Nobel Peace Prize in 1948. House, who also chaired OU's Department of Modern Languages from 1918 to 1942, somehow kept the journal afloat financially during the lean years of the Great Depression and World War II. His successors as editor, three European émigrés—Ernst Erich Noth (1949–58), Wolfgang Bernard Fleischmann (1959–61), and Robert Vlach (1961–66)—each put his personal stamp on the journal, gradually expanding *Books Abroad*'s coverage from an initial focus on the literatures of western Europe (for the most part, those literatures taught by House and his colleagues in the department).

When the Czech-born Vlach took over the helm as editor in 1961, he extended the journal's coverage to include "Books of Asia and Africa," in keeping with the catholicity of his interests and his wide-ranging talents as a poet, translator, journalist, and literary critic. In anticipation of *Books Abroad*'s fortieth-anniversary year (1966–67), Vlach urged McCarter to help underwrite a speaker series that would have brought "nine Nobel Prize winners or other world-famous foreign writers" to the university, and President George Lynn Cross endorsed a $25,000 application to the Ford Foundation to support the series.[3] Like the editors who preceded him, Vlach continually tried to impress upon the administration and his faculty colleagues the value of a journal like *Books Abroad* in bringing prestige to the university, even when the publication could barely make ends meet financially, like so many of the so-called little magazines of the modernist and postwar era. Bringing Nobel laureates to campus would have been an impressive coup for the young editor.

Unfortunately, the Ford Foundation turned down the grant request, then Vlach died suddenly in January 1966, at the age of forty-nine, so his dream never came to fruition.[4] Associate Editor Bernice Duncan, who had worked with every editor from House to Vlach, took over as acting editor in the wake of her predecessor's death. Soon enough, another European émigré would be hired as the journal's sixth editor: the polyglot Estonian-Latvian poet and frequent *Books Abroad* contributor Ivar Ivask, whom Duncan helped recruit for the position from his professorship at St. Olaf College in Minnesota. When Ivask arrived on campus in fall 1967, the issue featuring the Nobel Prize symposium—including Vlach's posthumous contribution on Slavic writers—had recently been published. Howarth's "Petition to the Swedish Academy," the first of nineteen essays in the issue, was frequently damning in its critique. "I would like to see the Swedish Academy less often fix the crown, and sometimes the death-mask, on fulfilled grandeur," wrote Howarth, "more often go ranging for the discovery and reinforcement of genius which is still on the advance."[5]

Howarth—who worked for the British government in Tel Aviv during World War II but resigned in protest over its policies in Mandate Palestine—went on to propose five changes to the academy's procedures, including, notably, a recommendation to "exert itself to discover writers outside the domains of the Big Powers and the current languages of diplomacy." Moreover, "Only with hesitation and restraint," he wrote, "should the Academy endorse a writer already widely recognized and rewarded." Ultimately, the literary world would be better served if the Nobel contributed to "the enlargement of the periphery of international vision."[6] While no doubt such criticisms stung the members of the academy, it nevertheless extended an invitation to four of the issue's contributors—Howarth, Manuel Durán, Albert H. Carter Jr., and Robert E. Spiller—to take part in a symposium in Stockholm in fall 1967 and included their talks in the subsequent proceedings volume, *Problems of International Literary Understanding* (1968).

Having grown up in the Soviet-controlled Baltics during the interwar years and experienced the Cold War as an exile in the West, Ivask knew that living on "the periphery of international vision" had real-world consequences. He took careful note of Howarth's critiques when formulating the original charter for the Books Abroad Prize, and he credited Howarth in the preamble to the 1969 announcement. Ivask signaled his intention that the new prize would rival the Nobel ("To date, there is no competition to the criteria set up by the Swedish Academy, with its attendant perquisites of professional status and monetary compensation"), and he was also careful to avoid the Stockholm model of a permanent jury, choosing instead to empanel a new group of writers every other year. Ivask envisioned a prize "representative of American concern for genuine achievement in world literature"—note the emphasis on "genuine achievement," not Old World perquisites. To the PEN delegates assembled in France, Ivask concluded with a hopeful question: "Is it not faith in the essential creative function of literature that has brought us together from all corners of the globe?"[7]

Almost inevitably, despite such a lofty international vision, not every pitfall could be avoided. Of the twelve jurors named to the first jury in 1970—Piero Bigongiari (Italy), Heinrich Böll (Germany), J. P. Clark (Nigeria), Frank Kermode (Great Britain), Jan Kott (USA), Juan Marichal (USA), Gaëtan Picon (France), A. K. Ramanujan (India, USA), Allen Tate (USA), Mario Vargas Llosa (Peru), and Andrei Voznesenski (USSR), plus Ivask—nearly half were Europeans, with the entirety of Africa, Asia, and Latin America represented by merely one writer each. And only six of the twelve took part in person when the panel convened at the University of Oklahoma in February 1970. The complicated logistics of prize-giving vexed Ivask so much that he would modify the original charter to account for some of the eventualities that might disrupt his lofty plans for an award that would compete with the Nobel.[7]

Too, Ivask's announcement of the first prize amount—$10,000—in September 1969 was something of a wish and a prayer. Earlier that summer, Vice President McCarter wrote to Ivask to inform him that "there now seems little or no prospect that the money for the projected *Books Abroad* prize can be raised this year. I am very sorry to send you this news, for I can understand what embarrassment it will cause you in notifying the distinguished people who, because of your own prodigious efforts, have agreed to serve on the Board [i.e., jury], and I can understand your own great personal disappointment, which I share. [Vice President Thurman] White tells me, however, that the list of prospective donors has now been exhausted, and no likelihood any longer exists of raising the money within the next two months."[8] Despite McCarter's dire prediction, Ivask was able to secure contingency funding from the office of then-President J. Herbert Hollomon Jr., thereby averting disaster.[9]

Ivask could finally breathe a sigh of relief when the jury arrived on the OU campus in February 1970 and emerged with a winner despite an initial deadlocked vote.[10] Ivask broke the tie, elevating Italian poet Giuseppe Ungaretti over the leftist Chilean poet Pablo Neruda. After hastily arranging travel plans for the eighty-two-year-old Italian poet, Ivask welcomed Ungaretti to Oklahoma on March 13, 1970. (For a fuller account of Ungaretti's visit to OU, turn to "The Old Captain's Last Voyage" on page 19.) At the banquet in Ungaretti's honor, President Hollomon echoed Ivask's lofty vision for this new award emanating from the Southern Plains of the United States:

This land and this place is for Western man, young, vital, unreasoning, irrational, hopeful, lustful, and youthful. We honor today and he honors us, a poet who at any age is young and hopeful, innocent, loving, and rational. It is this combination of the Dionysian and Apollonian that makes life have any hope at all. It does us great honor that he comes to us as the first laureate of a prize based upon a tradition of interest in literature at a university only a little more than half a century old, from a place and a time of great tradition from which all of our art, our music, our poetry, and much of our prose comes. It is, I believe, a signal beginning to what I hope will become a great tradition in Western European America as for the whole world: to award a prize to someone in literature without consideration of his background or ideology and without reference to political boundary.

Flushed with the success of having crowned the prize's first laureate, Ivask soon confronted the inevitable reality of coming up with funding for the next biennial award. Fortunately, a Maecenas—according to 1974 laureate Francis Ponge, evoking the Roman emperor Octavian's friend and adviser who was legendary for his patronage of Horace and Virgil—came to the prize's rescue: the Neustadt family of Ardmore, Oklahoma. The same week that Ivask was in France announcing the debut of the Books Abroad Prize, Boyd Gunning, executive director of the University of Oklahoma Foundation, wrote to Doris Westheimer Neustadt to formalize the Walter Neustadt Memorial Fund in honor of her late husband, Walter Neustadt Sr., who had served as a trustee of the foundation from 1951 to 1965. Gunning outlined his plans to utilize the memorial fund to underwrite acquisitions for the library, art museum, and natural history museum and to endow a professorship.[11] Walter Neustadt Jr., who had received his master's degree from OU in 1941, followed in his father's footsteps as a trustee for the OU Foundation beginning in 1965, joined the advisory board for the University of Oklahoma Press, and served on the OU Board of Regents from 1969 to 1976. Through the intercession of David A. Burr, who had served as President Cross's assistant and became vice president for university affairs in 1968, Neustadt recognized that the Books Abroad Prize presented a natural opportunity to realize his family's philanthropic ideals by endowing an award that would bring international renown to his beloved university.[12] President Paul F. Sharp announced the family's initial gift of $200,000 on May 17, 1972, with Regent Nancy Davies, Doris Westheimer Neustadt, Walter and Dolores Neustadt, and Allan and Marilyn Neustadt as honored guests in attendance.

With the endowment in place that spring, Ivask would publish a glowing "Progress Report" in the summer 1972 issue, in which he somewhat triumphantly claimed that "the faith in impartial literary evaluation on a worldwide scale, which this journal has championed now for forty-six years, has again been vindicated." After receiving the 1972 award, Colombian novelist Gabriel García Márquez wrote: "This is a prize that has taken shape in the fertile imagination of a native of Estonia who has attempted to invent—rather than dynamite—a literary prize that would be dynamite for the Nobel. It is a prize in the mythical Oklahoma of Kafka's dreams and the land of the unique rose rock, and has been awarded to a writer from a remote and mysterious country in Latin America nominated by a great writer from far-off Iceland." By the time French poet Francis Ponge was chosen as the 1974 laureate, it became clear that the Neustadt Prize represented a remarkable convergence between Ivask's global literary vision and the Neustadts' cultural patronage. In his acceptance speech, Ponge remarked:

> This gratitude—how shall I put it—is very complex, because I owe this honor and this award to the University of Oklahoma and to *Books Abroad,* to the chairman of the jury, to the jury itself, naturally, and to the Neustadt family who have made it possible for this prize to become something perfectly magnificent. It is so rare to find this combination that I do not know how to express myself. It is certainly extraordinary that almost fifty years ago the University of Oklahoma decided to support a publication like *Books Abroad* and to continue supporting it. With Mr. Ivask's assumption of the editorship came the creation of this prize, which is so original and

so unlike any other in the conditions of the deliberations, the jury which is renewed with each prize, and all the other very original things connected with it. This initiative is truly extraordinary, as is the family who supports it by playing the role one would expect of a truly cultured Maecenas, that is to say, of one who has a very devoted interest in activities other than sports.

The fledgling's wings had magnificently spread.

*

The twenty-five Neustadt laureates' acceptance speeches in the pages that follow offer five decades' worth of insight into the evolution of world literature since 1970. Moreover, the accompanying essays that introduce each of the laureates' speeches provide an evolving panorama of international literary tastes and critical judgments during that same time frame, distilling the collective will of the more than 250 writers, translators, and scholars who have served on the juries over the years. Each of the special issues of *Books Abroad* or *World Literature Today* devoted to the prizewinner may likewise be viewed as a time capsule offering a wealth of insights into the literary zeitgeist since 1970.

The predominant theme of the laureates' acceptance remarks is literature's relationship to the broader social, cultural, and political world of its time. For some laureates, writing offers an escape from the world into an aesthetic realm purified of worldliness, but for most, writing is inextricably engaged with reflecting or changing the world. Themes of freedom, tolerance, forgiveness, bearing witness, solidarity, justice, and outright revolt appear often in their reflections on the writer's role. Assia Djebar quotes Mario Vargas Llosa: "In the heart of all fiction, the flame of protest burns brightly." For Claribel Alegría, inheriting "the sword of poetry" obligates the writer to wield it on behalf of justice.

While some of the Neustadt winners in the pages that follow remain rooted in their country and language of origin, many of the writers pen their works from a place of geographic or linguistic exile, and even those who never left home (or eventually returned) frequently write from a position apart from the cultural mainstream. According to Duo Duo, "Poetry takes this periphery as a blessing and continues to offer rituals for the sick rivers, to offer readable landscapes for the heart." Often, authors will claim a literary genealogy over a national one: among European poets, an unmistakable line runs through the work of Ungaretti, Ponge, Miłosz, Tranströmer, and Zagajewski. In the New World, another line runs through the work of Bishop, Paz, Cabral, and Brathwaite. Yet both lines readily cross the Atlantic—and Pacific—as well.[13]

Questions of language abound in their meditations. The laureates frequently invoke both an oral tradition as well as scribal legacies and literary histories in their work. Some plumb the depths of their native tongue, while others, like Farah and Malouf, embrace a polyglot English that may be global in expanse but ultimately full of local "coloratura." Issues of translation—not only of linguistic transfer but cultural translatability—often arise. Ultimately, for a novelist like Raja Rao, how we use language reflects our humanity, and the writer engages in "radical questioning" to probe the human condition.

One of the perennial pleasures of that condition is the gift of storytelling, and many of the laureates claim that the enchantment of telling stories drives much of their work. Dubravka Ugrešić quotes Nabokov's *Lectures on Literature* in this regard: "There are three points of view from which a writer can be considered: he may be considered as a storyteller, as a teacher, and as an enchanter. A major writer combines all three—storyteller, teacher, enchanter—but it is the enchanter in him that predominates and makes him a major writer." Writers achieve "major" status by enchanting or challenging their readers, without whom they would be anonymous scribes, describing the shadows on the wall of the cave. For Mia Couto, "Literature and storytelling confirm us as relatives and neighbors in our infinite diversity."

Writers also confront the pressing questions of history in their work, from the Middle Passage (Brathwaite, Danticat), the Cold War (Miłosz, Zagajewski), and civil wars (Alegría, Couto) to the legacies of the postcolonial world. Writing about Patricia Grace's gift to the Māori people of New Zealand, Mvskoke writer Joy Harjo—the first Native American U.S. poet laureate—connects her work to a globalizing sense of pan-indigenous reckoning: "We understand that we have all been colonized, challenged by the immense story we struggle within. We are attempting to reconstruct ourselves with the broken parts." In 1973 Gabriel García Márquez announced that he was giving his $10,000 award to a defense fund for political prisoners in Colombia. And in protest against the Reagan administration's policies in Central America, Max Frisch donated his prize money to a local organization working to build schools in Nicaragua.

While each writer claims the right to absolute freedom in the aesthetic realm of the imagination, their work ultimately connects to the broader moral and ethical concerns of our age. In speaking to "the business of making in all its forms," David Malouf ponders "what we are seeking when we set out there in the world some artefact, some made thing, that was not previously part of nature but is now, so that nature is changed, enlarged by its presence." Such "forms of making," contends Malouf, reflect the power of the writer's craft to remake the world. In turn, 1984 laureate Paavo Haavikko offers a powerful reflection on the writer's task:

> Thus literature is always philosophical and always moral. It asks what is right in the final count, knowing that there is no reply. But it asks and it seeks, and it cannot be shackled by laws, social systems, technology or business. Using all the rich patterns in the world, literature constructs a form in which the following things can be found: the question of injustice and justice, the movement of events in the world, and darkness. The reader is invited, he is given an opportunity—but he may walk past if he will. It is the writer's lot to go on working, in the dark, in motion, free, alone, available. The value of this work is not in immutable, established classics; it is not in any completed book; it is in the endless work itself, the endless effort to remain free and unbound.

Djebar, Alegría, Danticat, and others take up "the question of injustice and justice" at an even deeper level, situating their work in the tradition of bearing witness, emerging from the solitude of writerly preoccupations to claim a sense of solidarity with the powerless. "What does the artist do to move the world?" asks Danticat. "I want to say we can begin by bearing witness. . . . Sometimes we cannot fully move the world, but it can move us with its vastness, its expanse, its limitlessness, its geography or geographies, its beginnings and endings, its injustices." In such a worldview, the writer's impulse is to work toward healing trauma and ensuring our collective survival. For Djebar, that work of healing is reciprocated by her readers, fellow writers, and like-minded artists, who offer her "the power of solidarity [in] the solitude of my exile."

The centrifugal pull of great literature, as embodied by the work of these twenty-five writers, draws us into a fuller realization of our humanity.

*

Looking back on the first half-century of the Neustadt Prize, has Ivask's dream of an award that would be "representative of American concern for genuine achievement in world literature" been fully realized? In his 1978 acceptance speech, Czesław Miłosz replied in the affirmative while at the same time marveling over the improbability of the Neustadt Prize: "The Neustadt literary prize belongs too, in my opinion, to those things which should not exist, because they are against the dark and immutable order of the world. . . . The decision of founding such a prize seems to me a wise one, not only because I am a recipient, but because it favors all those who in the game of life bet on improbability."

Octavio Paz, the 1982 laureate, echoes Miłosz in offering a broad-minded assessment:

> . . . very few literary prizes [. . .] are truly *international*. Among these a place apart is occupied by the Neustadt Prize. Two characteristics lend it a unique face: the first is that each jury is composed of critics and writers belonging to different languages and literatures, which means that it constitutes an *international* body, as international as the prize itself; the second characteristic is that the jury is not permanent but instead changes from one prize to the next—that is, every two years. These two characteristics translate

into two words: *Universality* and *Plurality*. Due to the first word, the prize has been awarded to poets and novelists in Italian, English, French, Polish, Spanish and Czech; due to the second word, Plurality, we find among the laureates not only writers of different languages but also of different literary and philosophical persuasions. In esthetic terms, Plurality is a richness of voices, accents, manners, ideas and visions; in moral terms, Plurality signifies tolerance of diversity, renunciation of dogmatism and recognition of the unique and singular value of each work and every personality. Plurality is Universality, and Universality is the acknowledging of the admirable diversity of man and his works. Considering all this, in the convulsed and intolerant modern world we inhabit, the Neustadt Prize is an example of true civilization. I will say even more: to acknowledge the variety of visions and sensibilities is to preserve the richness of life and thus to ensure its continuity. Hence the Neustadt Prize, in stimulating the universality and diversity of literature, defends life itself.

For Paz, a poet from the ancient cosmopolis of Mexico City who also served as a diplomat in Paris, Tokyo, Geneva, and Mumbai, that such a prize emanated from a small-town university less than a hundred years old must have been even more of a marvel. Decades before he was named a Neustadt laureate, Paz had discovered an Oklahoma-based journal that would open his literary awareness to the world: "In those days the literary isolation of Mexico was almost absolute, to the degree that when I read those pages I felt the opening of the doors of contemporary literature in languages other than my own. For a while *Books Abroad* was my compass, and foreign literatures ceased to be for me an impenetrable forest."

Two decades later, Adam Zagajewski would even make the audacious claim that "Norman, Oklahoma, has established itself as one of the undeclared capitals of modernity."[14] And William Gass, in calling the Neustadt Prize "the most important international award we have," noted that for a writer like Assia Djebar, the award "stands for this priceless connection which literature can

make between distantly separated places and far-off times, between a ceremony in Oklahoma and a city in Algeria." Finally, 2014 laureate Mia Couto
would echo Paz in claiming that "what we are celebrating here, in Oklahoma,
year after year, is more than literature. With the Neustadt Prize we all praise
the cultural diversity of our world and the cultural diversity of each one of us.
That is crucial in a moment where personal and national identities are constructed like fortresses, as protection against the threats of those who are presented to us as aliens."

Combining all these threads into a single appeal, 2016 laureate Dubravka
Ugrešić argues that those in positions of cultural power must preserve our
"Gutenberg civilization" for the generations that follow:

> . . . we should invest all our energies in supporting people who are
> prepared to invest in literature, not in literature as a way to sus-
> tain literacy but as a vital, essential creative activity, people who
> will preserve the intellectual, the artistic, the spiritual capital. I
> couldn't have dreamed that one day a student theater in Norman,
> Oklahoma, would be putting on the first-ever staging of my story,
> written thirty-three years ago. Literary continuity, therefore, does
> exist, and the fact that it describes an unexpected geographical tra-
> jectory only heightens the excitement.
>
> The literary landscape that has greeted me in Norman has
> touched me so deeply that I, briefly, forgot the ruling political
> constellations. I forgot the processes underway in all the nooks
> and crannies of Europe, I forgot the people who are stubbornly
> taking us back to some distant century, the people who ban
> books or burn them, the moral and intellectual censors, the bru-
> tal rewriters of history, the latter-day inquisitors; I forgot for a
> moment the landscapes in which the infamous swastika has been
> cropping up with increasing frequency—as it does in the open-
> ing scenes of Bob Fosse's classic film *Cabaret*—and the rivers of
> refugees whose number, they say, is even greater than that of the
> Second World War.

In a "convulsed and intolerant modern world" that increasingly demonizes "those who are presented to us as aliens," such pleas for cultural patronage and diversity, tolerance, and universality are needed more than ever. Since 1970, the Neustadt International Prize for Literature has helped preserve "the intellectual, the artistic, the spiritual capital" of the world, and one can only hope that the prize will continue to promote it for generations to come.

Norman, Oklahoma
August 2019

Daniel Simon *is* WLT*'s assistant director and, since 2008, editor in chief.*

1. McCarter's opinion was strongly informed by the counsel of Savoie Lottinville, director of the University of Oklahoma Press, which had handled the printing and distribution of Books Abroad since the journal's founding in 1927. While Vlach complained of working 60–70 hours a week in his budget request for 1965–66, Lottinville in turn questioned Vlach's competence in the business of publishing. In an August 1964 letter to McCarter, Lottinville—a former Rhodes scholar who earned a master's degree from Oxford and coached the university's boxing team—offers a lengthy analysis of the journal's editorial formula and circulation woes, then concludes by mentioning the prospect of replacing Vlach. See Savoie Lottinville to Pete Kyle McCarter, December 30, 1963, and August 29, 1964, Presidential Papers of George Lynn Cross, Western History Collections, University of Oklahoma, Norman (hereafter abbreviated WHC).

2. Robert Vlach to Pete Kyle McCarter, November 20, 1964, *World Literature Today* archives, WHC.

3. Robert Vlach to Pete Kyle McCarter, April 21, 1965, *World Literature Today* archives, WHC.

4. Joseph M. McDaniel Jr., secretary of the Ford Foundation, to George Lynn Cross, June 8, 1965, Cross Presidential Papers, WHC.

5. In accepting the 1972 award, García Márquez would comment, "the role of a literary award like the BA / Neustadt Prize is not only to crown the glorious achievements of the living past (or a dying one, even one that may be dead, for that matter) which has quite often been the case with the Nobel Prize, but also to reward and call attention to the remarkable things actually happening and bursting into creation now."

6. Herbert Howarth, "A Petition to the Swedish Academy," *Books Abroad* 41, no. 1 (Winter 1967): 4–7.

7. Ivask's "Revised Charter of the *Books Abroad* International Prize for Literature," with provisions to limit proxy and absentee balloting, appeared in the spring 1972 issue of *Books Abroad*. That charter also formalized the procedures of "elimination balloting," which became the gold standard for other juries in the future.

8. Pete Kyle McCarter to Ivar Ivask, July 10, 1969, *World Literature Today* archives, WHC.

9. See George Lynn Cross, *The Seeds of Excellence: The Story of the University of Oklahoma Foundation* (Transcript Press, 1986), 121–22.

10. Ivask recounts the details of the first jury's proceedings in "Giuseppe Ungaretti: Laureate of Our First International Prize for Literature," *Books Abroad* 44, no. 2 (1970): 191–94.

11. R. Boyd Gunning to Mrs. Walter Neustadt [Sr.], September 25, 1969, OU Foundation archives, University of Oklahoma, Norman.

12. An undated eight-page endowment proposal to Walter Neustadt appears in the 1972 Books Abroad folder, box 7 of the Presidential Papers of Paul F. Sharp, WHC. See also David A. Burr to Paul F. Sharp, "Books Abroad" memo, November 30, 1971, Sharp Presidential Papers, WHC; "Literary Prize Endowed" press release, May 11, 1972, Sharp Presidential Papers, WHC; and Carol J. Burr, *Because They Cared : A Chronicle of Private Support at the University of Oklahoma* (University of Oklahoma Foundation, 1975), 22.

13. The Chinese poet Duo Duo cites the influence of Charles Baudelaire, Federico García Lorca, Marina Tsvetaeva, and Ilya Ehrenburg on his poetry.

14. The French-born literary scholar Henri Peyre once wrote that "Norman, Oklahoma, sounded to many a European ear as Persepolis or Samarkand once may have done to Marlowe or to Keats" (*Books Abroad*, Autumn 1976).

A NOTE ON THE TEXT

Generic titles such as "Laureate's Words of Acceptance," "Presentation of...,"
and "Encomium for . . ." have been replaced in this collection with thematic
titles. Detailed biliographical information about all the pieces included here
can be found in the "Recommended Reading" section that begins on page
329. Elisions to the original texts are marked by bracketed ellipses, and occa-
sional typos, errors in fact, formatting inconsistencies, and stylistic infelicities
have been silently emended.

GIUSEPPE UNGARETTI
THE 1970 LAUREATE

Giuseppe Ungaretti (1888–1970) was born into an Italian family in
Alexandria, Egypt, where he was educated in French and began working
as a journalist and literary critic. He moved to Paris in 1912 but enlisted
in the infantry in World War I and fought in the trenches in northern Italy.
World War I served as the catalyst for Ungaretti's venture into poetry,
and he published his first collection in 1916. Among the many literary
affiliations that influenced his work were hermeticism (which he helped to
revolutionize in the 1930s), symbolism, and futurism. Ungaretti's books of
poetry include *L'allegria* (1931), *Sentimento del tempo* (1933), *Un grido
e paesaggi* (1952), and *Vita d'un uomo* (1969; Eng. *The Life of a Man*,
1958).

I am happy to be here not only on
account of the honor, but also for
having seen in a distant land, which
seems isolated from the world, how
much can be done for the support
of culture and for the diffusion
of poetry—with determination,
with grace, and with a well-guided
intuition.

—Giuseppe Ungaretti

The Old Captain's Last Voyage
Ivar Ivask

Balugina da un faro
Verso cui va tranquillo
Il vecchio capitano.

G.U.

Vacationing amidst the solitary Finnish woods and lakes, I am trying to order my impressions of the dramatic events that occurred in connection with Giuseppe Ungaretti between 7 February and 4 June of this year, and in which I was to a certain degree involved. True, I had very briefly met the Italian poet on 17 April 1969 after his highly successful reading at the Poetry Center in New York, where he was presented by Professor Luciano Rebay from Columbia, with English translations of his verse read by Isabella Gardner, Allen Ginsberg, and Louis Simpson. But little did I then surmise that about a year later, Ungaretti would be the first recipient of the just-established international literary award. My reaction to his exaggerated manner of reading— ranging from a barely audible whisper to a hoarse shout; now angelic-looking, now more like the grimace of a Kabuki actor—was ambiguous. This was probably the case because I then honestly preferred the often obscure complexities of Eugenio Montale to Ungaretti's sparse, essential lines. It was for this reason that Montale became one of my candidates when the jury met in Norman, 5–7 February 1970. (My other candidate was Jorge Guillén.) Since Montale had advance support by several other jury members, his chances were quite good. However, when he politely declined to accept any international literary prize at that time, this changed considerably the situation confronting the members of the jury who had gathered for their deliberations. Since the story of the first jury has already been told in these pages (see *BA* 44:2) and in the *Saturday Review* (see the issue of 21 March 1970), suffice it to recapitulate here that it was my vote as chairman which broke the tie between Pablo Neruda and Ungaretti in favor of the latter.

This was the first dramatic event. No less exciting was the visit of the eighty-twoyear-old patriarch of Italian letters to Norman and New York. Ungaretti arrived at Oklahoma City's Will Rogers Airport on Friday 13 March together with Professor Luciano Rebay and John Ciardi who had joined him in New York. The poet was totally exhausted from an uninterrupted flight all the way from Rome. No one had at that time any idea that he had not slept much even before leaving and that he had broncho-pulmonary troubles. I hardly recognized the poet whom I had met only last year in New York; he had let his white hair grow to shoulder-length locks and refused to shave his white stubble with the explanation that it was important to renew one's appearance from time to time. Ungaretti was furious, his cane flailing the air, because he believed that his suitcase had not arrived. Yet the one suitcase from Rome was vehemently disowned by him, and he only grudgingly accepted it when I demonstrated its obvious contents to him: several copies of *Vita d'un uomo* and a tuxedo (among other things).

Came Saturday morning 14 March, the day of the solemn presentation of the award, and Ungaretti said he did not feel up to reading his verse or giving any speeches. Understandably so, what with his prolonged sleeplessness, and the change in time from Rome to Oklahoma, his not too stable health at the advanced age of eighty-two. Yet it was also quite vexing to all organizers who had made infinite preparations, and already the guests were arriving, including a crew of *Radiotelevisione italiana* . . . The success of the evening was far from assured. Fortunately, in the afternoon things began to look up: the maestro had had a good nap and together with Ciardi and Rebay, the four of us sat down around a small table in one of the university cottages where Ungaretti was lodged. He went through his collected poems page by page in order to make a selection for the reading. "This one is not bad, is it?" Ungaretti generously consulted us. Mostly we nodded our "si, si" assent, although worrying a bit that this part of the program might both tire the laureate and exceed the allotted span of fifteen to twenty minutes, since after each original poem, Ciardi or I would read the English version by Andrew

Wylie. Ungaretti's final choice for the occasion was eighteen poems, which spanned half a century of productivity: "Agonia," "Veglia," "Sono una creatura," "Solitudine," "Girovago," "Caino," "Tu ti spezzasti," "Cori descrittivi di stato d'animo di Didone, I, IV, VIII, X, XVIII, XIX," "Variazioni su nulla," "Ultimi cori, nos. 12, 24," "Proverbi I–IV," and "Dunja." (The selection was determined, at least in part, according to which poems happened to be available in Wylie's translation, which Ungaretti obviously preferred.)

The evening program, a black-tie affair, began at 6:00 p.m. I have carefully leafed through the photographs of the poet reproduced in Leone Piccioni's *Vita di un poeta Giuseppe Ungaretti* (Rizzoli, 1970), a moving interpretive biography, but it seems to me that Ungaretti never looked better and more the magician that he always was than during the last months of his life—what with his beard and long white hair; the earlier severity was gone, a compassionate openness marked his face. I had the honor of saying the opening words. One of the real connoisseurs of Ungaretti's oeuvre, Professor Luciano Rebay, pronounced the encomium. Then J. Herbert Hollomon, at that time president of the University of Oklahoma, rose to present the hand-lettered certificate, bound in blue leather, to the first laureate of the *Books Abroad* International Prize for literature, and said:

This land and this place is for Western man, young, vital, unreasoning, irrational, hopeful, lustful, and youthful. We honor today and he honors us, a poet who at any age is young and hopeful, innocent, loving, and rational. It is this combination of the Dionysian and Apollonian that makes life have any hope at all. It does us great honor that he comes to us as the first laureate of a prize based upon a tradition of interest in literature at a university only a little more than half a century old, from a place and a time of great tradition from which all of our art, our music, our poetry, and much of our prose comes. It is, I believe, a signal beginning to what I hope will become a great tradition in Western European America as for the whole world: to award a prize to someone in literature without consideration of his background or ideology and without reference to political boundary. But recognizing someone somewhere who brings to man the hopefulness and the despair of man's short time alive. In a very deep sense, Ungaretti has brought to the world a sense of love and of hope and of feeling that lies, unspoken often, within all of us.

It therefore does me honor to be able to present to him, the first laureate, the *Books Abroad* University of Oklahoma Prize for Literature.

Giuseppe Ungaretti responded with the following words (translated here into English):

I am very moved by this ceremony in this distant land. It was exhausting to get here: it was far away, it was farther than I ever would have imagined, but finally I did get here to receive the honor that was bestowed on me this very moment, which is an honor surpassing my merits, and this honor was accompanied by most kind words. I find myself at a university which is a model of a university—a model for encouraging studies, but also for the diffusion of poetry. Hence I am happy to be here not only on account of the honor, but also for having seen in a distant land, which seems isolated from the world, how much can be done for the support of culture and for the diffusion of poetry—with determination, with grace, and with a well-guided intuition.

I was comforted to read in Piccioni's spirited account that microphones hardly ever work when Ungaretti reads his verse since his voice fluctuates so much. We had the same difficulty in Norman. But enough of the man's unusual intensity came through to move his audience, who listened intently to the hunched figure of the old poet seated in the pit of the amphitheater-like modern auditorium of the Oklahoma Center for Continuing Education. (I myself was strongly reminded of Vainamoinen, the Finnish god of song in the *Kalevala,* and indeed Ungaretti's forebears—the name means literally "Little Hungarian"—had migrated centuries ago from Hungary to Tuscany.) Suddenly the complete unity of his life and poetry became clear to me, the perfect overlapping achieved in such lines as "La morte / si sconta / vivendo," "Ora sono ubriaco / d'universo," "In nessuna / parte / di terra / mi posso accasare," "Cereo un paese innocente," or "Fui pronto a tutte le partenze." The immediate truth of "S'incomincia per cantare / E si canta per finire" became clear, alas, only in retrospect.

It was a moment of cordial simplicity in spite of all solemn appearances, potted palms, popping flashlights and whirring television cameras. It was Ungaretti's moment and he placed on it his unmistakably vigorous imprint. The standing ovation seemed so insignificant in the presence of this tiny, stooped, white-haired old man who almost seemed to have come to us from another reality, to which he had witnessed as the prophets of old. Two and a half months later this creature of myth was dead.

No one entertained seriously this possibility at that hour of fulfillment. The reading over, the crowd descended to congratulate the poet, have copies of his books autographed, take more pictures. Tired but obviously pleased, Ungaretti complied. He inscribed for me then and there the copy of *Vita d'un uomo* from which he had just read, combining Italian, Arabic, and French words, thus representing the three cultures which most decisively had shaped him.

At the banquet, toasts were made as candles fluttered: by President Hollomon, the Italian minister plenipotentiary, Giulio Terruzzi, John Ciardi (in the name of the American poets), Professor Lowell Dunham, chairman of the department of modern languages at the university, and Ungaretti was made an honorary citizen of Norman by the mayor's representative, Professor James Artman. I read some of the telegrams and greetings that had arrived for the occasion: from Governor Dewey Bartlett, Jorge Guillén, Francis Ponge, Octavio Paz, Professors Thomas Bergin (Yale), Glauco Cambon (Connecticut), Zbigniew Folejewski (British Columbia), etc. I would like to quote also here some of these messages. Jorge Guillén, hospitalized in Puerto Rico, wrote:

Ungaretti's presence always brings such a sharing of happiness, of vitality generously given, that to be with him always means a celebration and a joy. This time, Ungaretti's celebration will be in Norman, Oklahoma, because he is the poet who is being honored.

With all my heart I am glad that the light of this prize has focused on a truly illustrious figure, abounding in years and merit. The marvelous precision of Ungaretti's language has been for all of us an unsurpassable model of disciplined expression.

Francis Ponge gave this opinion in his letter to me dated 3 March 1970:

J'ai été ravi . . . que mon cher grand ami Ungaretti ait été désigné par votre jury ce qu'il est, effectivement: le plus grand poète vivant. Voilà qui rachète l'injustice stupidement commise par le jury Nobel. . . . Bravo donc!

Octavio Paz in his turn commented:

It was a great joy to know that Ungaretti was the first laureate, a most deserving and welcome choice. For once an international jury did the right thing. I hope you will manage to keep this high level in subsequent choices.

Glauco Cambon's telegram put it succinctly and memorably:

Dear Ungaretti, I wish I could share this happy occasion with you tonight, but your poetry makes it possible for me to be with you anywhere because poetry is the only antidote to exile.

Allen Ginsberg's short poem in tribute, "Ungaretti in Heaven," can be read in this issue; it, too, seems to have acquired a prophetic ring.

The feted poet expressed his thanks very simply, praising the beautiful women near him and again the university that went to such lengths to reward poetry. The mood remained festive and no one wanted to break it. President Hollomon summed it up by saying that it had been a perfect day which nevertheless had to end just as we have one day to die, yet the experience of these hours cannot be destroyed. Said it and extinguished grandly with his palm the candles on the candelabra in front of him. It seems strange that someone would bring up the subject of death at such an occasion, but it seemed right and, looking back, uncannily so. Later Ungaretti commented favorably that the president of a university should have those rarest of talents, wit and style. The poet withdrew to a deserved rest, while the other guests continued to celebrate his victory.

Although we hardly believed that Ungaretti would take up our suggestion to use the next day before returning to New York for a visit to Anadarko, the "Indian Capital of the World," he enthusiastically accepted. So we went there by car, Ungaretti, Rebay, my wife and I. It was a windy, cloudy Sunday afternoon with Ungaretti alternately taking naps and engaging in lively conversation, while the not very varied south Oklahoma landscape rolled by. We went first to the Indian Village, an open air museum of dwellings used by the various Southern Plains Indian tribes, faithfully reproduced by the Indians themselves. It is located a mile out of Anadarko on the Tonkawa hills near the site of an Indian massacre. Ungaretti was too tired to take the full guided tour by Miss Dolores Buffalo, an Otoe Indian, and so he just looked at some of the tepees, observed the landscape with typical stretches of red clay bleeding here and there. It was evident that he felt the almost sacral character of the place belonging to the original inhabitants of this red earth. When a group of Indians performed some of their authentic war dances, Ungaretti was as fascinated and delighted as a child. It later turned out that the leader of the group had been among the first American soldiers to liberate Rome from the Nazis and hoped to return there with his dancers as part of a European tour. In town, we visited the small but well-arranged Southern Plains Indian Arts and Crafts Museum. Ungaretti could not admire enough the exhibited samples of Indian beadcraft and silverwork. He commented that the Indians possessed the best sense of color in the world. This, coming from one who had lived in Paris and known most of the great modern painters there, was no superficial judgment.

He bought samples of bead and silverwork, as well as suede moccasins for his granddaughter Annina. That this encounter appealed strongly to the basically nomadic nature of Ungaretti, always open to new exotic adventures, be they in Egypt, Brazil, or Oklahoma, is reported by several people with whom he later talked about it, and was expressed in the last letter I received from him, dated 6 May: "La ricordo continuamente e ricordo la sua sposa e le loro straordinarie cortesie e gli incontri inaspettati con gli indiani."

Monday morning 16 March, Ungaretti boarded the plane for New York, accompanied by Luciano Rebay. He looked now really ill, complaining about various aches and pains. None of us had been easy about the state of his health during the past strenuous days, but now we were frankly worried. The medical diagnosis in New York confirmed the worst, and the poet was committed to the Presbyterian Hospital at Columbia University with bronchopneumonia and a congested heart. What a sad epilogue to the festive days in Norman! His son-in-law, the architect Mario Lafragola, flew in from Rome, and so did his good friend, Signora Nella Mirone from Milan. Fortunately, the poet's health responded well to the medical treatment, and he was permitted to return to Rome on 26 March—just before the erratic layoffs on account of the sick calls among the air control personnel. During April and May, Ungaretti was recuperating at Salsomaggiore. He sent several letters promising various contributions to the issue I was planning in his honor for the autumn. I was to discuss these matters with him personally during our stay in Rome early in June. We arrived in Rome on Monday, 1 June. 2 June was the day of the Italian Republic, marked by colorful military pageantry. During that day, I phoned the poet, who lived with his daughter Ninon, and was informed that Ungaretti was not at all in Rome, but in Milan; neither was his daughter available. I should call back on Wednesday, at ten in the morning. This sounded strange. The mystery was resolved when I learned Wednesday morning from the housekeeper that I could not see the "professore" because he had died in Milan, Monday night, 1 June, from a lung clot at the home of friends. . . . In my shocked disbelief I could only express amazement that the news had not yet been publicized anywhere. Could it really be true? Yes, yes, the news was to be released later that day and the burial services were to be held Thursday

4 June at the church of San Lorenzo fuori le Mura, the burial following at the cemetery of Verano.

It was still difficult to believe. None of the newspapers carried the front page news that Italy's greatest modern poet had died. I wandered into Rizzoli's bookstore to buy the second, enlarged edition of *Vita d'un uomo,* discovered Piccioni's just-published biography of the poet, and discreetly inquired from the clerks whether they had by chance heard the news. No, indeed, and how could it be true when nobody knew about it? Died on 1 June, and still the fact was unknown on the morning of 3 June? Thus I wandered around Rome, obviously belonging to the very few who were aware that the life of that great Roman poet had ended. Visiting in the afternoon the Spanish poet Rafael Alberti and his wife, the writer María Teresa León, in their Andalusian-looking apartment in the Trastevere district, it was I who had to break the news about their friend to them. Then, the afternoon and evening papers finally carried the news. Why was it withheld for two whole days? It seems to have been the poet's own wish that the announcement of his passing and his actual burial come as close as possible, to avoid elaborate preparations.

One would almost have expected a state funeral, just as de Gaulle ordered for Paul Valéry back in 1945, but the poet got his wish of a simple funeral by ordering the delay of the announcement. The Early Christian basilica of San Lorenzo fuori le Mura, several times rebuilt with its high ceiling of rugged wooden beams, was nevertheless filled with about one hundred of the poet's relatives and friends. Next to us sat the poet and critic Piero Bigongiari, who came to Norman with his wife to present Ungaretti as his candidate and saw him win. Among those who had come to pay their last respects were Carlo Bo, Mario Luzi, Giancarlo Vigorelli, Leone Piccioni, Oreste Macrí, Libero de Libero, Giorgio Bassani, Leonardo Sinisgalli, Carlo Levi, Natalia Ginzburg, Maria Bellonci, Alfonso Gatto, Murillo Mendes, Attilio Bertolucci, Vittorio Sereni, Renato Guttuso, and Guido Piovene. But also a number of students, even hippies, paying last homage to the poet who kept always close to the young and their aspirations, only recently reading a poem, "Greece 1970," at a rally directed against the regime of the Greek colonels. Cardinal Dall'Aqua blessed the casket and then it was carried out into the bright sunlight by Luzi, Piccioni, Bo, Vigorelli. No speeches in church and almost none at the tomb until the critic and longtime friend of the poet, rector of the University of Urbino, Carlo Bo, stepped forward to say a few words. He stressed that Ungaretti had not only been a poet, but poetry itself, and above all a companion, *the* companion. At the same time, he lamented the absence of any high government official. The coffin was placed in the tomb next to that of the poet's wife, Jeanne (who died in 1958), and the opening closed with concrete. Someone advanced and incised with a dry branch in large letters the name Ungaretti, and added a cross. Milena Milani inscribed the word "poet," somebody else wrote the poet's often-repeated self-characterization as "Uomo di pena"—man of sorrows. The crowd dispersed, casting one more look at the plain epitaph— even this spontaneously created, but later probably to be covered with a more finished marble plaque. The huge wreaths sent by the University of Rome, where Ungaretti taught for so many years, the Writers' Syndicate, the Italian premier, the Association of Italian Editors and Authors, the Editions Apollinaire (a friend from his first Paris years), shook in the breeze. I met the daughter of the poet, Signora Ninon Lafragola, who told me that I was probably the first in Rome to learn about her father's death. We walked away in the company of Ungaretti's last secretary, Ariodante Marianni and his wife. He told me how much our award had meant to Ungaretti, who came very close to getting the Nobel Prize in 1969. He returned full of excitement from his last American trip, planning to write down some of his impressions of Oklahoma for the issue of *Books Abroad* in his honor. It turned out to be his last great joy in life. We talked at length about the issue, now in memory of Ungaretti, and went to the railroad station to send off Carlo Bo and Piero Bigongiari with his wife Elena, who were returning to Florence. We did not feel like joining them and going from Florence on to Umbria as we had originally planned. Ungaretti's death had changed everything.

*

I had met Ungaretti briefly in 1969. Then followed those three incredible days spent in his company in Norman during March of this year. Our correspondence had lasted but three months. But never has someone won me over so completely and in so short a time, as a human being and artist, as did Giuseppe Ungaretti. Our encounter was of a rare intensity and openness; the loss the more cruel and real. Fortunately his life and poetry were and still are completely fused, Life of a Man, which communicates to us all that he was and always will be: "Poesia / è il mondo l'umanità / la propria vita / fioriti dalla parola / la limpida meraviglia / di un delirante fermento," as he wrote back in 1916 as a soldier in the trenches of World War I. He wrote and acted out of such a "delirious ferment" which made him travel like a restless nomad, made him try out every new way of poetic expression. Prudence was not part of his character. Who but Ungaretti would have literally risked his life, ill and eighty-two years old, to fly halfway around the globe just not to disappoint those friends who had gathered in Norman to hear him read his poetry and receive a new international literary prize? The present issue praises the poet for his original achievement and mourns the disappearance of an extraordinary human being from our midst: an almost equally grave loss for those who had the privilege to have been his friends of a lifetime and for those who knew him but a few years, months, or even days. For future friends, the man will be the poetry.

Born in Riga, Latvia, in 1927, **Ivar Ivask** *served as editor of* Books Abroad *and* World Literature Today *from 1967 to 1991. He inaugurated the Neustadt Prize in 1969.*

The Perennial Wanderings of the Nomad
Luciano Rebay

Caro Ungaretti, Mr. President, Ladies and Gentlemen:

In the years following the First World War, a group of leading Italian critics and writers expressed the belief that poetry was dead, and that henceforth the only medium through which a poet might communicate was prose. Apocalyptic statements of this kind are not entirely unusual—we have all heard time and again that the *novel* is dead—but the significant fact in this instance is that few predictions of doom uttered in recent times have proved to be so completely incorrect. Our very presence this March 14, 1970, in Norman, Oklahoma, thousands of miles from Italy, proves in the most spectacular manner not only that Italian poetry has managed to survive in our century, but that it has known a period of revival and greatness worthy of a long tradition of poetic excellence. For we are here to honor Giuseppe Ungaretti, a leading protagonist of this revival and in a real sense the father of contemporary Italian poetry, the master who, by daring to explore anew the hidden meanings as well as the most secret potentialities of the Italian language, was the first to revitalize a tradition that had threatened to become stagnant.

Clearly, however, the significance of his work today reaches far beyond the confines of Italy. Now in his eighty-second year, Ungaretti has won world fame for his poetic achievements, at the same time distinguishing himself as a challenging critic and scholar of poetry, ranging from Vergil to Dante, from Petrarch and Leopardi to Mallarmé, from Góngora and Shakespeare to Racine and Blake, from Valéry and Saba to Breton and Saint-John Perse, among others. Also, one must not forget, he has produced superb translations from Shakespeare, Blake, Góngora, Racine, Mallarmé, Perse. And in turn, his poems have been translated into every major Western language. He has been a frequent contributor to *La Nouvelle Revue Française*, where some of his major poems were published even before their appearance in Italy, and to such prestigious journals as *Commerce* and *Mesures*, which during the period between the First and Second World Wars kept alive an interest in what was new and vital in creative literature throughout the Western world. I expect that in the near future a scholar—a comparatist—will study the seminal influence that Ungaretti's poetry has had on his younger contemporaries and on later generations, both in Italy and abroad. The findings of such an investigation, it is easy to predict, will show ramifications throughout Europe and across the Atlantic Ocean as far as Brazil, where Ungaretti lived and taught for six years between 1936 and 1942, and in the United States, where, as he well knows, he has many friends and admirers. To anticipate but one example, I shall refer you to Robert Lowell's "Returning," a poem from *For the Union Dead*, which, as Lowell himself has indicated, could never have been written without the stimulus of Ungaretti's "Canzone" from *La terra promessa.*

The impact of Ungaretti's poetry—his sparing use of words, his capacity to bring language to unusual heights of lyric tension, his power to create illuminating images—has been acknowledged by the leading men of letters of our century. T. S. Eliot, who was also born in 1888, said of Ungaretti: "He is one of the very few authentic poets of my generation." Saint-John Perse has praised him for "having given universal meaning to the voice of European man." Robert Lowell has pointed out that "Ungaretti did something new, and stood like a human rock behind it." And Allen Tate, observing that as a result of the work of poets such as Ungaretti and Montale, the poetic center of continental Europe had shifted from France to Italy, stated: "I consider Giuseppe Ungaretti one of the great modern European poets, who since the death of Paul Valéry has no superior in Europe." But perhaps the best summary of what constitutes the essence of Ungaretti's contribution to modern poetry is to be found in a reflection by André Pieyre de Mandiargues: "If you want to know his equals," he wrote, "you must turn to Berg, Stravinsky, Picasso, men whose art partakes of the nature of lightning and who know, or knew, how to ally in their creations the greatest lucidity with the blind force of un-reason. Each of them has accomplished the prodigious feat of losing his head, yet keeping it."

Prodigious feat, indeed: for poetry is forever an adventure at the limit of reason and logic, "the exploration of a personal continent of hell," says

Ungaretti, in which the poet feels utterly alone, different and at times isolated from his fellow men, as though condemned by the weight of a very special responsibility: to discover a secret, and to reveal it. As far back as 1931 he wrote in the *Nouvelle Revue Française*: "Je suis un 'homme' qui a toujours brûlé sa vie pour quelque chose de bien plus grand que l'homme, et cela, en effet, c'est de la poésie." (I am a "man" who has always burnt his life for something much greater than man himself, and that is poetry.) We should note at this point that Ungaretti's complete works, just published in Italy by Mondadori, are fittingly titled *Vita d'un uomo*—Life of a Man.

Why did Ungaretti adopt for his *opera omnia* this inclusive title? Because, obviously, he does not believe that the poet is an abstract entity, separate from humanity, but on the contrary that even in his necessary, unavoidable, and at times tragic loneliness, he is an integral part, and often the most alive, most vigilant part of humanity. The poet is therefore first and foremost a "man," and his poetry cannot but convey his particular mode of being a man, cannot but express—to quote Glauco Cambon—his "search for the archetypal meaning of personal experience." In the preface to *L'allegria* (Joy), the definitive edition of the first volume of his collected verse, Ungaretti made a statement that is essential to the understanding of his approach to art and that places his entire poetic output in proper perspective. He wrote—and that was again 1931: "This old book is a diary. Its author has no other ambition than to leave a good biography of himself, an ambition which he believes is shared by the poets of all times." And only last year—in the eight-five-page appendix of newly written, candid "Notes," which to me constitutes the happiest surprise of *Vita d'un uomo*—recalling that he had composed his first poems in Milan during the autumn of 1914, he observed: "I wrote those poems in the only natural way known to me, trying to represent in them the environment that surrounded me, what aspects of my personality it reflected at that particular moment, and, as laconically as possible, the variations of my feelings. . . . Those first poems are exactly what all my subsequent poems will be, embedded in a psychological situation closely linked to my biography: never have I known a poetic dream that did not stem from a direct personal experience."

Ungaretti was born in Egypt, in that crucible of different races and religions that was Alexandria, the native city of another great poet, Constantine Cavafy, and also of Filippo Tommaso Marinetti, the flamboyant founder of futurism. Ungaretti's family (he was the younger of two sons) was of humble stock, had emigrated from Lucca, in Tuscany, at the time of the construction of the Suez Canal, where the poet's father had found work as a laborer. He died when his son Giuseppe was only two years old. His widow, a strong-willed, deeply religious woman, raised their two children alone with the income provided by a bakery she and her husband had managed to open in the poor district of Moharrem Bey. Ungaretti spent the first twenty-four years of his life in Alexandria—a crucial formative period that not at all surprisingly left a lasting imprint on his poetry. One of the constantly recurring themes in his work—the desert—is in fact the result of his direct contact with the Sahara. For Ungaretti, the desert means distance, light, freedom, sensuousness, the piercing melancholy of Bedouin songs and, above all, dreams, mirages—the dreams and mirages of the nomad who becomes for him the symbol of the poet in his perennial wanderings in search of innocence, happiness, love. In a three-line poem titled "Tramonto" (Sunset) we read: "Il carnato del cielo / sveglia oasi / al nomade d'amore" (The flesh-colored sky / awakens oases / for the nomad of love). This was written in 1916 on one of the battlefields of the First World War. Although the sunset described here is not an African one, the images it evokes by analogical counterpoint unmistakably are. The nomad reappears later as the protagonist of a longer poem, written in 1918, "Girovago" (Wanderer), a metaphor for the poetic quest. The last lines convey in an inspired synthesis the poet's longing for purity and innocence: "Godere un solo / minuto di vita / iniziale // Cerco un paese / innocente." (To enjoy only one / minute of life primeval // I seek a country / innocent.)

In a 1926 article, "Innocenza e memoria" (Innocence and Memory)—which, incidentally, provided the title for his book of essays in French translation, *Innocence et mémoire*, published last year—Ungaretti characterized poetry as an insatiable longing for innocence ("una speranza inappagabile d'innocenza"), a brilliant definition that Marcel Raymond quoted in his well-known study *From Baudelaire to Surrealism*. Ungaretti later elaborated on it in his fundamental essay, "Ragioni di una poesia" (Reasons for My Poetry, 1949), now to be found at the beginning of his collected works. "Poetry," he wrote, "enables man to create an illusion of youth reconquered, and to believe in this illusion; to become, as Rimbaud wanted, *voyant*—a seer; . . . to bring forth an illusion of innocence, the illusion of the perfect freedom man enjoyed before his fall." This "illusion," this feeling of freedom, lightness, joy is one of the precious gifts that Ungaretti's poetry has to offer, a gift available to any of us if only we open *Vita d'un uomo.*

In 1912 Ungaretti left Egypt for Europe. He did not at first, as one might expect, choose to live in Italy. Rather, he settled in Paris, with friends and schoolfellows from Alexandria who had gone to the French capital to complete their studies. In Paris he enrolled at the Sorbonne, studied under famed professors, such as Henri Bergson, and even began work on a doctoral thesis on the nineteenth-century poet Maurice de Guérin. But most important, he found his way to bohemia and frequented some of the leading exponents of the literary and artistic avant-garde: Picasso, Braque, Léger, Salmon, Jacob, Cendrars, and especially Apollinaire, with whom he quickly developed a deep and devoted friendship.

Ungaretti remained in Paris until the outbreak of the First World War, at which time he moved to Italy to volunteer in the army. He served as a private in the infantry, first on the Italian front in the Carso Mountains and later on the French front in the Champagne region. It was out of that conflict that his first major poetry was born, although it would be most inaccurate to label any of his lyrics "war poems." "In my poems there is no trace of hatred for the enemy, or for anyone," says Ungaretti, "there is simply an acute awareness of the human condition, of the brotherhood of men in their suffering, and of the extreme precariousness of human life." In the trenches, during lulls between battles, or at night in his tent, Ungaretti wrote what later he was to call his "diary," on scraps of paper which he would stuff into his pack. A literary-minded lieutenant, Ettore Serra, one day discovered them by accident and later in 1916 published them at his own expense in an eighty-copy edition. The slender volume—Ungaretti's first book of verse—was called *Il porto sepolto* (The Buried Port) and revolutionized Italian poetry. The title was suggested to Ungaretti by the sunken Pharaonic harbor of his native Alexandria. In the book, however, the buried port is an allegory for poetry itself, whose orphic secrets are brought out from the depths into the light by the poet: "Vi arriva il poeta / e poi torna alla luce con i suoi canti / e li disperde // Di questa poesia / mi resta quel nulla / d'inesauribile segreto." (The poet reaches [the buried port] / and then returns to the light with his songs / and scatters them around. // Of this poetry / there remains to me the nothingness / of an inexhaustible secret.)

Most of the poems of *Il porto sepolto* were short, the lines were not regular ones, there was no rhyme, no punctuation, no attempt at D'Annunzian grandiloquence; the general versification represented a complete break with tradition. Yet those lyrics had a freshness, an intensity, a regenerating strength that was uncannily captivating and moving. Italian poetry was never the same after them. Their compressed power continues to fascinate those who read them today.

Il porto sepolto was incorporated in 1919 into a larger collection of poems, *Allegria di naufragi* (Joy of Shipwrecks). This title, echoing as it does the celebrated last line of Leopardi's "L'infinito" ("E il naufragar m'è dolce in questo mare"—And to shipwreck is sweet for me in this sea), indicates, as later poems revealed, that Ungaretti was then already seeking to get back into the mainstream of Italian lyric tradition (Leopardi had been, with Mallarmé, the poet who had presided over his youth while he was still living and studying in Egypt), and that he was rediscovering for himself the meters of the old Italian masters, especially the hendecasyllabic line and the septenary. It was a new "season"—to use the word Ungaretti has adopted for each progressive stage in his poetic development—that culminated in the publication in 1933 of *Sentimento del tempo* (Sentiment of Time), the book of summer and sensuality, and, in its second part, of a tormenting religious crisis.

Beginning in the mid-thirties, Ungaretti then worked on his next book in which he intended to reflect the autumn of his life, "an autumn," he wrote, "which bids farewell to the last signs of earthly youth, to the last carnal appetites." But the publication of this work, to be called *La terra promessa* (The Promised Land), was delayed until 1950 by supervening tragic events. These events—the death of his nineyear-old son in Brazil in 1939, followed by the horrors of the Second World War—led instead to the printing in 1947 of *ll dolore* (Grief), "of my books the one closest to me," says Ungaretti. "I wrote it during terrible years, half-choking. I cannot speak of it except to say that that grief will never cease torturing me." *ll dolore* includes some of the most powerful poems Ungaretti has written—I have in mind one in particular, "Tu ti spezzasti" (You Were Shattered), in which the cosmic sense of bereavement caused by the loss of his son is recorded in heart-rending, unforgettable lines.

In the course of the last two decades Ungaretti has published three new volumes of collected verse: *Un grido e paesaggi* (A Shout and Landscapes, 1952), which includes "Monologhetto" (Little Monologue), a lyric chronicle of some of the most significant moments in his life, as well as new poems for Antonietto, his dead son; *Il taccuino del vecchio* (The Old Man's Notebook, 1960), a collection of poems in the metaphysical vein of *La terra promessa*; and, in 1967, *Marte delle stagioni* (Death of the Seasons), which many thought was his swan song. But then, in 1968, the year of his eightieth birthday, the unpredictable "vecchio" surprised everyone by bringing out with characteristic coquettishness yet a new book, *Dialogo*, a love dialogue of dazzling verbal virtuosity and youthful confidence, perhaps best epitomized by a single line: "Ancora mi rimane qualche infanzia," which approximately translated means "Some infancy is still left to me." Observed Ungaretti in a recent interview, as reported by Leone Piccioni: "I believe that in the poems of old age the freshness and illusion of youth are gone; but I also believe that they encompass so much experience that if one succeeds in finding the right words, they represent the highest form of poetry one may leave." *Vita d'un uomo*, I may add, does not close with *Dialogo*. The last composition, "Dunja," again a love poem, but inspired—one should note—by a different lady, was begun in Rome on April 2, 1969, and I can still see Ungaretti's triumphant expression when he showed it to me in New York two weeks later.

This makes me realize that I have said nothing of what Ungaretti means to me personally. But tonight is not the time for personal recollections. Were I to follow them, they would take me back to Rome where I first met Ungaretti fourteen years ago while he was still teaching at the University; or to Paris with Jean Paulhan; or to Milan with Jean Fautrier; or, especially, to New York in 1964 when he spent a semester as visiting professor at Columbia and charmed students and colleagues alike with the warmth of his personality. As I conclude this tribute of my affection and admiration, I believe that the paramount fact to be stressed here, on this evening of the award to him of such a distinguished prize, is that, thanks to Giuseppe Ungaretti and his work, Italian poetry early in this century regained a universality of language through which have found exemplary expression the innermost anguish, dreams, and hopes of modern man.

March 14, 1970
University of Oklahoma

P.S. As I reread this encomium two and a half months after Ungaretti's death, I have before me the typewritten text of what I believe to be his last poem, "L'impietrito e il velluto" (The Petrified One and Velvet)—the second inspired by Dunja. He handed it to me after the award ceremony in Norman. This poem was then still unpublished (it has now been included in the second printing of *Vita d'un uomo*), and I remember being struck and very moved by its unmistakable images and visions of death. Ungaretti watched me as I read it; then he took a pen and slowly wrote along the margin a few words, which I translate: "A poem like this I may never be able to write again, perhaps it is my last poem. To Luciano Rebay with great affection. Ungaretti."

Luciano Rebay *(1928–2014), a leading postwar critic of Italian literature, was the Giuseppe Ungaretti Professor (emeritus) at Columbia University.*

GABRIEL GARCÍA MÁRQUEZ
THE 1972 LAUREATE

Gabriel García Márquez (1927–2014) was born in Aracataca, Colombia, where his maternal grandparents raised him for the first nine years of his life. He began his career in writing as a journalist while studying at the University of Cartagena, writing columns for the university's paper. In 1955 García Márquez published his first novella, *La Hojarasca* (Eng. *Leaf Storm*, 1972), a stream-of-consciousness story about a young boy's first encounter with death. But it would not be until the publication of *Cien años de soledad* (1967; Eng. *One Hundred Years of Solitude*, 1970) that he would become the literary figure he remains to this day. García Márquez's publications include the novels *In Evil Hour* (1970), *Love in the Time of Cholera* (1985), and *The General in His Labyrinth* (1989). His novellas include *Chronicle of a Death Foretold* (1981) and *Of Love and Other Demons* (1994), and his nonfiction includes such titles as *The Story of a Shipwrecked Sailor* (1970) and *News of a Kidnapping* (1996).

His final publication was the novella *Memories of My Melancholy Whores* in 2004. García Márquez was the recipient of the 1982 Nobel Prize in Literature and is widely considered one of the most significant authors of the twentieth century.

These circumstances suffice to make of the . . . Neustadt International Prize for Literature the one great international prize for highly deserving writers who are not yet well known.

—Gabriel García Márquez

Allegro Barbaro, or Gabriel García Márquez in Oklahoma
Ivar Ivask

García Márquez has studied and read more English than French or Italian, yet perfectly fluent in the latter two, he is hesitant to speak English. Why? "Because the English sentence is too simple," he explains. As to his tastes in music (he is quite a stereo-buff), he prefers the period from the late Beethoven to the last Bartók. He admires in particular Bartók's way of breaking up the melodious line to which the eighteenth- and nineteenthcentury masters have accustomed us. There is a lesson here for the modern novelist: "The Spanish prose sentence falls almost inevitably into hendecasyllabic or alexandrine verse which I want to avoid. One of the main tasks in polishing the text of my new novel, *El otoño del patriarca*, a complicated work, will be to break this flow of my sentences. By the way, the double meaning in the English translation of the novel's title, 'The Fall of the Patriarch,' is more apt than the original title but unfortunately cannot be duplicated in Spanish."

An aversion to simple sentences, a wish to achieve greater rhythmic complexities in the prose of his fiction: it all fits the complicated, intense, cordial character of the Colombian novelist who had come to Oklahoma to accept his prize (see *BA* 47:1, pp. 7–16). He made his stopover of barely two days, 27–28 June 1973, on his way from New York to Los Angeles and from there to a longer vacation with his entire family in Mexico. The best manner of characterizing this brief encounter would be in terms of one of Bartók's compositions, "Allegro barbaro." However, for Bartók—one of García Márquez's most admired human beings—"everything came too late." Fortunately this is not true in the case of García Márquez, who by forty-five has produced a world-wide bestselling novel and was awarded in 1972 both the prestigious Latin American Rómulo Gallegos Prize as well as the *Books Abroad* / Neustadt International Prize for Literature.

He had come to accept the *Books Abroad* / Neustadt award at an informal presentation "with an absolute minimum of witnesses." Crowds and public spectacles frighten him, hence his insistent request that we dispense this one time with a public ceremony. A few sentences were pronounced by Mrs. Walter Neustadt, who presented the symbolic silver eagle feather (in a box made of three woods native to Oklahoma—cherry, pecan and walnut); Huston Huffman, President of the University of Oklahoma Board of Regents, spoke briefly in Spanish and presented the check for ten thousand dollars along with the hand-lettered leather-bound certificate—in the absence of vacationing University president Paul F. Sharp—while thunder and lightning were raging outside and we looked out to see it raining in Macondo. Two photographers illuminated the scene inside. García Márquez's thanks came later in the form of a short written statement released to the press:

> This is a prize that has taken shape in the fertile imagination of a native of Estonia who has attempted to invent—rather than dynamite—a literary prize that would be dynamite for the Nobel. It is a prize in the mythical Oklahoma of Kafka's dreams and the land of the unique rose rock, and has been awarded to a writer from a remote and mysterious country in Latin America nominated by a great writer from far-off Iceland. These circumstances suffice to make of the *Books Abroad* / Neustadt International Prize for Literature the one great international prize for highly deserving writers who are not yet well known.

To be quite honest, the image of dynamite and dynamiting never would have occurred to me; it belongs to García Márquez's own resourceful imagination. Furthermore, since things are not supposed to be too simple, another news release was simultaneously made in New York by García Márquez's American publishers Harper & Row, explaining that he intends to establish with his prize money a defense fund for political prisoners in his native Colombia.

In retrospect I am still amazed at how many matters we were able to talk about before the presentation! He related to me, for example, that Pablo Neruda, the runner-up for the 1970 *Books Abroad* Prize, had expressed his great satisfaction to him in Paris about Giuseppe Ungaretti winning our award a few months before his death. What would García Márquez do in Los Angeles? Talk about Ray Bradbury. Science fiction aside, he thought Bradbury had written three or four of the most amazing pages in all modern prose. And Borges had dedicated some of his finest pages to a Spanish edition of Bradbury, as García Márquez informed me, immediately adding: "There are very few authors whom I have read completely; Borges is one of them." Spending an evening in the company of two poets, my wife and I, it was inevitable that his expressed dislike of—or better, lack of interest in—poetry had to come up. No, it actually was not quite exact, he considered himself a "clandestine poet," who liked, among twentieth-century poets, most especially Pablo Neruda, Pedro Salinas, Luis Cernuda, and Jorge Guillén. What about the roman nouveau, structuralism? A dead end.

So the hours passed, with García Márquez alert to everything: food and wine being served, music in the background, questions about literature past, present and future. Too bad I thought of playing the record with Bartók's "Allegro barbaro" only long after he had left. By now he is surely in Mexico, where his sons Rodrigo and Gonzalo were born, trying to break the backbone of the all-too-natural Spanish prose sentence. But how can you possibly turn the noun "otoño" of Latin origin into anything resembling the Anglo-Saxon "fall"? And I remembered Borges meditating in a similar vein about the advantages of writing in English. No doubt, the major Spanish-language writers today are less provincial than their English-speaking peers who hardly ponder the subtle shades of meaning offered them by the Castilian tongue.... Yet isn't this what Goethe's world literature is all about: the creative contact between the intensely local and universal relevance and responsibility? García Márquez will stop in Colombia on his way back to Barcelona from Mexico. He promised to return to Oklahoma because of its spaces, silence, and simple sentences.

The Fabulating Gifts of Gabriel García Márquez
Thor Vilhjálmsson

I do not feel inclined to join with those who hold that the poet should be relieved of his shamanistic duties, unburdened of his responsibility and role in enchanting his fellow man. The poet cannot be reduced to the task of merely collecting facts to feed the cybernetic monsters that are taking over, running and rounding our little lives and that are making us all identical moles striving to fill our quota of anthill chain-labor tasks and chain-life functions, where all shades of tergiversation are anathema and high treason, regardless of whether they are impelled by inner needs and nobly motivated; the creed in the shadow of the cybernetic tyrannosaurus rex of the encroaching brave new world is threatening to take over: mole stay mole. What then are our arms against the sea of robotification troubles and mechanization that threaten to suck out our souls and spit them into the void or onto garbage-dumps on the moon, there to wander undancing and bodiless among broken spaceships, surplus H-bombs, cyclonic gas. containers and exiled warfare-germs as spirits ambulating from crater to crater over the lunar sands while the earth-bound bodies continue to do the blind St. Vitus dance to the untuned commands of robots who may one day acquire whims and suddenly delight in crushing legions of our frail kind of ants with their unticklish toes?

One is fantasy. And therefore my choice of candidate in the present race is a writer eminently endowed with a gift of speech animated by dynamic fantasy. Gabriel García Márquez is one of those writers who enchants us as he deals with those perennial forces that rule our lives and cast us hither and thither. He also represents a highly encouraging phenomenon in world literature, which has been designated as the South American boom in literature. In an age when more and more often we hear that the novel is dying or dead, as the fish in the sea and life in Lake Erie, under the threat of *Menschendämmerung* it is worthwhile, I feel, to find such a countercurrent of fantasy and to bewingedly reflect thus upon the human lot awhile, and refreshed, thence to renew our efforts and even gingerly resume taking arms against a sea of troubles, and by opposing. . . .

García Márquez does not fail to deal with the dark forces, or give the impression that the life of human beings, one by one, should be ultimately tragic, but he also shows every moment pregnant with images and color and scent which ask to be arranged into patterns of meaning and significance while the moment lasts.

For: "You are the music / while it lasts." (T. S. Eliot)

It seems to me that García Márquez marries realism and objectivity with a most singular sense of the fantastic and delicious fabulating gifts, often employing surrealistic clairvoyance to paint frescoes full of moral indignation and anger protesting against oppression and violence, degradation and deceit. Extolling pride, he clearly depicts certain ludicrous, even grotesque aspects, such as quixotic bravery and intransigent single-mindedness of purpose. It is a joy to encounter a poet who revels in his seductive powers as García Márquez does. And yet he is so exact in his formulation and precise in his composition. In juxtaposing the twin elements of humor and tragedy García Márquez often achieves contrapuntal heights where language and image are thoroughly fused.

It is my opinion that the role of a literary award like the *BA* / Neustadt Prize is not only to crown the glorious achievements of the living past (or a dying one, even one that may be dead, for that matter) which has quite often been the case with the Nobel Prize, but also to reward and call attention to the remarkable things actually happening and bursting into creation now. I have the impression that in the case of García Márquez we have a writer at the height of his productivity, and I feel it would be fascinating to award this distinction while that creativity is at its full flow. A book such as *Cien años de soledad* (*One Hundred Years of Solitude*), a masterpiece, makes García Márquez indubitably one of the most important writers of fiction today.

In awarding García Márquez the *BA* / Neustadt Prize which he so well merits, I also feel that the great boom of South-American literature is saluted. This is a remarkable phenomenon of contemporary literature which revives optimism about the future of the novel. It is a fascinating body of literature that encompasses such varied and impressive writers as Asturias, Carpentier, Lezama Lima, Julio Cortázar, Vargas Llosa, Guimarães Rosa and Carlos Fuentes, and it induces me to revive the use of the word "South-American" instead of the term "Hispano-American" literature. Not forgetting the great poetry bred in this hemisphere, let me mention Neruda and Octavio Paz. Most of those just mentioned would also qualify for the present prize, but we should bear in mind that two of them have already been given the Nobel Prize, making it an act of redundancy to heap other prizes upon them.

García Márquez has invented a fantastic imaginary country of his own with its pertinent mythology of persons and events, recurrent in all his books, linked by allusion, with themes taken up and carried from one book to the other and elaborated upon, causing García Márquez's mythological world to emerge and expand, addicting readers to a fantasy and humor that titillates the imagination and makes the reader eager for more. Nor should we forget its ubiquitous poetry.

Reykjavík, Iceland

Novelist, short-story writer, poet, essayist, and translator **Thor Vilhjálmsson** *(1925–2011) was a leading exponent of Icelandic modernism. His awards included the Nordic Council Literature Prize and the Swedish Academy Nordic Prize.*

FRANCIS PONGE
THE 1974 LAUREATE

Francis Ponge (1899–1988) was a French essayist and poet. He was born in Montpellier and studied at the world-renowned Sorbonne. His first poems were published as early as 1923, and it would be through these publications that he introduced his distinct poetic style. His style of prose poetry (he often referred to this style as *proêms*) features meticulous descriptions of natural, everyday objects in lyric prose form. Ponge's collections of poetry include *La Rage de l'expression* (1952; Eng. *Mute Objects of Expression*), *Pour un Malherbe* (1965), *Le Savon* (1967; Eng. *Soap*, 1969), and *La Fabrique du Pré* (1971; Eng. *The Making of the Pré*, 1978). In 2005 Gallimard Press published *Pages d'atelier, 1917–1982*, a text encompassing Ponge's entire life's work, including some pieces that had previously never been published. In addition to the Neustadt Prize, Ponge received the French National Poetry Prize in 1981 and the Grand Prix of the Société des Gens de Lettres in 1985.

It is . . . rare to find a university which dedicates itself to and gives what is necessary for culture, for something which is probably more important than sports and does not risk becoming an opiate of the young.

—Francis Ponge

Master of the Still Life in Poetry
Michel Butor

Francis Ponge is certainly one of the greatest living poets. His specialty is the prose poem in the tradition of Baudelaire, Mallarmé, Jules Renard and Paul Claudel. The subject matter is always very commonplace—ordinary things or landscapes—and the idea is not only to describe but to extract a learning, a wisdom from the contemplation of nature. So he writes various kinds of prose fables in many ways reminiscent of Lafontaine. He can be called the master of the still life in poetry; but in that still life, the work, the effort of the painter is always reflected. Each poem, then, is a meditation upon life and art, and especially upon language. His prose style, extremely rich and diverse, is also very controlled, always chaste ("châtié" as we say in French); he is in that regard typically French.

His quiet influence has been decisive on three periods of French literature: existentialism (one remembers the essay of Sartre in *Situations*), the nouveau roman (with the still-life concern) and *Tel Quel* (with the linguistic trend). And through these movements, of course, he has been influential in all the important literatures of the world today. Ponge tries to be as classical as possible, as is quite manifest in a first reading of his book on Malherbe, but he cannot help being adventurous, and the result is that his experimentation is always at once daring and deeply justified, discreet and decisive. He has, as could have been predicted, given wonderful examples of the art of the book, of the way to handle its physical components. Of course he is a first-class essayist on painting, in the tradition of Claudel and Breton, but here again he is more restrained and delicate than they.

All his works were originally collected in three volumes called *Le grand recueil* (lyres, méthodes, pièces), but a first tome was later added, *Tome premier,* in which we find his earliest publications, the ones he may consider youthful pieces (though they are not); and it's there that we find what is today his best-known collection: *Le parti pris des choses (Taking the Side of Things)*. Subsequently, a fifth volume has appeared, called *Nouveau recueil*. There are also a radio-script called *Le savon*, a book explaining how he tried to write a book about Malherbe for a commercial series ("Ecrivains de Toujours," Éditions du Seuil) and couldn't, and a very intensive and meandering meditation about the fact of writing, *Pour un Malherbe*. Finally, I would mention *La fabrique du pré* (published in the beautiful series "Les Sentiers de la Création" by Albert Skira), one of Ponge's most interesting innovations in the art of bookmaking, which includes all the stages of manufacture of the piece in *Nouveau recueil* called "The Prairie."

Translation from the French by Ivar Ivask

French novelist, poet, and essayist **Michel Butor** *(1926–2016) was the 1981 Puterbaugh Fellow at the University of Oklahoma (see* WLT, *Spring 1982). He received many literary awards for his work, including the Prix Renaudot and the Grand Prix of the Académie Française.*

What Is Necessary for Culture
Francis Ponge

Merci beaucoup, thank you very much. I am very moved. This is a great day for me. Perhaps it is because I have been enclosed within *my* own language that I am listening now, hearing encomiums, compliments and receiving praise and an important prize, in a language that I cannot understand. I am not saying that there is a lesson to be learned here. I think that it is excellent to know many languages, but I am also convinced that *we* work amidst our ignorances.

One must work, defend oneself against too much knowledge and enclose one-self in one's language.

Now I would like to convey my emotion, my gratitude. This gratitude—how shall I put it—is very complex, because I owe this honor and this award to the University of Oklahoma and to *Books Abroad,* to the chairman of the jury, to the jury itself, naturally, and to the Neustadt family who have made it possible for this prize to become something perfectly magnificent. It is so rare to find this combination that I do not know how to express myself. It is certainly extraordinary that almost fifty years ago the University of Oklahoma decided to support a publication like *Books Abroad* and to continue supporting it. With Mr. Ivask's assumption of the editorship came the creation of this prize, which is so original and so unlike any other in the conditions of the deliberations, the jury which is renewed with each prize, and all the other very original things connected with it. This initiative is truly extraordinary, as is the family who supports it by playing the role one would expect of a truly cultured Maecenas, that is to say, of one who has a very devoted interest in activities other than sports. Naturally I am not against sports. I am very capable of liking them. I was even a high-jump champion in the French military and a semi-finalist in the 400 meters. I like sports.

It is, however, rare to find a university which dedicates itself to and gives what is necessary for culture, for something which is probably more important than sports and does not risk becoming an opiate of the young. I am not saying that sports are an opiate. But I think that one must also know "Mens sana in corpore sano." Both are good. It is in a healthy body that the mind becomes clear. Now, I have talked too much and I have spoken in a way that many people may find clumsy, but it is the clumsiness of sincere emotion. Thank you, I am too moved to say more.

Translation from the French by Jo Ann Chesnut

from "Notes toward a 'Francis Ponge in Norman,'" by Ivar Ivask
Books Abroad 48, no. 4 (Autumn 1974): 647–51

ELIZABETH BISHOP
THE 1976 LAUREATE

Elizabeth Bishop (1911–1979) was born in Worcester, Massachusetts. Her father died when she was very young, and as a result of the heartbreak, her mother was committed to an institution in 1916. Bishop never reunited with her mother and was subsequently raised by her grandparents. Though she dabbled with poetry while in school, Bishop left home to study music composition at Vassar College in 1929. After suffering a bout of stage fright, she changed her focus to English literature. Following her graduation from college, Bishop spent the rest of her life traveling, writing poetry, and teaching at various colleges around the United States. Her body of work includes the poetry collections *North & South* (1946), *A Cold Spring* (1956), and Farrar, Straus, and Giroux's "definitive edition," *Poems* (2011). In addition to the 1976 Neustadt Prize, Bishop was honored with the American Academy of Arts and Letters Award in 1950, the Pulitzer Prize for Poetry in 1956, and the National

Book Award for Poetry in 1970. From 1949 to 1950 she served as Poet
Laureate of the United States.

I find it extremely gratifying that, after having spent most of my life timorously pecking for subsistence along coastlines of the world, I have been given this recognition from so many different countries, but also from Norman, Oklahoma, a place so far inland.

—Elizabeth Bishop

The Optical Magic of Elizabeth Bishop
Marie-Claire Blais

Elizabeth Bishop is my choice for the *Books Abroad* award because to me she is one of the finest living poets, well known in the United States but not sufficiently recognized internationally. The body of her work is relatively small, yet one cannot read a single line either of her poetry or prose without feeling that a real poet is speaking, one whose sense of life is as delicately and finely strung as a Stradivarius, whose eye is both an inner and an outer eye. The outer eye sees with marvelous objective precision, the vision is translated into quite simple language, and this language with the illuminated sharpness of an object under a microscope works an optical magic, slipping in and out of imagery, so that everything seen contains the vibration of meaning on meaning.

One scarcely knows how to choose an example, there are so many. In "The Armadillo," for instance, there is the baby rabbit on whose peaceful world a fire balloon falls: "So soft!—a handful of intangible ash / with fixed, ignited eyes." Bishop makes such an image stand for a whole world of violence, vulnerability, helpless terror and protest. One cannot read the poem without quivering with a sense of the pain inherent in every form of beauty. Or she can say something that seems to mean exactly what it says, such as "we are driving to the interior," in "Arrival at Santos," although we have been prepared earlier by "Oh, tourist, / is this how this country is going to answer you" for the idea that every great personal change is a country waiting to be explored in its interior.

Yet Bishop is not personal as Lowell or Plath or Berryman is personal. Everything we know about her from her poetry comes through images that transform her particular suffering or loneliness or longing into archetypal states of being. "Four Poems," for example, is a sequence about the pain of the loss of love in which there is a flow of energy between the interior and exterior landscapes, the latter imitating the shape, color and anguish of the former. Somehow Bishop performs the miracle of fusion without ever altering her exterior truth. The fourth stanza makes one think of Donne in its mingling of physical and metaphysical, in the preciseness of the last lines: "a separate peace beneath / within if never with." No poet has ever spoken more concisely of the state of loving someone who is no longer there, of willing good to crystallize out of the pain.

Much of Bishop's poetry is the result of this struggle for accommodation with what is intolerable in life. Some poets turn their struggle to rage and hate, but she has arrived at a kind of pure nostalgia that is both past and present and at the peace "beneath" and "within" (but not necessarily "with") which I consider essential to great poetry.

Montreal

Marie-Claire Blais *(b. 1939) is a French Canadian novelist, poet, and playwright. Her many honors include the Governor General's Award and two Guggenheim Fellowships.*

The Ecstasies of Elizabeth Bishop
John Ashbery

To call Elizabeth Bishop a writer's writer is to pay her an ambiguous compliment. We all know about writers' writers, though we are perhaps incapable of really defining that term. But we perhaps do feel, even as we say it admiringly, that it somehow diminishes the writer. Should he be placed so far above the mass of readers, not to mention the mass of writers? Mightn't such exaltation be harmful for him, even taking into account the fact that he himself hasn't asked for it and may not know precisely what to do with it?

To call Elizabeth Bishop a writer's writer's writer, as I once did in a review of her *Collected Poems*, is perhaps to compound the audacity of the compliment, to imply that her writing has sophistication—that somehow unfortunate state of felicity in whose toils most of us wallow from time to time even as we struggle to cast them off. Yet this is the first thing that strikes me about Miss Bishop's unique position among American poets, one might even say among American writers. That is, the extraordinarily intense loyalty her work inspires in writers of every sort—from poets like myself, sometimes considered a harebrained, homegrown surrealist whose poetry defies even the rules and logic of surrealism, and from a whole generation of young experimental poets to experimenters of a different sort and perhaps of a steadier eye, such as Robert Duncan and James Tate, and to poet-critics of undeniable authority like Marianne Moore, Randall Jarrell, Richard Wilbur and Robert Lowell. It shouldn't be a criticism leveled at Miss Bishop that her mind is capable of inspiring and delighting minds of so many different formations. We must see it as her strength, a strength whose singularity almost prevents us from seeing it.

I first read Elizabeth Bishop's book *North & South* when it was published in 1946, and I had the experience in the very first poem, "The Map," of being drawn into a world that seemed as inevitable as "the" world and as charged with the possibilities of pleasure as the contiguous, overlapping world of poetry. Here, as in so many of her poems, the very materials—ink and paper—seemed to enlarge the horizons of the poem as they simultaneously called it back to the constricting dimensions of the page, much as a collage by Schwitters or Robert Motherwell triumphs over its prosaic substance by cultivating its ordinariness and the responses it can strike in our minds, where in a sense everything is ordinary, everything happens in a perpetual present which is a collage of objects and our impressions of them. [...]

In the last line ("More delicate than the historians' are the map-makers' colors") of this first poem in her first collection Elizabeth Bishop has, I think, given us the nucleus from which the dazzling variety of her poetry will evolve. Like the highest kind of poetic idea, it presents itself in the form of a paradox. How could the map-makers' colors be more delicate than the historians'?

How could the infinity of nuances and tones which is finally transformed into history, a living mosaic of whatever has happened and is happening now, prove more delicate—and not in the sense of softness or suavity but in the sense of a rigorously conceived mathematical instrument—than the commercial colors of maps in an atlas, which are the product, after all, of the expediencies and limitations of a mechanical process? Precisely because they are what is given to us to see, on a given day in a given book taken down from the bookshelf from some practical motive.

As the critic David Kalstone has said, Bishop's poems "both describe and set themselves at the limits of description. . . . Details are also boundaries for Miss Bishop. . . . Whatever radiant glimpses they afford, they are also set at the vibrant limits of our descriptive powers. [The poems] show us what generates that precarious state, and what surrounds us. 'From this the poem springs,' Wallace Stevens remarks, 'that we live in a place that is not our own and, much more, not ourselves, and hard it is in spite of blazoned days.' Miss Bishop writes under that star, aware of the smallness and dignity of human observation and contrivance. She sees with such a rooted, piercing vision, so realistically because she has never taken our presence in the world as totally real."

It is this continually renewed sense of discovering the strangeness, the unreality of our reality at the very moment of becoming conscious of it as reality, that is the great subject for Elizabeth Bishop. The silhouette of Norway unexpectedly becomes the fleeing hare it resembles; the names of cities conquer mountains; Labrador is yellow on the map not by chance but because the Eskimo has oiled it so as to make it into a window for an igloo; the universe is constantly expanding into vast generalizations that seem on the point of taking fire with meaning and contracting into tiny particulars whose enormous specific gravity bombards us with meaning from another unexpected angle. [. . .]

In a group of memorable poems about Brazil, Miss Bishop, like Darwin whom she admires, has sought not so much to come to grips with the frightening, teeming discipline of nature as it can be experienced raw in the South American landscape as to let herself be permeated and perhaps ultimately ordered by the lesson of that swarming order. Speaking of what the act of writing might be, she has said: "Dreams, works of art, (some) glimpses of the always-more-successful surrealism of everyday life, unexpected moments of empathy (is it?), catch a peripheral vision of whatever it is one can never really see full-face but that seems enormously important. I can't believe we are wholly irrational—and I do admire Darwin—but reading Darwin one admires the beautiful solid case being built up out of his endless, heroic observations, almost unconscious or automatic—and then comes a sudden relaxation, a forgetful phrase, and one feels that strangeness of his undertaking, sees the lonely young man, his eye fixed on facts and minute details, sinking or sliding giddily off into the unknown. What one seems to want in art, in experiencing it, is the same thing that is necessary for its creation, a self-forgetful, perfectly useless concentration"—a formulation not unlike Gauguin's "placing oneself in front of nature and dreaming." Only out of such "perfectly useless concentration" can emerge the one thing that is useful for us: our coming to know ourselves as the necessarily inaccurate transcribers of the life that is always on the point of coming into being.

In many of her poems Bishop installs herself as an open-minded, keen-eyed, even somewhat caustic observer of the life that is about to happen, speaking in a pleasant, chatty vernacular tone which seeks in no way to diminish the enormity of it, but rather to focus on it calmly and unpoetically. In the three short prose poems spoken from the point of view of three creatures much lower on the scale of human consciousness—"Giant Toad," "Strayed Crab," "Giant Snail"—she gives us the mystery of awareness as filtered through the mystification of an elemental eye that is being steeped in it to the point of bemused utterance. [...]

In another poem where, as in "The Map," Miss Bishop shows a series of pictures which are sometimes illustrations in an old gazetteer (the poem is entitled "Over 2000 Illustrations and a Complete Concordance") and sometimes real scenes remembered from an actual voyage—memories and illustrations overlap inextricably here—she elaborates the dilemma of perception versus understanding in a sustained, almost painfully acute argument that is one of the summits of her poetry. "Thus should have been our travels:

/ serious, engravable," she begins. But "The Seven Wonders of the World are tired / and a touch familiar, but the other scenes, / innumerable, though equally sad and still, / are foreign." Throughout the poem, which dips freely back and forth from a steel-etched "Holy Land" to the coast of Nova Scotia to Rome to Mexico to Marrakesh, we are never sure that the landscape we are in is the real world or the "engravable" one. Finally travel, the movement on which so much of her poetry hinges, dissolves into a bewildering swarm of particulars.

Everything only connected by "and" and "and."
Open the book. (The gilt rubs off the edges
of the pages and pollinates the fingertips.)
Open the heavy book. Why couldn't we have seen
this old Nativity while we were at it?
—the dark ajar, the rocks breaking with light,
an undisturbed, unbreathing flame,
colorless, sparkless, freely fed on straw,
and, lulled within, a family with pets,
—and looked and looked our infant sight away.

In the almost twenty years since I first read this poem I have been unable to exhaust the ambiguities of the last line, and I am also convinced that it somehow contains the clue to Elizabeth Bishop's poetry. Just as the crumbling gilt of the books seems, disturbingly, to pollinate our fingers, endow them fleetingly with life, so is flame—freely fed on straw (in the illustration)—colorless, sparkless, unbreathing and undisturbed. It would have been nice, at this point, to have seen the nativity, and not only to have seen it but to have participated in it to the point of self-effacement—to have looked our infant sight away.

David Kalstone has glossed the line thoughtfully and pointed out the similarity to a line in another key poem in Bishop's oeuvre, "The Imaginary Iceberg," where she describes the monstrous perfection of the iceberg as "a scene a sailor'd give his eyes for," mentioning that both lines convey a mysterious yearning to stop observing, which they also guard against. "What will it mean," he asks, "to look and look our infant sight away?" Where or when is away? Is it a measureless absorption in the scene? Or on the contrary, a loss of powers, as in "to waste away"? Or a welcome relinquishment, a return to "infant" sight, keeping its Latin root of "speechless"?

It is no doubt all these things, and a perfect summation of the poet's act—the looking so intense that it becomes something like death or ecstasy, both at once perhaps. Behind the multiple disguises, sometimes funny, sometimes terrifyingly unlike anything human, that the world assumes in Elizabeth Bishop's poetry, this moment of almost-transfiguration is always being tracked to its lair, giving the work a disturbing reality unlike anything else in contemporary poetry.

Brooklyn College, CUNY

John Ashbery *(1927–2017) was the author of more than twenty books of poetry and served as a Chancellor of the Academy of American Poets. His many honors included the Pulitzer Prize, a National Book Award, and the Bollingen Prize.*

The Inland Coast of Recognition
Elizabeth Bishop

Thank you, Mrs. Neustadt, President Sharp, Mr. Ivask, and Mr. Ashbery. The night before I left Boston to come here, I had dinner at a Chinese restaurant. I thought you might be interested in hearing the fortune I found in my fortune cookie. Here it is. It says: YOUR FINANCIAL CONDITION WILL IMPROVE CONSIDERABLY.

However, I don't want to express my gratitude *only* for the "improvement" in my "financial condition," grateful as I am for that. Mr. Ivask has selected a poem called "Sandpiper" to be printed on the program today, and when I saw that poem, rather old now, I began to think: Yes, all my life I have lived and behaved very much like that sandpiper—just running along the edges of different countries and continents, "looking for something." I have always felt I couldn't *possibly* live very far inland, away from the ocean; and I *have* always lived near it, frequently in sight of it. Naturally I know, and it has been pointed out to me, that most of my poems are geographical, or about coasts, beaches and rivers running to the sea, and most of the titles of my books are geographical too: *North & South, Questions of Travel* and one to be published this year, *Geography III*.

The first time I came to Norman, Oklahoma—in 1973—it was the farthest I had ever been inland in my life. I enjoyed myself very much on that first visit, and of course I am enjoying myself on this second, and very special, visit. I find it extremely gratifying that, after having spent most of my life timorously pecking for subsistence along coastlines of the world, I have been given this recognition from so many different countries, but also from Norman, Oklahoma, a place so far inland. Thank you again.

Norman, Oklahoma
April 9, 1976

CZESŁAW MIŁOSZ
THE 1978 LAUREATE

Czesław Miłosz (1911–2004) was a poet, writer, and translator born in the village of Szetejnie in a district that today is part of Lithuania. His first book of poetry was published in 1934. After World War II, which he spent in Warsaw, Miłosz defected to Paris in 1951, and the Communist government of Poland banned his works. In 1960 he immigrated to the United States, where he began teaching at the University of California at Berkeley. It was not until the Iron Curtain fell that Miłosz was able to return to Poland, and he split the remaining years of his life between Poland and the United States. Among his very long list of works, the most well known are *Zniewolony umysł* (1953; Eng. *The Captive Mind*), *Zdobycie władzy* (1955; Eng. *The Seizure of Power*), *The Witness of Poetry* (1983), and *Nieobjęta ziemia* (1984; Eng. *The Unattainable Earth*, 1986). Miłosz's *Selected and Last Poems, 1931–2004* (Ecco Press), selected by Robert Hass and Anthony Milosz, were published in 2011. In addition to the Neustadt Prize, Miłosz received the Nobel Prize in Literature in 1980. Additionally, 2011 was named "The Miłosz Year," and many literary festivals were organized around the world in honor of Miłosz's contributions to world literature.

The Neustadt literary prize belongs too, in my opinion, to those things which should not exist, because they are against the dark and immutable order of the world.

—Czesław Miłosz

The Whispered Guilt of the Survivor
Joseph Brodsky

I have no hesitation whatsoever in stating that Czesław Miłosz is one of the greatest poets of our time, perhaps the greatest. Even if one strips his poems of the stylistic magnificence of his native Polish (which is what translation inevitably does) and reduces them to the naked subject matter, we still find ourselves confronting a severe and relentless mind of such intensity that the only parallel one is able to think of is that of the biblical characters—most likely Job. But the scope of the loss experienced by Miłosz was—not only from purely geographical considerations—somewhat larger.

Miłosz received what one might call a standard East European education, which included, among other things, what's known as the Holocaust, which he predicted in his poems of the late thirties. The wasteland he describes in his wartime (and some postwar) poetry is fairly literal: it is not the unresurrected Adonis that is missing there, but concrete millions of his countrymen. What toppled the whole enterprise was that his land, after being devastated physically, was also stolen from him and, proportionately, ruined spiritually. Out of these ashes emerged poetry which did not so much sing of outrage and grief as whisper of the guilt of the survivor. The core of the major themes of Miłosz's poetry is the unbearable realization that a human being is not able to grasp his experience, and the more that time separates him from this experience, the less become his chances to comprehend it. This realization alone extends—to say the least—our notion of the human psyche and casts quite a remorseless light on the proverbial interplay of cause and effect.

It wouldn't be fair, however, to reduce the significance of Miłosz's poetry to this theme. His, after all, is a metaphysical poetry which regards the things of this world (including language itself) as manifestations of a certain superior realm, miniaturized or magnified for the sake of our perception. The existential process for this poet is neither enigma nor explanation, but rather is symbolized by the test tube: the only thing which is unclear is what is being tested—whether it is the endurance of man in terms of applied pain, or the durability of pain itself.

Czesław Miłosz is perfectly aware that language is not a tool of cognition but rather a tool of assimilation in what appears to be a quite hostile world— unless it is employed by poetry, which alone tries to beat language at its own game and thus to bring it as close as possible to real cognizance. Short-cutting or, rather, short-circuiting the analytical process, Miłosz's poetry releases the reader from many psychological and purely linguistic traps, for it answers not the question "how to live" but "for the sake of what" to live. In a way, what this poet preaches is an awfully sober version of stoicism which does not ignore reality, however absurd and horrendous, but accepts it as a new norm which a human being has to absorb without giving up any of his fairly compromised values.

New York

Born in Leningrad, **Joseph Brodsky** *(1940–1996) was awarded the Nobel Prize in Literature in 1987. He immigrated to the United States in 1972 and taught at several universities, including Mount Holyoke, Yale, Columbia, Cambridge, and Michigan. He was named U.S. Poet Laureate in 1991.*

Against the Dark and Immutable Order of the World
Czesław Miłosz

One of the essential attributes of poetry is its ability to give affirmation to things of this world. And I think with sadness of the negation which has so strongly marked the poetry of my century and my own poetry. When our historical and individual existence is filled with horror and suffering, we tend to see the world as a tangle of dark, indifferent forces. And yet human greatness and goodness and virtue have always been intervening in that life which I lived, and my writings have some merits to the extent that they are not deprived of a feeling of gratitude.

Logically, I should not have preserved my identity as a poet faithful to his native tongue throughout thirty years of exile. I explain it by a mysterious influence of a land where I was born, Lithuania, and of a city where I went to school and to university, Wilno. My high school teachers have been present in my poetry, either invoked by name or as invisible guests. It is probable that I would not have become a poet without what I received from them. Particularly, I was shaped by seven years of Latin and by exercises in translating Latin poetry in class. If the names of those teachers are forgotten, I, for one, remain their grateful pupil.

For many years I have been meditating upon zones of silence covering many events, deeds and names of our age. To quote myself: "I would have related, had I known how, everything which a single memory can gather in praise of men." *Had I known how*—in fact, writing praise is a struggle against the main current of modern literature. But now, in the last quarter of the twentieth century, looking back to the time of war and political terror, I think less of crime and baseness and more and more of human capability of the purest love and sacrifice. Had I to live much longer, I would search for means of expressing my humble respect for so many anonymous and heroic men and women.

The Neustadt literary prize belongs too, in my opinion, to those things which should not exist, because they are against the dark and immutable order of the world. Normally, it should be given to film stars or at least authors of best sellers. In my case it goes to a poet who can be read only in translation and whose poems do not translate well because of many cultural-linguistic allusions in their very texture. It goes to an author who, measured by the market standard, is a permanent flop and is read by a very small public only. The decision of founding such a prize seems to me a wise one, not only because I am a recipient, but because it favors all those who in the game of life bet on improbability.

The endeavors of Ivar Ivask are an example of human will interceding against the normal and the usual. There is no reason for survival of such a magazine as *World Literature Today* and no reason for the University of Oklahoma's attracting the attention of literary communities all over the world, as it does, because of that periodical and an international prize. Yet the order of the world has to inscribe that fact as one of its components.

Norman, Oklahoma
April 7, 1978

JOSEF ŠKVORECKÝ
THE 1980 LAUREATE

Josef Škvorecký (1924–2012) was a Czech author and publisher. After receiving his PhD in philosophy, Škvorecký began to write novels, which were banned by the Communist government of Czechoslovakia. Many of his works espoused democratic ideals that threatened the state, but his novels helped to usher in the Prague Spring in 1968. When the Russian army invaded Czechoslovakia that same year, Škvorecký and his wife sought asylum in Canada, where the pair founded a publishing house that printed banned Czech and Slovak books. Škvorecký resided in Canada for the remainder of his life. Among his numerous published works are novels, novellas, essays, and screenplays. His novels include *Zbabělci* (1958; Eng. *The Cowards*, 1970), *Lvíče* (1969; Eng. *Miss Silver's Past*, 1974), *Tankový prapor* (1969; Eng. *The Republic of Whores*, 1992), and *Příběh inženýra lidských duší* (1977; Eng. *The Engineer of Human Souls*, 1984).

I feel that the prize granted to me honors all my literary rivals and dear friends in Czechoslovakia, people who in conditions inconceivable to writers in the West have not abandoned their trade, which is, as Hemingway once said, to tell the truth.

—Josef Škvorecký

Josef Škvorecký, the Literary King
Arnošt Lustig

Ladies and gentlemen, it is a privilege for me to speak to you briefly about the winner of the 1980 Neustadt Prize, one of the best contemporary Czech writers, Josef Škvorecký. This is a very pleasant occasion. Škvorecký, who is here today to receive the prize in person, was born in Czechoslovakia fifty-five years ago and is living now in Canada, in his new home, like many exiles from Central Europe, where the storms of wars and revolutions come sooner and last longer. Škvorecký is the author of more than a dozen books, five screenplays and some beautiful poems. He is also the author of one of the best-known books on the golden age of Czech cinema, the new film wave of the sixties, and is a broadcaster for the Voice of America to Czechoslovakia on contemporary American literature, just as he was a translator of American culture to his people while he lived in Prague. He is also our colleague, a professor of English.

Like Franz Kafka, Josef Škvorecký is a man who writes in a minor language and has become, in translation, the spokesman for the mind and soul of people in far greater numbers than the original language could have reached. I would like to discuss with you some of the reasons why Škvorecký—as the critic of the *New Yorker*, George Steiner, put it, "a novelist of the first rank"— has become a writer of world importance.

As I was looking for a key for presenting the personality and work of Josef Škvorecký, another great Czech artist came to mind: the world-famous composer Antonín Dvořák, about whom Škvorecký is currently writing a novel and who was the composer of the *Symphony from the New World*. I like this comparison not only because Dvořák lived here in America from 1892 to 1895, but also because he was so much in love with the inspiration he found in America, like African American music or the cultures of the American Indians. This was the principal approach of Dvořák. While receptive to the influences of the world and able to open his mind and soul to everything, he also was able to absorb it and then to express it in his own fashion, in a creative amalgam, the unique magic of art in his very personal way. He expressed his view of the world in a manner never used either before him or after. While his way of looking at things was universal, cultivated by the world, it was also very original. His expression was undeniably his own, and yet was Czech at the same time.

Škvorecký too is open to all the influences of the world with his entire heart and soul, and still remains undeniably original, very Czech, very personal. There is an Italian proverb which states that a man who changes the stars above his head doesn't change his nature. Perhaps he enriches his point of view. Perhaps he is able to see more stars, and from a more important point of view. And sometimes, as in the case of Škvorecký, he can report what he has seen.

Škvorecký is a writer from a country which begat and gave birth to writers like Comenius, Franz Kafka, Jaroslav Hašek, and Karel Čapek, or writers such as Vladislav Vančura, Jiří Langer, and Jiří Weil and many others—some good and some very, very good. They say that Prague is a very good place for writers, that there is something which cannot die, in spite of the fact that it—from time to time—cannot even live. And in that group of writers, Škvorecký means to Czech literature something akin to what the name Joseph Conrad means to English literature, Gunter Grass to contemporary German writing or J. D. Salinger to American letters.

In the late fifties Škvorecký became known in Prague overnight. This sounds a little as if it were a phrase made for the American public, but here we know that an overnight success is never really overnight, that it is a result of talent, hard work, and, only in the last place, luck as well. The scandal of Škvorecký was also similar to French history's case of Gustave Flaubert, who was tried because of his offense to the double standards of French society, whereby one could not behave at home as in public. But Flaubert's Emma Bovary was an innocent woman compared to Škvorecký. The literary perversions of Josef Škvorecký were of a different nature.

Nothing can match the very originality or, if you wish, the very absurdity of the literary conditions in the empire of the greatest hope on earth before it becomes the greatest disappointment. While the mighty literary establishment was roaring with official optimism and revolutionary promises, with the romance of the future based on the heroic past, Škvorecký, like a young, inexperienced boy from the countryside, came to Prague to publish his first novel. It was a personal account of the revolution, numbering 370 printed pages and bearing the title *The Cowards*. There was not a book in Prague more discussed than this one. The English television film *Death of a Princess* and the resulting Saudi Arabian protest are only a faint echo of what the Czech "sheiks" did to Škvorecký s book. The nation was divided overnight. The Politburo could not believe that a single book would do it to them.

Škvorecký wrote in his first—and, as many say even today, his best—book about eight days in the revolution against the Germans in a small Czech city, about a group of boys and girls who were quite happy that with the end of the war everything else was going to burn out, to be changed, and that they would be able to start a new life. He did not speak about the idols. He did not pay attention or even polite honor to those who were now in charge. His hero and the storyteller, in one voice, expressed his lack of understanding of the world, built and managed so absurdly by the fathers. He alone had the courage to say that he didn't understand, that he didn't know. This hero was not easy to understand. He was more complicated than the heroes of Czech literature before him. That was the crime of Josef Škvorecký.

The book was, of course, banned immediately. The fate of the young writer was up in the air. Škvorecký was described as a counterrevolutionary, as an anti-Soviet, petit-bourgeois element, as a man who, in his book, says more about himself than about his hero, about his own approaches, his own qualities. He was described as an agent of decadence, an agent provocateur, and the official press labeled him everything from a conventional to an immoral writer, a perverted author who tries to turn the clock of history backward. To be described as foreign to the spirit of people was an accusation whose equivalent in prison terms could be as much as a life sentence, if not worse. Today this is all evidence of Škvorecký's courage, of his honesty, of his democratic feeling. When he is described today in the *New York Times*, the

Washington Post or *Le Monde* as "a fearless writer, a symbol of free writing," it must be traced to his very first book, *The Cowards.*

Fortunately, Škvorecký was luckier than his book. After he had become a "non-person," the better times of the era of liberalization enabled him to publish his "Legend of Emöke," a beautiful story, so highly praised last year all over the world as one of the best novellas of our time. Some say that "Emöke" is about a chance a man gets only once in his life; others assert that it is a myth, a real legend, powerful and beautiful, that it is a book about courage, about the greatness and sacrifice of man, about his desire to be a man, about relating to a woman, which means relating to the entire world. It is a tale which imparts a feeling that man has a chance, that he may hope to change a bad life for a better one, that it is in his hands.

In all his books Škvorecký attacks the cowardice of life, the brutality of life, the smallness of life. What makes him such a good writer is his sense of tension, his awareness of the duty of a writer to write interestingly, with wit and suspense. The proof is his novel *Miss Silver's Past.* I like this book more than the others, and not only because it is a book about a lonely Jewish girl who, with the help of a man who now courts her beauty, challenges the postwar world alone, all her people killed and her family destroyed. Škvorecký was one of those writers with conscience, one who remembered Hitler's remark that what is Jewish is perverted and crippled, that the human conscience cripples the mind just as circumcision cripples the body.

Škvorecký wrote a beautiful story about Rebecca, "The Menorah." He did not look left, nor did he look right when searching for his themes. As a democrat with a writer's heart, he was always on the side of the underdog, and it was more than a statement when Škvorecký, a non-Jewish author, wrote in Prague about the Jewish children—of the approximately 15,000 living in Czechoslovakia before the war, only 100 survived. When the secretary general of an anti-Fascist organization in Czechoslovakia claimed that nobody in Prague was interested in glorifying those who went to their death without fighting, Škvorecký understood better than this official that it is somehow difficult for babies, for boys and girls without weapons, for old women to fight a German army which had defeated, in a few days, France, Poland and almost all the rest of Europe.

Škvorecký is a very creative person. It was a fitting choice that the judges voted to include him in a select field of writers such as Czesław Miłosz, Gabriel García Márquez, and Giuseppe Ungaretti. Not only is he rightly compared to those writers, but more, he has an extra sense of humor that is very Czech, unique, and is the core of what the established "sheiks" of socialist-realist literature fear most. Škvorecký not only makes us cry, but he makes us smile too. This is, in this crumbling world of ours, an essential contribution. He pays attention to the mysteries of life, and his observations of strange reality are marvelous. [...]

Ladies and gentlemen, I had ten reasons for nominating Josef Škvorecký for the 1980 Neustadt Prize. I was proud to do it. But I never quoted the letters of Graham Greene, and I would like to do this today.

7 October 1968

Dear Josef Škvorecký,

I have this moment finished reading *La Légende d'Emöke*. It is masterly and can stand comparison with Chekhov's *The Lady with the Dog*. *The Game in the Train* is magnificent, but perhaps the most moving phrase to me came at the end: "Cette indifférence qui est notre mère, notre salut, notre porte." Anyway it's a master work. I would be glad to have news of you. Are you going to England? I am told that Sir Gerald Barry has formed a committee to help Czech writers and intellectuals. He knows me and if you feel like communicating with him do use my name and say that I suggested it. I am dictating this letter to my secretary in England and I will ask her to add his address.

Yours ever,

/s/ Graham Greene

20 March 1974

My dear Škvorecký,

I've read the two stories you sent me and I shall now forward them on to Max Reinhardt. *The Bass Saxophone* I found superb—it made as great impression on me as a few years back *The Legend of Emöke. Pink Champagne* interested me less, but to make a volume it is certainly needed. Forgive a hasty line but I wanted to get a message off to you as quickly as possible and to sense my great admiration for the Saxophone.

Yours ever,

/s/ Graham Greene

I would like to add only a few comments. An award for Josef Škvorecký means an award for all of Czech literature: to that part of it which must be silent at home, and to her sister, the literature in exile. It is also proof that literature cannot be silenced. But it is not always so easy.

Literature is, unfortunately or fortunately, connected in our age with history, politics, philosophy, with everything in which man is involved. During Škvorecký's lifetime so many things have happened, and so many happened so close. A writer who comes from our country—which was given in appeasement by Chamberlain to Hitler in 1938, a country where children were listening to the news of how Mussolini was bravely defeating the barefooted Ethiopians with his tanks and how the Spanish Republic was lost because of Western indifference—the writer is up to his neck in politics. A writer in that part of the world has a taste of history involving human fate, like those children who are ill with a sickness that comes to them from their mothers' breasts without anyone's knowing it; years afterward, when they know, it is too late for a cure.

Why am I saying this? Because to listen to a writer means to know and maybe to be able to prevent. Kafka saw the penal colonies before they covered Europe like a plague. To recognize a writer sometimes takes a lifetime and sometimes centuries. Some writers, never discovered, disappear in the abyss of the forgotten, as does their work—sometimes in an abyss, sometimes in flames, sometimes in silence. The lives and works of some writers disappear so completely, it is as if they had never been alive, had never written. That is why recognition of a writer is so important—just like the conquest of a new continent, the finding of a secret treasure or the discovery of a new star.

There is an old proverb which states that a king who is not accepted by his people is not yet a king. Today Josef Škvorecký, the voice of Czech literature at home as in exile, opposed by the authorities in his native land and welcomed and loved by people abroad, is a king. Kings of literary realms are, contrary to other rulers, not dangerous to living creatures. They are threats only to the minds of those who claim the ownership of people as if it were the ownership of goods, those who—as in the dark times of history—are today trading and selling people for money, goods and political gain, especially writers. Literary kings do not kill their enemies; they do not kill people at all, with the exception of themselves.

Literary kings are, in comparison with the real kings of the world, more gentle, more silent, more generous, in spite of the fact that literary kings, like all kings, must fight from time to time. Josef Škvorecký is not one of those people who, by claiming that they are fighting the last battle of man, are ready to bury not only man but his world as well. It is a beautiful privilege to say that Josef Škvorecký is a winner today, and to know that he wins in the name of, and for, all of us. It must be marvelous to be a literary king. Thank you.

Norman, Oklahoma
May 17, 1980

The Jewish Czech writer **Arnošt Lustig** *(1926–2011) survived the Theresienstadt, Auschwitz, and Buchenwald concentration camps. After the Prague Spring (1968), he eventually immigrated to the United States, where he taught at American University in Washington, D.C., before returning to Prague after the Velvet Revolution (1989). The author of novels, short stories, plays, and screenplays, he was awarded the Karel Čapek Prize in 1996 and the Franz Kafka Prize in 2008.*

Truth-telling and Literary Freedom in Czechoslovakia
Josef Škvorecký

Twenty-two years ago, when my first novel *The Cowards* was published in Prague and a month later banned by the censor and confiscated from bookshops by the police, a well-orchestrated band of hired Communist Party critics pounced upon me, and at the very top of a long list of the sins and crimes I had allegedly committed in that novel, they placed the sin—or the crime—of individualism. It was indicative of the literary erudition of those critics that they deduced this individualism chiefly from the narrative mode I had chosen: the first-person singular. They had no notion of what is generally well known in the writers' trade, that the I-form is usually the least individualized of all forms, and that therefore the narrator is usually the least vivid character in the book.

This also presented an interesting paradox, which I am acutely aware of whenever I think back on the 1960s in Prague. At that time Czech literature was rapidly recovering from the almost mortal blow it was dealt by the imported socialist realism of the 1950s. Suddenly, against the collective background of hack writers who practiced that establishment literary method, a few magnificently individual authors began to appear. Along with the safely dead classics, people began once more to buy contemporary prose, and thus competition developed among those authors who had laid aside—or who had simply never adopted—that uniform mask of socialist realism. They were all able, at last, to show their own faces.

Yet—and here is the paradox—whenever I think of the 1950s, a decade branded by the establishment's notion of a collective *we*, it is always in terms of "I," whereas I never think of the 1960s, when individualism was flourishing, in any terms other than "we"—"we" referring to us Czech writers who, having painted our world in rosy hues for so long, desired to show the face of our native land and its people exactly as we saw them and loved them, without the pink makeup.

When I learned that I had been awarded the Neustadt Prize, that grand old notion of "we" came to mind, and my first thought was about my literary rivals from the sixties, those dear friends of mine: Václav Havel, who is now in prison and will remain there for another five years; Jiří Lederer, who once defended my *Cowards* and lost his job because of it, now just recently returned from four years in jail; Jiří Pištora, a poet who committed suicide after the Soviet divisions invaded my native land. And many others who are without work and cannot publish.

Why was I chosen? Why not one of them? Am I better than they are? And are they genuinely good in relation to the notoriety they have gained through persecution?

The cultural establishment of Czechoslovakia today is trying in every way it can to make cultivated westerners think that such writers are not good at all, but merely notorious; they would have you believe there is no such thing as a "Biafra of the spirit" in Czechoslovakia, as Aragon once wrote, or a "graveyard of culture," as Heinrich Böll has said. If you wish, the cultural attaché of the Czechoslovak Socialist Republic will willingly send you statistics that measure culture by the weight of paper used to make books and that try to overwhelm you with the number of books published by contemporary authors living in Prague.

It is extremely difficult to explain to westerners, who are separated from an understanding of the real situation by an ignorance of foreign languages that are far more widely used than Czech, just what kind of authors these people are. Nor do I claim that everyone who can publish legally in Prague today is an ordinary hack writer. But a kind of fanciful analogy occurred to me. Let us imagine that Mark Twain had written his *Huckleberry Finn* some thirty years before he did and tried to have it published in his native South. We must also imagine, however, that the southern slave-owners in the first half of the nineteenth century had a literary censorship equally as strict as today's socialist Czechoslovakia has. Mark Twain would undoubtedly have known that trying to publish, in a slave-owning society, a novel about the inhumanity of slavery would have been—as we might say today—unrealistic. But his great talent and the desire to write would remain. So instead of trying to publish that novel about the inhumanity of slavery, he would write another one instead, one, let's say, about the decline of table manners in the Deep South, about how people pick their teeth while eating and don't always hit the spittoon when they spit. No doubt it would be a very amusing, masterfully written and absolutely truthful humoresque about life in the slaveholding South.

The best novels coming out of Prague today are precisely of that type. The ones that do not get published, that are merely copied on typewriters for the *samizdat* Padlock Editions, are novels about the friendship of a poor white boy and an equally poor black slave. I flatter myself that even though my work can be published—because I live in the West—I still belong in a certain sense to those unpublished authors for whom human freedom is a more urgent literary theme than picking one's teeth. I feel that the prize granted to me honors all my literary rivals and dear friends in Czechoslovakia, people who in conditions inconceivable to writers in the West have not abandoned their trade, which is, as Hemingway once said, *to tell the truth.* The truth, that is, about Nigger Jim, and not about tobacco-chewers who can't hit a spittoon.

Norman, Oklahoma
May 17, 1980

OCTAVIO PAZ
THE 1982 LAUREATE

Octavio Paz (1914–1998) was born and raised in Mixcoac, part of present-day Mexico City. His family supported Emiliano Zapata, and after Zapata's assassination they were forced into exile in the United States. Paz was only nineteen when he published his first collection of poetry, entitled *Luna Silvestre* (1933). During his long career, Paz founded the literary journals *Barandal* (1932) and *Taller* (1938) and the magazines *Plural* (1970) and *Vuelta* (1975). In 1945 he began working as a diplomat for the Mexican government in such places as Paris, Tokyo, Geneva, and Mumbai. His travels influenced much of his work, and he published many of his books while working abroad. Paz's numerous collections of poetry include *Entre la piedra y la flor* (1941), *Piedra de sol* (1957; Eng. *Sun Stone*, 1991), and *Renga* (1972). Additionally, Paz wrote many essays, short stories, and plays, including *El laberinto de la soledad* (1950; Eng. *The Labyrinth of Solitude*, 1961), *Corriente alterna* (1967; Eng. *Alternating*

Current, 1973), and *La hija de Rappaccini* (1956). In addition to the
Neustadt Prize in 1982, Paz was awarded the 1981 Miguel de Cervantes
Prize and the Nobel Prize in Literature in 1990.

Considering all this, in the
convulsed and intolerant modern
world we inhabit, the Neustadt
Prize is an example of true
civilization.

—Octavio Paz

The Turning House
Octavio Paz

for Ivar and Astrid

There is a wooden house
on the plain of Oklahoma.
Each night the house turns
into an island of the Baltic Sea,
a stone that fell from a fabled sky.
Burnished by Astrid's glances,
ignited by Ivar's voice,
the stone slowly turns in the shadow:
it is a sunflower and burns.
                              A cat,
returned from Saturn,
goes through the wall and disappears
between the pages of a book.
The grass has turned into night,
the night has turned into sand,
the sand has turned into water.
                              Then
Ivar and Astrid lift up architectures
—cubes of echoes, weightless forms—
some of them called poems,
others drawings, others conversations
with friends from Málaga, Mexico
and other planets.
                    These forms
wander and have no feet,
glance and have no eyes,

speak and have no mouth.
          The sunflower
turns and does not move,
               the island
ignites and is extinguished,
                    the stone
flowers,
          the night closes,
the sky opens.
          Dawn
wets the lids of the plain.

(1982/83)

Translation from the Spanish by Ivar Ivask

Octavio Paz: The Poet as Philosopher
Manuel Durán

The poet Derek Walcott remarked recently, "The greatest writers have been at heart parochial, provincial in their rootedness. . . . Shakespeare remains a Warwickshire country boy; Joyce a minor bourgeois from Dublin, Dante's love of Florence was very intense. Hardy's place, of course, was rural Essex: 'I can understand / Borges's blind love for Buenos Aires, / How a man feels the veins of his city swell in his head' (Midsummer '81)."[1] There are many books and poems by Paz that proclaim his rootedness, his intimacy with Mexican traditions, landscapes, people. Books like *The Labyrinth of Solitude,* for instance, or *Posdata* could not have been written by anyone outside the mainstream of Mexican culture. No foreign observer could have given such books the impact and urgency they possess. Paz is not content with describing some of the deepest and most relevant aspects of Mexican psychology; he involves the reader in the system of values he describes because he is himself involved in it for better or for worse, inescapably. It is ancient Mexican culture with its circular patterns that molds a long poem such as *Sun Stone;* it is the experience of being an adolescent in and around Mexico City that imparts distinctive flavor to Paz's "Nocturno de San Ildefonso."

Yet very often at the conclusion of Paz's sustained efforts to explore his roots and the origins of his culture, a change of mood and of ideas begins to emerge. From the poet's direct and intimate experience he leads us toward a deeper knowledge of what it is to be a Mexican living and working in the present century, within a culture as tragic and fragmented as it is rich and complex. But the poet's experience allows him to express also much that belongs to our experience. His exploration of Mexican existential values permits him to open a door to an understanding of other countries and other cultures. What began as a slow, almost microscopic examination of self and of a single cultural tradition widens unexpectedly, becoming universal without sacrificing its unique characteristic.

This is a special gift, a gift few poets possess. The inescapable conclusion is that Paz belongs to a select group of poets who can expand the limits of poetry until they invade the realm of philosophy. Paz is a poetphilosopher, a philosophical poet. Such a gift has never been widespread. Among the classics, for instance, Lucretius would qualify, but not Catullus. Dante was a philosophical poet, and so were Shakespeare and Milton, Donne and Eliot. In each of these instances we find a persistent exploration of nature, of the place of human beings in nature. What is our place in the cosmos? Are we, as we often think in our pride, the masters of nature, the almost perfect creation of a protecting and loving God? Are we intruders barely tolerated? Are we, as Shakespeare claims in a somber moment, no more to the gods than flies are to wanton children, flies which they kill as a pastime? Or are we enveloped by the very same love which, as Dante explains, is the force that moves the Sun and the other stars? Philosophical poets may differ widely with respect to the answers they give to the riddles of life. What they have in common, however, is a mixture of curiosity and awe, and this is much more important than what separates them.

The philosopher-poet is always ready to travel with his mind and his body, through time and through space. Octavio Paz has traveled as widely as he has written, and as Anna Balakian has said, he "belongs to that new breed of humans, more numerous each day, who are freeing themselves of ethnic myopia and walking the earth as inhabitants of the planet, regardless of national origin or political preferences."[2]

It is entirely possible that all human beings are born poets, born philosophers, born scientists, but that circumstances and a poor education shrink or atrophy the imagination and the curiosity that would sustain such activities. Fortunately for us, Paz was a poet and a curious observer since childhood and has managed to retain a child's heart and vision. A sense of being open to the world was among his childhood's more precious gifts. Paz has said about himself:

> As a boy I lived in a place called Mixcoac, near the capital. We lived in a large house with a garden. Our family had been impoverished by the revolution and the civil war. Our house, full of antique furniture, books, and other objects, was gradually crumbling to bits. As rooms collapsed we moved the furniture into another. I remember that for a long time I lived in a spacious room with part of one of the walls missing. Some magnificent screens protected me inadequately from wind and rain. A creeper invaded my room. . . . A premonition of that surrealist exhibition where there was a bed lying in a swamp.[3]

I see in this room invaded by rain, wind and plants a symbol of the poet's career, always open to the wind coming from every direction of the compass, always exposed to the outside world and the forces of nature—a room quite the opposite of a fortress or an ivory tower. From this exposed vantage point the poet ventures forth. His goal is not only to see infinity in a grain of sand, as William Blake proposed, but at the same time to describe the texture and color of the grain of sand, to see its reflection in his eye—and ours.

Paz knows that human beings have many roots, not a single taproot, fibrous roots that connect them with many cultures, many pasts. The themes, meanings, images by which poetic imagination seeks to penetrate to the heart of reality—the permanence and mystery of human suffering, human hope, joy and wonder—reach the poet from many sources. The poet sees existence with the double vision of tragedy, the good and the evil forever mixed. He is constantly under strain, admitting dire realities and conscious of bleak possibilities. Yet he is aware that love, knowledge, art, poetry allow us to experience the unity and final identity of being.

Ultimately Paz as a poet is a master of language, yet one who recognizes that language is also our shaper and ruler. If the German philosopher Ernst Cassirer defined man as the animal who can create language and myths, we can also state that it is language, myths, poetry that have created man, that have made man into a speaking, mythmaking, poetry-writing animal. It is through language that Paz faces the world, sees the world as a unity, confronts the diversities of culture and explains their apparent oppositions and contradictions, their conjunctions and disjunctions, as different responses to the same identical questions. To understand is to see correspondences and patterns, structures of symmetry and dissymmetry, constellations of signs in space and in time—yet anything can be expressed and related through words. In Paz's manysplendored vision the poet is capable of flying through space and time, because like the magical monkey of Hindu legend, Hanumān, he has invented grammar and language.

From above, in his vertical flight, drunk with light and with love, the poet contemplates the fusion of opposites, the marriage of Heaven and Hell, the radiance of the void, the dark luminosity where life and death meet. The movements of planets, the patterns of seasons and nature, are circular, yet the circle becomes a spiral pointing toward vaster spaces where everything becomes possible, where I become the Other, where the labyrinth of mirrors fuses into a single blinding light. We learn to say "no" and "yes" at the same time, because through poetry we reach the certain knowledge that Becoming and Being are two facets of the same reality. As Paz describes it, "The spirit / Is an invention of the body / The body / An invention of the world / The world / An invention of the spirit" (*Blanco*).[4] Within this is language, poetic language, the language of myths and of passion that has made us what we are. Language is a huge shuttle going back and forth, weaving our world, and the poet is at the center of this operation. "By passion the world is bound, by passion too it is released," reads the epigraph from Buddhist tradition *(The Hevajra Tantra)* that frames what is perhaps Paz's most famous poem, *Blanco*. As a poet, Paz is the master of words. Word of passion, words of wisdom. They can create our ultimate vision; they can also erase it.

*

An English poet-philosopher, John Donne, wisely warns us that when we hear the bell toll for someone's death we should realize that it tolls for us, that someone else's death in a subtle but certain way diminishes us, partially kills us, for we are part and parcel of the fabric which this death unravels. I would like to point out a reverse situation: when a poet's work is heard, understood, applauded, it is a triumph for life, a celebration of Being, and therefore it is *our* victory, *our* glory, that is heard in the joyous pealing of the bell.

This celebration of Being is instinctively clear to the philosophical poet because he or she is often conscious of speaking, feeling, writing not only for himself or herself, but for all of us. Sympathy unites the philosophical poet to other human beings that he or she may not know and with whom he or she may superficially have little in common. A capacity for generalized feelings, visions, ideas is another feature of the philosophical poet that makes his or her voice different from the voices of other poets. The philosophical poet sees and describes a specific flower, a yellow rose or a purple iris, and at the same time there is a space in his mind, in his imagination, in his soul, where the rose and the iris come closer and closer to a perfect flower, the Platonic flower described by Mallarmé as "l'absente de tout bouquet"—the flower that is the essence of all flowers and therefore absent from any real bouquet.

Unless the description given above sounds too precious, we should agree on a few basic points. Aristotle stated that there can be no scientific description, no scientific knowledge, until and unless it is generalized description, knowledge, statement. The efforts of the pre-Socratic Greek philosophers were already moving in the same direction. Poetry is a personal statement, the most individualistic and intimate statement if we mean by *poetry* what most readers accept as its basic definition: that is to say, lyric poetry. How can any writer bridge the gap between the individual vision and the generalized overview of our world?

Octavio Paz gives us the answer in almost every one of his books. An analysis of his techniques as related to both his style and his ideas would become lengthy if applied to all his texts. It is reasonable to choose two individual texts, one old and one relatively new, one a prose book and the other a poem. The first is perhaps Paz's most celebrated and widely read book, his obvious best seller, *The Labyrinth of Solitude*, whereas the second, chosen in order to show how Paz is a consistently philosophical poet, is *Blanco*, a philosophical poem which both rivals and complements—perhaps *contradicts* would be a better word—T. S. Eliot's *The Waste Land*.

In *The Labyrinth of Solitude*, Paz approaches a difficult problem: how to define and explain the feelings of identity and lack of identity of today's Mexicans, especially of those Mexicans who are conscious of living, thinking and feeling according to a Mexican system of values. He uses the vocabulary and the stylistic resources of poetry: images, metaphors, oxymorons, conceits, all the figures of speech. Images and symbols, however, cluster around certain basic observations, which are often derived from a comparison with other sensitivities, other systems of values, whether American, west European or from the Orient. Early enough in the book Paz avows that most of what he has to say about being Mexican came to his mind during the two years he resided in the United States. In order to define what is Mexican, he had to understand and define several other cultural traditions and value systems: only then, profiled by the ways of life that are different, the geographical and temporal space where Mexican values are to appear begins to emerge.

This is so because the identity of an individual or a group assumes the "otherness" of the individuals and groups that surround them. The world is incredibly rich and complex: we can find our place in it only after acknowledging its thousand faces. As Paz puts it in his words of acceptance of the Neustadt International Prize for 1982:

> In esthetic terms, Plurality is a richness of voices, accents, manners, ideas and visions; in moral terms, Plurality signifies tolerance of diversity, renunciation of dogmatism and recognition of the unique and singular value of each work and every personality. Plurality is Universality, and Universality is the acknowledging of the admirable diversity of man and his works. . . . To acknowledge the variety of visions and sensibilities is to preserve the richness of life and thus to ensure its continuity.

Paz knows by instinct what German philosophers of the Romantic era— Fichte, Schelling, Hegel—found out through arduous reasoning and what in our own time Martin Buber has restated successfully: there is no *I* without a *Thou;* there is no individuality without an "otherness," a plurality. We know everything, we are everything and everybody if, and only if and when, we acknowledge our diversity, engage in a dialogue with everybody else, create bridges between human beings and their own past, their traditions and hopes. A dialogue between ourselves and nature, between human history and the history of the cosmos.

It goes without saying that when a poet invades the realm of philosophy, the impact is bound to be strong and enduring. Philosophers deal with questions that we all care about, but they often are clumsy and obscure in the way they state them and in the way they make their conclusions explicit. Few philosophers are forceful writers. So few, in fact, that their lack of expertise about language and communication is perhaps the major factor that has brought philosophy into disarray and ineffectiveness in our time. Plato was a first-rate writer; so were Nietzsche, Bergson, Ortega y Gasset.

A concern with language, a concern about language, is what poets and philosophers have most in common. Modern philosophy from Descartes to the present has paid constant attention to the tools that have helped us reach toward knowledge, and foremost among these tools is language, which brings us knowledge in such a grasping, intimate way that we receive both knowledge and language at the same time, closely intertwined. Young Emerson points out in his journals, "The progress of metaphysics may be found to consist in nothing else than the progressive introduction of apposite metaphors."[5]

Paz is committed to language, not only because he is a poet, but also because as a thinking man he sees in language a meeting place of space and time, essence and existence. "The word is man himself. We are made of words. They are our only reality, or at least, the only testimony of our reality," Paz assures us in *The Bow and the Lyre*. Moreover, as Paz writes in *Alternating Current*, "The problem of meaning in poetry becomes clear as soon as we notice that the meaning is not to be found outside, but rather inside the poem; it is not to be found in what the words have to say, but rather in what the words *have to say to each other*" (". . . en aquello que *se dicen entre ellas*").

It is perhaps in *Blanco*, a long poem published in 1966, that Paz reaches his highest level as a philosophical poet. *Blanco* is a text that unfolds in several ways. We can read it as a whole, from beginning to end, or we can read first the central column, which deals with the birth of words, the birth of language. To the left of this central column is another column, a poem in itself if we choose to read it as such, an erotic poem divided into four sections which stand for the four elements in the physical world. To the right of the central column we find another column, another poem, also divided into four parts: it deals with sensation, perception, imagination and understanding. Read as a whole, *Blanco* can be baffling and exasperating if we do not understand that it is the interaction of the different parts across time (the time it takes to read the poem) and space (the printed page with its white spaces surrounding the texts as silence surrounds our words) that conveys the message. Language cannot be born, Paz seems to say in this poem, unless we combine into one single unit space, time, sensuousness, passion and silence.

It is through language that we can approach the world around us, Paz seems to tell us, and each new word created by us enriches us with a new treasure—with the joy which this victory produces we find new strength to go on

and invent new words. This is the way he describes the creation of the word
sunflower:

> Survivor
> Among taciturn confusions,
> It ascends
> On a copper stalk
> Dissolved
> In a foliage of clarity,
> Refuge
> Of fallen realities.
> Asleep
> Or extinct,
> High on its pole
> (Head on a pike)
> A sunflower
> Already carbonized light
> Above a glass
> Of shadow.
> In the palm of a hand
> Fictitious,
> Flower
> Neither seen nor thought:
> Heard,
> It appears
> Yellow
> Calyx of consonants and vowels
> All burning. (177–79)

Flashes of light and color, metaphors, images, synesthesia precede and follow
the word sunflower (*girasol*), helping in its birth, reinforcing its presence and
its meaning. Everything begins and ends in words. Words, on the other hand,
need us, need our senses, our passion, in order to be born. In an audacious

reverse movement similar to the flight of a boomerang, Paz compels poetic language to turn around and examine itself, examine words and sentences, in order to seize the second in which a sensation becomes a word.

As Ricardo Gullón has stated, "Paz, like André Breton, understands that the language of passion and the passion of language are on good terms with one another, that they are the recto and verso page of the same attitude. Moreover, language is where song happens. There is no song without words, even though a song can be diminished to a susurration or concealed in a number."[6] Poetry, language, passion: these are key words for anyone approaching Paz's texts. It is the way he relates and combines them that makes his message a universal one, no matter how closely related many of his poems and essays are to the Mexican soil and culture that shaped him. By approaching language through poetry and passion he deals with a universal fact—there is no culture without language, and language belongs to all of us—through feelings (sensuousness, sexual passion) that are also our common heritage. An intellectual and philosophical quest has been carried out through experiences that can be shared by all. Can there be a greater achievement for a philosopher-poet?

Yale University

Editorial note: Durán's essay is an expanded version of the encomium that he delivered at the 1982 Neustadt Prize award ceremonies on 9 June at the University of Oklahoma.

1. James Atlas, "Derek Walcott, Poet of Two Worlds," *New York Times Magazine,* 23 May 1982, 32.
2. Anna Balakian, "Focus on Octavio Paz and Severo Sarduy," *Review* 72, Fall 1972.
3. Rita Guibert, "Paz on Himself and His Writing: Selections from an Interview," in *The Perpetual Present: The Poetry and Prose of Octavio Paz,* ed. Ivar Ivask (Norman: University of Oklahoma Press, 1973), 25.
4. Octavio Paz, "Blanco," trans. Charles Tomlinson and G. Aroul, in *Configurations* (New York: New Directions, 1971), 193.

5. Quoted in "Emerson in His Journals," *New York Times Book Review*, 20 June 1982, 20.

6. Ricardo Gullón, "The Universalism of Octavio Paz," in *The Perpetual Present*, 80.

Manuel Durán *(b. 1925, Barcelona) is an emeritus professor in the Department of Spanish and Portuguese at Yale University and a longtime editorial board member of* World Literature Today. *After publishing an essay on Spanish and Spanish American writers in the "Nobel Prize Symposium" issue of* Books Abroad *(Winter 1967), the Swedish Academy invited him to take part in a symposium in Stockholm in September 1967.*

Literature as a Compass on the Navigable Sea
Octavio Paz

Dr. William S. Banowsky, President of the University of Oklahoma; Mrs. Doris Neustadt; Ladies and Gentlemen.

In all languages there are limpid words which are like air and the water of the spirit. To express such words is always marvelous and furthermore necessary, like breathing. One such word is *gracias*, thank you. Today I pronounce it with joy. Also with the awareness of being the object of a happy confusion. The truth is that I am not very certain of the value of my writings. On the other hand, I am certain of my literary passion: it was born with me and will die only when I die. This belief consoles me. The jurors were not completely mistaken in awarding me the Neustadt International Prize for 1982: they wanted to reward, in my case, if not excellence, then obstinacy. . . . I shall not say more about my feelings. I am no more than the incidental (or accidental?) cause, and so what should count, however deep my gratitude, is not my person but the significance of the Neustadt Prize. It is worth reflecting upon this for a moment.

Situated in the center of the United States and surrounded by immense
plains, Oklahoma seemed destined due to geographic fate for interior activity and historical apartness. However, the relation of every society with its
surrounding physical reality is one of contradiction: men who inhabit a valley climb mountains which separate them from the world, and men of the
plains move along the endless expanse as if it were a navigable sea. These
are opposite and reversible metaphors: the desert is a sea for the Arab, and
the sea is a desert for the sailor. In each case the metaphor is a challenge and
an invitation: the horizon remains at the same time a call and an obstacle. In
the domain of literary communication, Oklahoma has overcome isolation and
distance through a series of exemplary initiatives.

The first was the founding of the journal *Books Abroad* in 1927 by Roy
Temple House. I remember how many years ago, when I was studying for the
bachelor's degree and was beginning to discover literature for myself, a copy of
the journal came into my hands. In those days the literary isolation of Mexico
was almost absolute, to the degree that when I read those pages I felt the opening of the doors of contemporary literature in languages other than my own. For
a while *Books Abroad* was my compass, and foreign literatures ceased to be for
me an impenetrable forest. *Books Abroad* no longer exists, not because it has dis-
appeared but because it has been transformed, enlarged and rejuvenated. Under
the energetic and intelligent editorship of Ivar Ivask, a poet who himself is a
lucid and intrepid literary explorer, the review has grown. It is now called *World
Literature Today* and has become an indispensable periodical for all those who
want to keep up with contemporary literature on a worldwide scale. I stress the
word *worldwide*, which must be understood literally: *World Literature Today*
is not dedicated only to the analysis of literature from the major European languages, but it also follows with genuine and admirable sympathy, not lacking in
rigor, the development of letters in the so-called minor languages. It is no secret
that these languages are often rich in notable works and original talents.

Following the example of *World Literature Today* and inspired by it,
there have emerged during these last few years other activities which exhibit
the same universal calling. One of these activities has been the series of
symposia which are convened periodically at the University of Oklahoma

honoring writers in Spanish or French. In these conferences critics from both the Americas and from Europe participate, and the papers and discussions represent, in many cases, essential contributions in the field of contemporary Hispanic and French literature.

Another manifestation, no doubt the most important to date, has been the establishment in 1969 of the Neustadt International Prize for Literature. In many countries there exist national literary prizes to single out a writer in a common language of several nations. On the other hand, there are very few literary prizes indeed which are truly *international*. Among these a place apart is occupied by the Neustadt Prize. Two characteristics lend it a unique face: the first is that each jury is composed of critics and writers belonging to different languages and literatures, which means that it constitutes an *international* body, as international as the prize itself; the second characteristic is that the jury is not permanent but instead changes from one prize to the next—that is, every two years. These two characteristics translate into two words: *Universality* and *Plurality*. Due to the first word, the prize has been awarded to poets and novelists in Italian, English, French, Polish, Spanish and Czech; due to the second word, Plurality, we find among the laureates not only writers of different languages but also of different literary and philosophical persuasions. In esthetic terms, Plurality is a richness of voices, accents, manners, ideas and visions; in moral terms, Plurality signifies tolerance of diversity, renunciation of dogmatism and recognition of the unique and singular value of each work and every personality. Plurality is Universality, and Universality is the acknowledging of the admirable diversity of man and his works. Considering all this, in the convulsed and intolerant modern world we inhabit, the Neustadt Prize is an example of true civilization. I will say even more: to acknowledge the variety of visions and sensibilities is to preserve the richness of life and thus to ensure its continuity. Hence the Neustadt Prize, in stimulating the universality and diversity of literature, defends life itself.

Norman, Oklahoma
June 9, 1982

PAAVO HAAVIKKO
THE 1984 LAUREATE

Finnish poet and playwright **Paavo Haavikko** (1931–2008) was born in
Helsinki and lived there until his death. He published his first collection
of poetry in 1951 at the age of twenty. After three more verse collections,
two three-act plays, and two novels, Haavikko's first English-translated
piece was published in 1961. Haavikko embraced the modernist
movement in Finland and, through his prolific works, influenced many
other genres of Finnish literature in his lifetime. Through his literary
achievements, Haavikko became the leading writer of his generation and of
the postwar period in Finland. Haavikko's poetry collections include *Tiet
etädisyyksiin* (1951), *Talvipalatsi* (1959; Eng. *The Winter Palace*, 1967),
Kaksikymmentdja yksi (1974; Eng. *One and Twenty*, 2007), and *Sillat:
Valitut runot* (1984). His works of drama include the titles *Agricola ja
kettu* (1968; Eng. *Agricola the Fox*, 1985) and *Kuningas Idhtee Ranskaan*
(1974; Eng. *The King Goes Forth to France*, 1984).

It is the writer's lot to go on working, in the dark, in motion, free, alone, available. The value of this work is not in immutable, established classics; it is not in any completed book; it is in the endless work itself, the endless effort to remain free and unbound.

—Paavo Haavikko

Paavo Haavikko's History of an Unknown Nation
Bo Carpelan

Already in his first collection of poetry, *The Ways to Far Away* (1951), Paavo Haavikko at the age of twenty emerged as a poet with a personal and original profile. As a matter of fact, his debut represented the final breakthrough of Finnish modernism. Ten years and five volumes later, in 1961, he was characterized as a "classic of modernism." Now, in 1984, he stands as the foremost living Finnish writer. Like every author of importance, he has created his own world of expression, not only linguistically but also in terms of ideas. This universe comprises, in addition to poetry, a good many short stories, novels, aphorisms and plays for stage and radio. To this should be added a controversial and brilliant history of Finland, *The National Line*, subtitled *Comments on the History of an Unknown Nation, 1904–1975*. This "unknown nation" is also a part of Haavikko's poetry. Internationally, however, he is best known for his librettos to operas by Aulis Sallinen (*The Horseman, The King Goes Forth to France*).

Haavikko's first books of poetry are characterized by a language of striking originality, particularly in *The Ways to Far Away* and *On Windy Nights* (1953). Outer and inner experiences are inseparable in a poetic landscape transformed by the changes of seasons and time; the intervals of meditation are a part of the whole. In the subsequent volumes there is a change in the language: it becomes dramatic, with great inner tensions. Irony and wit, warmth and coldness, proximity and distance, a striving for objectivity and simultaneously a strong personal engagement make *Birthplace* (1955), *Leaves, Pages* (1957) and especially *The Winter Palace* (1959) central works in Finnish literature of the 1950s.

In *Trees in All Their Verdure* (1966) Haavikko summarizes his themes—love, human relationships, loneliness, survival, the desire for political power—into a work of great intensity and depth. This central work in Haavikko's oeuvre is followed by longer poems such as *Fourteen Rulers* (1970), in which Michael Psellus's *Chronographia* of eleventh-century Byzantium serves as a source of themes. Many of the pieces in *Poems from a Voyage across the Sound* (1973; the "sound" here is the Bosporus) are also concerned with power and its uses. Still, Haavikko does not cut his ties to his home country, his "forest land." In the epic poem *Twenty and One* (1974) he gives his personal interpretation of the myth of the *sampo,* found in the *Kalevala.* In *Wine, Writing* (1976) he returns to universal themes in a short, composed and clear style free from decorations.

In his poetry, with great linguistic vigor, Haavikko creates a form of intense skepticism, or rather, a matter-of-fact relativism. His pessimism is never cynical; his humor is not always recognized but is as important as his clarity of vision. The inconstancy of feeling, the harsh conditions of a fragile life, hidden fears and the hidden longing for power are described in language that is close to the spoken word. In an interview in *Books from Finland* (1977) he summarizes his opinions about poetry: "I think the important thing with poetry is *not* to write it: keep it in your head, where it can live and grow What I've always aimed at, I think, is what I call normal expression, a sentence that is as clear and lucid as it can possibly be and is the best possible expression of what has to be said. In my own poetry I have always tried to conform to the rhetoric of speech. I've always been quite clear in my mind about this, ever since I was quite young. I try to shape it into speech: I try it out, and listen, until it really sounds like speech, like someone talking."

In answer to a question about the difficulties of language, Haavikko concludes: "I'm not terribly interested in language as such, but what does interest me is its power to usurp reality. What is language, after all? A set of symbols; and these symbols are apprehended as reality. Yet in fact these symbols lead a life of their own: you use them, but they dictate their own terms. They do whatever they like; or whatever the context wants them to do, or whatever some person wants them to do. They become totally divorced from reality. It's really a most frightening process. You can say anything, develop any idea, in such a way that it sounds like reality; what is even more dangerous, it can sound logical and wise. This is something that anyone who writes—anyone who thinks, for that matter—has to reckon with. Reckoning with it is in fact his job; it's what a writer's problems are all about: how to take these treacherous symbols and shape them into the truth."

For his views of the past, Haavikko could use a proverb attributed to the great Finland-Swedish modernist Gunnar Björling: "History—to be written anew. Always." The variations between past and present are characteristic both in Haavikko's poetry and in his paradoxically expressed aphorisms, with political economy as a starting point: "Speak, Answer, Teach" (1972), "The Human Voice" (1977) and "Time of Eternal Peace" (1981). In power he sees destruction, especially in the form of ideological blindness and exploitation of nature. His world of myths is interwoven with intense personal feeling and with the same clearly constructed objectivity.

Haavikko's poetry is most striking in its cleanness and harmony and in its absence of symbols and allegories: "The world itself, it is not an allegorical creature." Clearness, vitality, intensity are for him the essential components of poetry. He also adds a word of great importance for himself and his poetry: *hillitön,* meaning "unrestrained," "unbridled." This unbridled quality demands its own careful patterns. The task of the poet is to form the symbols of language into universal truth. This truth involves the grotesque and the contemplative, darkness and light. Above all, it is a question of penetrating language and moving toward an unaffected spoken idiom.

And my breath, I blew it out, let it hang dumb,
so as not to pollute the spot with bawling.

But in fact I asked it back on loan to say goodbye,
and stole it, and it's what I'm carrying to the country that isn't a place
right out of this poem.
("The Winter Palace XII ," trans. Herbert Lomas)

Helsinki

Bo Carpelan *(1916–2011) was a Finnish writer who wrote in Swedish. The author of poetry, novels, short stories, plays, and literary criticism, he won the Swedish Academy's Nordic Prize in 1997 and twice won the Finlandia Prize. He also translated Greek classics, works by Osip Mandelstam and Marina Tsvetayeva, and a number of Finnish writers, including Paavo Haavikko.*

Paying the Price of Freedom
Paavo Haavikko

Dr. William S. Banowsky, President of the University of Oklahoma; Mrs. Doris Neustadt; Ladies and Gentlemen.

More than a formal word of thanks is due to the University of Oklahoma for the work that has again gone into the preparation of this ceremony. Nor am I merely expressing thanks on my own behalf; I believe that all writers must appreciate the fact that there is an institution so dedicated to keeping up with the flow of world literature and to finding an author on whom to confer its award. I also believe that all writers, at least, realize that this choice must be appropriately subjective, since art is not a measurable activity like sport. And finally, thanks are due to the family who made this prize possible, the Neustadts. I believe that this prize will not be fully appreciated until decades from now.

The writer must work alone. In a small country he can do this with the reassuring knowledge that his readers are few and close at hand. A writer from a small country and a small linguistic area is at once confined and free. He cannot, indeed he need not think of anything wider than his own environment. He can even be free of popularity, for which he hardly has any use. He is left with very few excuses. He cannot be destroyed by money or fame or the lack of either. All that he is left with is the naked truth of how he sees himself, his potential—and literature.

It is easy to write when one knows that the significance of writing is in the work itself, in the examination of eternal issues. The inevitable consequence of this work is the realization that the only significant problems are those to which there are no answers or solutions. They must be examined constantly; they contain the limits of the possible and of human capacity. Only through the unanswerable questions can the world be depicted, constantly, unendingly.

Thus literature is always philosophical and always moral. It asks what is right in the final count, knowing that there is no reply. But it asks and it seeks, and it cannot be shackled by laws, social systems, technology or business.

Using all the rich patterns in the world, literature constructs a form in which the following things can be found: the question of injustice and justice, the movement of events in the world, and darkness. The reader is invited, he is given an opportunity—but he may walk past if he will. It is the writer's lot to go on working, in the dark, in motion, free, alone, available. The value of this work is not in immutable, established classics; it is not in any completed book; it is in the endless work itself, the endless effort to remain free and unbound. It is said that art brings nations closer together, since through art they come to know each other. Many work toward this end. I believe that it is much more important for art to bring a man closer to himself. If a man knows one person—himself—he is closer to others than if he knows many people by name, including himself.

The idea of art as a bridge between nations goes with the optimistic belief that everything can be solved in the long run, that problems were made to be solved. This may hold for practical problems. Real problems were not made to be solved, but rather to be borne with, lived with, in all countries and seasons, as time passes and changes the terms of life.

The writer has no expert help or institution as surety or support. He has only himself. There is no alternative. Everything else in developed societies is already so guaranteed, subsidized, secured, reliable and isolated from all reality—science is so exploited and subjected—that there is no alternative left but the individual, set adrift and free.

The writer needs a measure of attention and recognition. He must fight to obtain it. At the same time he must fight against turning or allowing himself to be turned into an institution, who must think of everything, including next year's income. And though I use the word *writer*, I do not wish to differentiate between this activity and the battle each individual must fight. This battle too lasts only one lifetime: it begins in medias res, it ends in medias res; it is final and inevitable.

The only meaningful freedom is that of the individual. Every system desires to offer every other kind of freedom except this one. Every organized society tends toward increasing organization: arranging, caring, protecting and guaranteeing. Every system, regardless of ideology, wishes to distribute the optimum amount of good to everyone. No system believes that man cannot endure so much good, and every system believes that all problems were made to be solved. Here is the source of the happiness and destruction of systems and political institutions alike.

To an outsider's eyes, America is a uniform, closed concept; it symbolizes a dream, and goals. Coming here as a European, I am aware that Europe is too incoherent for anyone to explain. There can be no comprehensive image of it, except that it is disrupted and broken. And Finland, a remote corner of Europe, is even less comprehensible. It is one of Europe's few neutral countries between East and West. Many think it is merely an all too small country in quite the wrong place to exist, if only in the light of recent European history. In the form that it does exist, it is a relic from a bygone age when there were still small, separate principalities in Europe. I am not trying to sell any conception or description of what the country is. It has been difficult enough even for European statesmen to fathom during a whole lifetime. All I can say, without resorting to a false comparison, is that in the light of historical wisdom, the Finns evidently have not had the sense to draw the correct conclusions about the price it is worth paying for freedom. This small nation has never set a price on freedom; it has merely paid, and for this reason it has received an excessive return on its absurd investment.

Lastly, I would like to express my thanks to Ivar Ivask for the enormous task he has accomplished as editor-in-chief of *World Literature Today*, bringing together on the pages of his review what has been written in seventy-two languages.

Norman, Oklahoma
May 31, 1984

Translation from the Finnish by Philip Binham

MAX FRISCH
THE 1986 LAUREATE

Max Frisch (1911–1991) was a Swiss novelist and playwright. Frisch's father suddenly passed away while he was studying at the University of Zurich, and Frisch had to abandon his studies and take up a job as a journalist, thus beginning his lifelong career as a writer. His first novel was published in 1934. In 1936 he returned to school and graduated with a degree in architecture, but he continued to write even as his studio thrived. By 1947, Frisch had filled more than one hundred notebooks with work, but his most active writing period occurred during the 1950s and '60s. Among the major themes in Frisch's writings are identity, individuality, and political commitment. This body of work includes the novels *Stiller* (1954; Eng. *I'm Not Stiller*, 1958) and *Homo faber: Ein Bericht* (1957; Eng. *Homo Faber*, 1959). Frisch also penned several plays, many of which have been included in various collections: *Andorra: Stück in zwölf Bildern* (1961; Eng. *Andorra*, 1964), *The Fire*

Raisers: A Morality without a Moral (1962), *The Great Fury of Philip Hotz* (1967), and *Man in the Holocene* (1980).

The art of radically questioning himself—and the reader—is perhaps the most consummate, and the most permeating, in Frisch's works, right up to his last novel.

—Adolf Muschg

The Radical Questioning of Max Frisch
Adolf Muschg

Indisputably, Max Frisch, now seventy-four, must be counted among the major writers of modern German and European literature. Together with Friedrich Dürrenmatt, he is the only living Swiss writer of world renown, translated into more than twenty languages, acknowledged as one of the authoritative voices of Western civilization, cultural values, and political conscience, and endowed with prestigious literary distinctions—short of the Nobel Prize, for which he has been a candidate for many years, and, of course, the Neustadt Prize, for which I should like to present him as a candidate.

Max Frisch, born on 15 May 1911 in Zürich, graduated in architecture from the Swiss Federal Institute of Technology in his hometown and worked in this profession well into the fifties. His early novels that appeared before the war show the extraordinary sensibility of a widely traveled young man in pursuit of his identity—a quest that, on a different level of psychological and artistic insight, would become something like the leitmotiv or hallmark of the one work that assured his international breakthrough in 1954, the novel *Stiller*. By every standard of judgment, this masterpiece of self-searching wit, with its literary strength and imaginative irony, opened a new chapter of German postwar literature, breaking away from both the self-indulgent, inward-looking privateness and the "threadbare" *(Kahlschlag)* style of the fifties in Germany. It was as though "feeling had returned to limbs numbed by a state of shock," as one contemporary critic put it.

Before, Frisch had already made his mark as an acute observer of the critical issues of his generation—the generation of "existentialism"—both in his famous *Tagebuch 1946-1949* and in several successful plays such as *Santa Cruz* (1944), *Nun singen sie wieder* and *Die chinesische Mauer* (1946), *Als der Krieg zu Ende war* (1948), and *Graf Öderland* (1951), the last anticipating the unrest of a youth at variance with bourgeois values that would manifest itself almost two decades later. *Biedermann und die Brandstifter,* his most successful play internationally, was widely interpreted as a parable of political weakness in the face of totalitarian subversion; it has stood the test of time by *not* lending itself to any single interpretation. *Andorra* (1961) succeeded by poignantly exposing the mechanism that turns a minority—Jewish or otherwise—into a scapegoat for collective frustration and common guilt.

Frisch's plays, including *Don Juan* (1952) or *Biographie: Ein Spiel* (1967), could be labeled moralistic in the sense that they confront the individual with choices on which hinges his personal credibility; they are pessimistic in the sense that the will to choose turns out to be less than free and very much defined by the fate—or fatality—of one's character. The art of radically questioning himself—and the reader—is perhaps the most consummate, and the most permeating, in Frisch's works, right up to his last novel, *Blaubart.* Under the guise of a highly critical observer of democracy—which has not endeared Frisch to the powers-that-be in his home country—hides a more basic concern with, and distrust of, human games, particularly the games of power and the games between man and woman. If Frisch is one of the most brilliant chroniclers of the vicissitudes of love, he is also one of the most self-critical analysts of masculinity, as in his novel *Montauk* (1975), where he takes stock of his "life as a man" with as much personal frankness as artistic discretion. His concern with playing roles has been pursued methodically and translated into a new form of novel-writing in *Mein Name sei Gantenbein* (1964), which has been a source of professional inspiration for many younger writers beyond the German-speaking world.

One of the basic concerns of Frisch's work has long been death—as an ultimate challenge to the "art of living." In a more somber and a more subtle way than in his earlier works (such as the provocative *Tagebuch 1966–1971*), the issue governs Frisch's writing in *Triptychon,* a play in which the universe of human relations has frozen into an underworldly standstill, or in *Der Mensch erscheint im Holozän,* the diary of a quiet catastrophe: aging.

Frisch is a man of personal and public courage; he has never shied from making his voice heard in matters of common concern and has never sided with the high and the mighty. He has displayed an exceptional gift for finding the right word at the right time. Even the enemies he has made by speaking up have always been indebted to the level of his arguments and the depth of his insights. If he has become less controversial in his later years, it is because the facts have in time justified his concerns. His influence on contemporary European sensitivity—not only of fellow writers—can hardly be overstated; his works have accompanied young readers in their personal growth much like those of Hermann Hesse. The true legitimacy of the questions that Frisch raises rests with the credibility of his art in raising them—always stopping short of answers that can only be given by the reader's total honesty toward himself.

Swiss Federal Institute of Technology, Zürich

Adolf Muschg *(b. 1934) is a Swiss writer. He taught German and German literature at ETH University in Zürich and also served as president of the Akademie der Künste in Berlin. His many awards include the Herman Hesse Prize, the Georg Büchner Prize, the Grimmelhausen Prize, the Grand Prix de Littérature (Switzerland), and the Hermann Hesse Gesellschaft Prize.*

Building a School in Nicaragua
Max Frisch

Ladies and Gentlemen,

I am grateful—as I wrote in my letter some months ago—very grateful, and I have to tell you in a few words: grateful for what? . . . Your country spoiled me quite a lot: thirty-five years ago, with a Rockefeller Grant that gave me the chance to live in New York and San Francisco over one year (on a modest standard, but free to write every day or night). Some other recognitions followed, recognitions by American academies and American universities, and today this final decoration.

I think my ambivalence, in regard to your great country, has its origin not in personal frustration; my criticism is not an expression of personal resentment. That means it certainly is not what some like to call *Anti-Amerikanismus*. It only concerns my criticism of politics wherever politics becomes inhuman-inhumane. That's what it's all about, and I am grateful for your generous understanding. I also thank you for your kindness in traveling from Oklahoma to Zürich; your visit here, ladies and gentlemen, is an honor for our town. Dafür danke ich als Zürcher.

As to the money, you know my decision to support with these funds a nonmilitary organization in Nicaragua, a nonprofit organization. It is a Swiss group of younger volunteers working there for development, which means aid to the people of Nicaragua in their long and painful struggle for independence. Two of those volunteers, Maurice Demierre and Yvan Leykraz, were killed last year. Compared to the one hundred million US dollars for military equipment on the other side, my support is very modest indeed—twenty-five thousand dollars—but it is said to be sufficient for one of the projects presented by the Asociación de Trabajadores del Campo: a school in a village with sixty farm families who want their children to learn the alphabet. The place (so I have been informed) is not far from the region where the terrorists known as contras are using their US military equipment to destroy bridges, power plants, homes, et cetera, hunting down farmers with gunfire and killing civilians from time to time before escaping across the border to Honduras, where they are trained by US advisors. The name of the modest project: Escuela Santa Emilia. The construction time: six months, assuming that the contras do not launch a sudden attack. It will be a simple building for three classes: Escuela Santa Emilia.

Zürich, Switzerland
May 16, 1987

RAJA RAO
THE 1988 LAUREATE

Raja Rao (1908–2006) was born in Hassan, in what is now Karnataka in South India. Though his father taught Kannada at a Hyderabad college, Rao graduated from the University of Madras with degrees in English and history; he then traveled to France for postgraduate studies. Most of his publications were written in the English language, though some of his earliest publications were written in his native Kannada. His first stories began appearing in various magazines and journals in 1931, and he published his first book, *Kanthapura*, in 1938. Upon his return to India in 1939, Rao became involved in the emerging nationalist movement. From 1966 to 1983 he relocated to the United States and taught philosophy at the University of Texas at Austin. Rao's works of fiction include *Kanthapura* (1938), *The Serpent and the Rope* (1960), *The Cat and Shakespeare* (1965), and *The Chessmaster and His Moves* (1988). Much of his writing appeared in various periodicals, including "A Client" (*Mercure de France*, 1934),

"The Cow of the Barricades" (*Asia*, 1938), "The Policeman and the Rose" (*Illustrated Weekly of India*, 1963), "Jupiter and Mars" (*Pacific Spectator*, 1954), and "The Writer and the Word" (*Literary Criterion*, 1965).

> The writer or the poet is he who seeks back the common word to its origin of silence, in order that the manifested word become light.
>
> —Raja Rao

The Moves of the Chessmaster
Edwin Thumboo

Once in a while the Chessmaster, who, for some, arranges the universe, enters it—at times dramatically, at times through the heart of silence—to remind man of the possibilities of the Absolute, of the ways it, the unmoving, moves us through knowledge to truth. The Chessmaster is but a label for the essence beyond that complex of form, substance, space, and energy which is the basis of life. Those who have seen the light, as it were, and are therefore free to con-jugate the word because they have moved beyond it, understand the need for temporary metaphors which those still in the process of knowing mis-take for reality; for man makes language after his own image, after his own hunger, inventing a discourse, a code without which he cannot relate either with himself or with others or give meaning to the unities and the contradic-tions in the flow of his thought and his experience. The sense of the Absolute, or of the most high, if you prefer, is enshrined in God, the Infinite, Allah, Olodumare, the Lord of the Universe, Kronos, Zeus, Yahweh, and a thousand other names. We also recall Buddha, Mahavira, Zoroaster, Confucius, Lao-Tzu, Christ, Krishna, and Mohammed, who together offer an infinity of ways or a Way, Tao, with different routes.

That is the spiritual history of man, marked by recurring search for the numinous, for the Absolute, and concurrently for his true, indestructible, immortal self. It is a search that is ultimately personal, undertaken on and through different levels where inner compulsions confront and are strength-ened by the doctrine, the dogma, and the ritualistic prescription of a partic-ular religion in a particular milieu at a particular time. You pray to and/or meditate upon Christ, the Buddha, or Krishna. Saint, sinner, and sage cor-roborate and reaffirm. Moreover, both the level and the way are directed or occur in two broad traditions, dominated respectively by duality and non-duality. Religions characterized by a duality rest on the belief that God—or the Absolute, if you prefer—is external to man. He creates, is compassionate, lays down. He judges, punishes, forgives. Out of such sets of beliefs arises an ethos, a way of life governed by the sacred and the secular, a distinction that deeply influences morality and action; you render unto God and you render unto Caesar. Thus the potential of conflict, in which the overriding anxiety is whether soul or spirit, immortal and God-given, redeemed from sin, whether original or incurred, is protected from evil and therefore damnation. A state of grace for life, a state of grace for death, for without grace there is everlasting darkness instead of eternal joy in the presence of God.

In contrast, the Vedantic tradition is nondual. As embodied in the Vedas, commented upon, expanded, and given greater precision by Sankara (788–820 A.D.) and other sages-gurus-teachers, including Rao's own guide Sri Atmananda, it is the basis of all his thinking and, consequently, of all his writings. To refer to his *thinking* and to his *writing* is to posit a dichotomy, a duality almost, which is not there, for the two activities are intrinsically bound, singular and seamless, as they are in Vedanta, which, Rao asserts in *The Serpent and the Rope*, "must become real again before India can be truly free." Its creative, linguistic, stylistic, ideational, psychological, analytical, social, philosophical, metaphysical nature, power, and reach derive from the totality of resources that are Indian, tested and refined over some four thousand years. It is underpinned by two key features: the conviction of nonduality, and the capacity to note the concrete in order to move beyond it to abstractions. Axles upon which the circles of Rao's epistemology turn, both are intimately linked to lie compacted at the core of his efforts "to move from the human to abhuman" through a dialectic defined and propelled by the continuities of the Indian tradition. There are fundamental consequences as well. First, the primary and secondary notions of the numinous in nonduality, such as the pantheon of Hindu deities, would appear exotic and/or confusing to those committed to a thoroughgoing monotheism—God above man—whose strictly parceled morality is likely to misjudge the true, abstract relationship between, for example, Krishna and his Gopis. Such monotheism posits a duality, separating the numinous from the human. On the other hand, in Vedantic nonduality man contains divinity; religions of duality shut him out. This leads to Rao's distinction between what he calls the horizontal and the vertical.

> There are, it seems to me, only two possible perspectives on human understanding: the horizontal and (or) the vertical. They could also be named the anthropomorphic and the abhuman. The vertical movement is the sheer upward thrust toward the unnamable, the unutterable, the very source of wholeness. The horizontal is the human condition expressing itself as concern for man as one's neighbour—biological and social, the predicament of one who knows how to say, I and you.
>
> The vertical rises slowly, desperately, to move from the I to the non-I, as the Buddhists would say—the move towards the impersonal, the universal (though there is no universe there, so to say) reaching out to ultimate *being*—when there is just being there are no two entities, no I and you. The I then is not even all, for there is no other to say I to. It is the nobility of *sunyata,* of zero, of light. ("On Understanding")

Societies and psyches are identified accordingly: India is vertical, China horizontal in *The Chessmaster and His Moves,* in which Siva is vertical and JeanPierre horizontal, whereas Suzanne attempts the vertical but fails because she cannot go beyond horizontal gestures and excursions. Neither is birth into a vertical setting an automatic advantage—Raja Ashok is still a Turk, his self, his "I" unreleased because he is captive to the sensualities of the concrete, in contrast to Ratilal, who has left these behind. The distinction is crucial, as it helps, for instance, to clarify and reassert the centrality of the feminine principle in Rao's thinking/works. Woman is essential to man's progress up the vertical, for only with and by woman can man and woman find the Absolute. The relationship is deeply intrinsic, not poised, complementary, or balanced as in yin and yang, which represent a horizontal relationship, one not integrated. It is Savithri who makes Rama holy in *The Serpent and the Rope,* Jayalakshmi Siva in *The Chessmaster and His Moves,* and they through them.

Rao's circles of understanding enlarge as he absorbs and fills out his possession of the Indian tradition, whose thrust and amplitude are depicted in his essay "The Meaning of India," with an oblique brevity so characteristic of Rao, through a rare combination of beast fable (how diminishing a description when the hare turns out to be the Bodhisattva, the Buddha-to-be); a passage on the supreme Swan who symbolizes Truth, Consciousness, and Liberation; disquisitions on Consciousness and the true nature of sacrifice as "the purification of the instruments of perception"; quotations from sacred texts; accounts by European, Muslim, and Chinese travelers and scholars attesting to the wisdom, splendid order, and well-being of India. The passage Rao quotes from Max Muller is particularly appropriate.

> If I were asked under what sky the human mind has most fully developed some of its choicest gifts, has most deeply pondered on the greatest problems of life and has found solutions to some of them, I should point to India. And if I were to ask myself from what literature we, in Europe, may draw that corrective which is most wanted in order to make our life more perfect, more comprehensive, more universal, in fact more truly human, a life not for this life only, but a transfigured and eternal life—again I should point to India.[1]

If we replace India the macrocosm with Raja Rao the writer of novels, short stories, meditations upon the word, and Puranas with poems and Jatakas embedded in them, we have a comprehensive statement of his intentions and achievement. The enlarging circles of his understanding are paralleled by his work over fifty-five years, from the first stories published in 1933 to *The Chessmaster and His Moves*, which appeared this past April. That long odyssey commences with his discovery of India, leading to the increasingly confident projection of her and the taking of her with him as he visits or lives in and seeks to understand other societies and cultures and those who inhabit them and who are equally concerned with life. It is this breadth and depth which makes *The Chessmaster and His Moves* the most international novel we have.

*

I eschew any brief summary of Rao's individual works. Those who have read *The Serpent and the Rope*, *The Cat and Shakespeare*, and *The Chessmaster and His Moves* know how rapidly they defeat such attempts. The expansion and deepening of his fiction centers on the search by the self for a self capable of fulfillment in a world shaped by a tradition that is alive, inexhaustible, subtle, and on the move, a broad and complex continuum whose matrix consists of metaphysics, religion, and ritual as embodied in texts ranging from the Vedas to the emblematic tales from the *Ramayana* that carry, as appropriate to the capacity of reader or listener, religious, social, and political linguistic instruction and reaffirmation. Key texts and narratives are shared, pan-Indian, and connect with those that are regional—such as the collection of *vacanas* in Kannada—down to ones associated with the rhythms of life presided over by a village deity, a village history. The continuum is marked at one end by the most abstract, taxing metaphysics, at the other by humbler religious practices. It has the mutually reinforcing power of written and oral traditions—the retelling of episodes from the *Ramayana* or the stories of the gods by traveling narrators of *harikathas*—that instruct and nourish priest and villager.

Characters in search of self on various levels offer the major fictional foci and energies. More often than not they must contend with change arising from the pressure of events or the challenge of understanding the ethos of another culture. The young orphan Narsa in "Narsiga" (from *The Cow of the Barricades and Other Stories*), who herds sheep and goats and is abused by some but protected by the master of the ashram and whose growing awareness of the image of the Mahatma is described with deep insight and precise delicacy, belongs to the large Rao cast of characters that includes Rama *(The Serpent and the Rope)* and Comrade Kirillov, who both rise to the challenges but at an infinitely more sophisticated level and in a much broader, more universal, international context. The fictional ground between is established by characters such as Little Mother, Catherine, Savithri, Madeleine, Georges *(The Serpent and the Rope);* Moorthy, Rangamma, and Ratna *(Kanthapura);*

Ramakrishna, Pai, and Govindan Nair *(The Cat and Shakespeare);* and Siva, Suzanne, and Jayalakshmi *(The Chessmaster and His Moves).*

Rao's themes include the metaphysical apprehension of God, the nature of death, immortality, illusion and reality, duality and nonduality, good and evil, existence and destiny, Karma and Dharma; the quest for self-knowledge, the place of the guru, the influence of religion and social concepts and patterns and prejudices on individual and group behavior, corrupt priests; the ideal and meaning of love and marriage, the impact of tradition on the individual and collective life and the meaning of India's real and symbolic content, and the historical or contemporary meeting of East and West in religious, political, and psychological terms tested against the vertical/horizontal distinction. The list is by no means exhaustive. Neither does it suggest the way themes conflate, complement, or construct oppositions depicted through the increasing psychological authority of the characters from the early short stories, through *Kanthapura, The Serpent and the Rope,* and *The Cat and Shakespeare,* to the firm, monumental authority of *The Chessmaster and His Moves.* This listing belies Rao's achievement of bringing into the life of each character and his or her relationships the extraordinarily complex worlds they each occupy—Indian, French, Greek, Hebraic, African, Chinese—and which overlap and contain, in a single moment, the mundane and the metaphysical.

That is a major achievement, as is Rao's remarkably successful reorientation of a language and his assembling of a narrative mode to articulate life fully within the continuum of tradition and change in which life is played out against the larger movements of personality, situation, and environment.

Rao's choice of English as his linguistic medium has had implications, the chief of which are disclosed in his foreword to *Kanthapura.*

> The telling has not been easy. One has to convey in a language that is not one's own the spirit that is one's own. One has to convey the various shades and omissions of a certain thought-movement that looks maltreated in an alien language . . . yet English is not really an alien language to us. It is the language of our intellectual make-up— like Sanskrit or Persian was before—but not of our emotional

make-up. . . . We cannot write like the English. We should not. We cannot write only as Indians. We have grown to look at the large world as part of us. . . .

After language the next problem is that of style. The tempo of Indian life must be infused into our English expression, even as the tempo of American or Irish life has gone into the making of theirs. We, in India, think quickly, we talk quickly, and when we move we move quickly. . . . We have neither punctuation nor the treacherous "ats" and "ons" to bother us—we tell one interminable tale. Episode follows episode, and when our thoughts stop our breath stops, and we move on to another thought. This was and still is the ordinary style of our story-telling. I have tried to follow it myself in this story. (vii–viii)

The uniqueness of Raja Rao's style is its apt flexibility, demonstrated in how it incarnates the thoughts and emotions of characters ranging from relatively "simple" peasants to the Brahmin prone to disquisitions. His prose is resonant, bare, or poetic as required. His language accords with the Indian spirit, its speech, gestures, proverbs, and metaphysical thrust. Still, this rootedness in the Indian scene and the Indian tradition does not circumscribe his language. In fact, the sharp management of syntax, of sentence structure, the revealing use of its symbolic and metaphorical resources, gives both clarity and power.

Rao's basic narrative structure, particularly in *Kanthapura*, a majority of the short stories, and *The Cat and Shakespeare*, derives from Puranas, *sathalapuranas*, and *harikathas*, which between them bring together, inter alia, religious and metaphysical discourse, folklore, local legend and quasi-history, straight description, dramatic insets and well-managed digressions. In *Kanthapura* the first-person narrator (a favorite Rao device) is a villager. The style is fluid and simple, with the flow of narrative relieved by digression. The structure which carries the narrative voice is determined to a considerable extent by the status of the narrator himself or herself. Though this may seem obvious, it is considerably less so in that merging of a new language to an old environment. Consequently, in *The Serpent and the Rope,* narrated by Rama the young Brahmin, we find a combination of Indian and "Western" modes. It blends the scope of the notebook and the quest, both of which offer room for autobiographical excursions. The Indian elements derive from the Puranas, which mix religion, philosophy, history, and literature. Given its theme of the discovery of self and illumination through the apparently tangential instruction of a "guru," *The Cat and Shakespeare* reverts to the style of the *sathala-puranas.* The comedy and whimsy are deceptive because the message is fundamental, put across with subtlety and an indirection that is clarified by the concluding paragraphs.

Rao's greatest achievement, which I suspect only he can surpass, is the degree to which his works, especially *The Chessmaster,* contain the insights, emblems, mantras, metaphors, and other carriers of meaning and instruction that enable the individual to achieve, through his own meditations, a better understanding of self through Knowledge and Truth. They lead us, in Rao terms, from the human to the abhuman, to the Absolute or, if you will, from god to God to GOD, thus moving from the horizontal to the vertical. E. M. Forster felt the horizontal Chessmaster in *Howard's End.* In *A Passage to India,* the Chessmaster turns vertical. Walt Whitman had meditated upon a passage to more than India. Forster went further, beyond the doctrinaire religions, chiefly those which rested upon a dualism and which had helped define and maintain the horizontal. The vertical Chessmaster was at work through Godbole, especially in his disquisition on good and evil and his participation in the Gokul Astami rites at Mau, and through the experiences of Mrs. Moore and Adela in the Marabar Caves, and through the Punkawala in the courtroom scene.

> The Court was crowded and of course very hot, and the first person Adela noticed in it was the humblest of all who were present, a person who had no bearing officially upon the trial: the man who pulled the punkah. Almost naked, and splendidly formed, he sat on a raised platform near the back, in the middle of the central gangway, and he caught her attention as she came in, and he seemed to control the proceedings. [. . .]

Then life returned to its complexities, person after person
struggled out of the room to their various purposes, and before
long no one remained on the scene of the fantasy but the beautiful naked god. Unaware that anything unusual had occurred, he
continued to pull the cord of his punkah, to gaze at the empty dais
and the overturned special chairs, and rhythmically to agitate the
clouds of descending dust. (217, 231)

Forster had made the move from the horizontal to the vertical, but the weight
of his deeply entrenched liberalism prevented contact with a forceful liberating
tradition such as Vedanta that could help him rise up to the vertical. He had a
number of unanswered questions which related to the nature of Hinduism or
whether "God is love" is the final message of India. Raja Rao goes beyond such
questions in the sense that he provides answers not to the questions but to the
uncertainties that lie behind them. It is there in his metaphysics, converted from
and into experience, taken from and returned to life, in a language that connects
emotion and spirit, a language restored, made central again in the life of man.

How does one end an encomium for a writer, a Purana-maker who insists
with honesty and fervor that he is not their creator? Fortunately, Raja Rao the
chessmaster provides a rescue which is a fitting conclusion. It is there in the
first excerpt that Ivar Ivask so aptly chose for the printed program of this evening's Neustadt Prize ceremony and which reveals the roots of Rao's art and
his deep compassion for mankind.

I write. I cannot not write. Yet he who writes does not know *that*
which writes. So, does one write? If so who? Which?

Why write? Two birds, says the Ramayana (our oldest epic)
were making love, when a hunter killed the male bird. The cry of
the widowed bird, says the text, created the rhythm of the poem.
The hero Prince Rama freed his wife Sita, abducted and imprisoned by the monster Ravana, King of Ceylon. Monkeys and bears
helped in freeing Sita, seated in sorrow under the Asoka tree. . . .

Why publish? That others may hear the cry of the bird hunted and killed whose mate is lost in sorrow. Uncovering the vocables is a poetic exercise. The precise word arises of love, that is pure intelligence. That is why in Sanskrit the word Kavi means the poet— and the sage.

Norman, Oklahoma
June 4, 1988

1. Raja Rao, "The Meaning of India," in *The First Writers Workshop Literary Reader,* ed. P. Lal (Calcutta: Writers Workshop, 1972), 40–41.

Poet, critic, academic, anthologist, and literary activist **Edwin Thumboo** *(b. 1933) is considered "one of Singapore's most distinguished poets and is widely regarded as the unofficial poet laureate of Singapore" (National Library Board). In 2006 he was awarded one of Singapore's highest honors, the Meritorious Service Medal.*

Words Manifested as Light
Raja Rao

I am a man of silence. And words emerge from that silence with light, of light, and light is sacred. One wonders that there is the word at all—*Sabda*—and one asks oneself, where did it come from? How does it arise? I have asked this question for many, many years. I've asked it of linguists, I've asked it of poets, I've asked it of scholars. The word seems to come first as an impulsion from the nowhere, and then as a prehension, and it becomes less and less esoteric— till it begins to be concrete. And the concrete becoming ever more earthy, and the earthy communicated, as the common word, alas, seems to possess least of that original light.

The writer or the poet is he who seeks back the common word to its origin of silence, in order that the manifested word become light. There was a great poet of the West, the Austrian poet Rainer Maria Rilke. He said objects come to you to be named. One of the ideas that has involved me deeply these many years is: where does the word dissolve and become meaning? Meaning itself, of course, is beyond the sound of the word, which comes to me only as an image in the brain, but *that* which sees the image in the brain (says our great sage of the sixth century, Sri Shankara) nobody has ever seen. Thus the word coming of light is seen eventually by light. That is, every word-image is seen by light, and that is its meaning. Therefore the effort of the writer, if he is sincere, is to forget himself in the process and go back to the light from which words come. Go back where? That is, those who read or those who hear must reach back to their own light. And that light I think is prayer.

My ancestors and, yes, the ancestors of some of you or of most of you who speak the English tongue, came from the same part of the world thousands of years ago. Was it from the Caucasus or the North Pole? One is not certain yet. They spoke a language close to my own language and close to your language. There is in America a remarkable dictionary called the *American Heritage Dictionary*. It offers almost a hundred pages (at the very end) of the Indo-European roots of many of our words. Most of you are of European origin. At least your thinking has been conditioned by European thought. There is thus a common way of thinking, an Indo-European way of thinking, between us, so that we are not so far from each other as we often think we are. And beyond the Indo-European way of thinking in Asia, Africa, Polynesia, is *that* same human light by which all words become meaning. Finally, there is only one meaning, not for every word, but for all words *where* the word, any word, from any language, dissolves into knowledge. It is only there at the dissolution of the sound of the word or of the image of the word that you say you understand. And *here* there is neither you nor I. That is what I have been trying to achieve. That I become no one, that no one shines but It.

Many good things have been said by distinguished speakers—about me—this evening. But I want to say to you in utter honesty: I would like to be completely nameless, and just be that reality which is beyond all of us who hear me—that reality which evokes in me you, and I in each one listening to me this evening, that there be no one there but light. And it is of that reality the sages have spoken. The sage is one, someone beyond the saint. He is no one. He is the real seer. In fact, we are all sages, but we don't recognize it. That is what the Indian tradition says. In the act of seeing—that is, of the seer, the seen, and the seeing—in seeing alone is there pure light. Where this comes from, nobody can name. I once asked Dr. Oppenheimer, the scientist, who told me his hands were soiled by the atom bomb: Have you ever seen an object? And he answered: Never. If a scientist like Dr. Oppenheimer says he has never seen an object—yet I am hearing him say what he has in all honesty declared—it is that level of knowledge I would like to reach from where I truly write. It is to that root of writing I pay homage. The Neustadt Prize is thus not given to me, but to That which is far beyond me, yet in me—because I alone know I am incapable of writing what people say I have written.

Norman, Oklahoma
June 4, 1988

TOMAS TRANSTRÖMER
THE 1990 LAUREATE

Tomas Tranströmer (1931–2015) was a Swedish writer, poet, and translator whose poetry has been translated into over sixty languages. In his life, he was considered the premier postwar Scandinavian poet. He published thirteen volumes of poetry in Swedish, from *17 dikter* (1954) to *Den stora gåtan* (2004). His books of poetry in English include *New Collected Poems* (2011), *The Sorrow Gondola* (2010), *The Half-Finished Heaven* (2001), *For the Living and the Dead* (1995), *Baltics* (1975), *Windows and Stones* (1972), and *20 Poems* (1970), among others. In addition to the Neustadt Prize, Tranströmer was honored with the 1991 Swedish Academy Nordic Prize and the 2011 Nobel Prize in Literature.

The poem as it is presented is a manifestation of another, invisible poem, written in a language behind the common languages. Thus, even the original version is a translation.

—Tomas Tranströmer

Oklahoma
Tomas Tranströmer

I

The train stalled far to the south. Snow in New York,
but here we could go in shirtsleeves all night.
Yet no one was out. Only the cars
sped by in flashes of light like flying saucers.

II

"We battlegrounds are proud
of our many dead . . ."
said a voice as I awakened.

The man behind the counter said:
"I'm not trying to sell anything,
I'm not trying to sell anything,
I just want you to see something."
And he displayed the Indian axes.

The boy said:
"I know I have a prejudice,
I don't want to have it, sir.
What do you think of us?"

III

This motel is a foreign shell. With a rented car
(like a big white servant) outside the door.

Nearly devoid of memory, and without profession,
I let myself sink to my midpoint.

Translation from the Swedish by May Swenson with Leif Sjöberg

Editorial note: Tranströmer took the train from Chicago to Tulsa and drove around eastern Oklahoma in 1965. From *Windows and Stones: Selected Poems,* copyright © 1972 by the University of Pittsburgh Press, reprinted by permission of the publisher. Tony Hoagland writes about "Oklahoma" in "Tranströmer: The Power of Disarray," in *Twenty Poems That Could Save America* (Graywolf, 2015).

Tomas Tranströmer's Poetic Depth of Vision
Jaan Kaplinski

My candidate for the 1990 Neustadt International Prize for Literature is the Swedish poet Tomas Tranströmer. I consider him one of the most outstanding poets of our time, a poet whose work can say much to every one of us, especially to people living in northern Europe and North America. In his work Tranströmer has succeeded in achieving a synthesis between the modern and the traditional, between art and life. He has been able to breathe life into the most uninspiring realities of modern existence and in this way has significantly broadened the scope of our poetic vision of the world. He is thus a contemporary poet in the true sense of the word.

In our world that is often so confused by all kinds of ideologies and doctrines, Tranströmer has always remained a politically nonengaged humanist who understands he has no right to forget the sufferings of other people, be it in the West or in the East, but who knows that there are no quick and simple solutions to the grave problems of our time. Despite many pressures, he has refused to believe in political slogans and participate in mass movements, giving proof of a remarkable courage and clarity of vision. At the same time, he has worked for more than thirty years as a practicing psychologist, helping people, giving them something of his remarkable integrity and strength, and achieving a depth of vision into our human condition that he is able to express in his poems.

Tranströmer has published ten volumes of poetry in Swedish, from *17 dikter* (1954; 17 poems) to *För levande och döda* (1989; Eng. *For the Living and the Dead*, 1995). His oeuvre is not large but has been very influential in Scandinavia and even in North America. Among the English versions of his poetry in book form are the following: *Twenty Poems of Tomas Tranströmer* (1970), translated by Robert Bly; *Night Vision* (1971, US; 1972, UK), translated by Bly; *Windows and Stones* (1972), translated by May Swenson and Leif Sjöberg; *Selected Poems* (1981), translated by Robin Fulton; and *Baltics*, translated by Samuel Charters for the US edition (1975), by Robin Fulton for the UK edition (1980). A special issue of the journal *Ironwood* (1979) was dedicated to Tranströmer's verse, and many translations of his poems and articles about him have appeared in various other publications. His poems have been translated into numerous languages, including German, Spanish, Hungarian, Bulgarian, and the other Scandinavian tongues. Tranströmer has received many literary prizes at home and abroad, and in my opinion his work deserves the distinguished Neustadt Prize.

Tartu, Estonia

Jaan Kaplinski *(b. 1941, Tartu) is an Estonian poet, playwright, essayist, journalist, linguist, sociologist, and ecologist. He has translated a number of poets from French, English, Spanish, Chinese, and Swedish into Estonian, including a verse collection by Tomas Tranströmer.*

The Invisible Poem behind the Poem
Tomas Tranströmer

My warm thanks to *World Literature Today*, the unique magazine with its visionary editor, to the University of Oklahoma, and to the Neustadt family, which with rare generosity has taken on the task of lending literature a helping hand.

I want to draw attention to a fairly large group of men and women who share this prize with me, without getting one single cent: those who have translated my poems into different languages. No one mentioned, no one forgotten. Some are my personal friends; others are personally unknown to me. Some have a thorough knowledge of Swedish language and tradition, others a rudimentary one (there are remarkable examples of how far you can get with the help of intuition and a dictionary). What these people have in common is that they are experts in their own languages, and that they have translated my poems because they wanted to. This activity has brought them neither money nor fame. The motivation has been interest for the text, curiosity, commitment. It ought to be called *love*—which is the only realistic basis for poetry translation.

Let me sketch two ways of looking at a poem. You can perceive a poem as an expression of the life of the language itself, something organically grown out of the very language in which it is written—in my case, Swedish. A poem written by the Swedish language through me. Impossible to carry over into another language.

Another, and contrary, view is this: the poem as it is presented is a manifestation of another, invisible poem, written in a language behind the common languages. Thus, even the original version is a translation. A transfer into English or Malayalam is merely the invisible poem's new attempt to come into being. The important thing is what happens between the text and the reader. Does a really committed reader ask if the written version he reads is the original or a translation?

I never asked that question when I, in my teenage years, learned to read poetry—and to write it (both things happened at the same time). As a two-year-old child in a polyglot environment experiences the different tongues as one single language, I perceived, during the first enthusiastic poetry years, all poetry as Swedish. Eliot, Trakl, Éluard—they were all Swedish writers, as they appeared in priceless, imperfect, translations.

Theoretically we can, to some extent justly, look at poetry translation as an absurdity. But in practice we must believe in poetry translation, if we want to believe in World Literature. That's what we do here in Oklahoma. And I thank my translators.

Norman, Oklahoma
June 12, 1990

JOÃO CABRAL DE MELO NETO
THE 1992 LAUREATE

João Cabral de Melo Neto (1920–1999) was a Brazilian poet and diplomat. After moving to Rio de Janeiro in 1940, he published his first collection of poems, *Pedra do Sono*. In 1945 he was assigned to his first diplomatic post in Spain, where he continued to write. Most of Cabral's life was spent as a diplomat, which afforded him the opportunity to travel the world. Through all of his travels, he continued to write poetry, and at the end of his life, he had published more than fifteen collections. He is considered one of the greatest Brazilian poets of all time. Cabral's body of work includes *O Engenheiro* (1945), *O Cão sem Plumas* (1950), *A Educação pela Pedra* (1966; Eng. *Education by Stone*, 2005), and *Sevilha Andando* (1990). His most famous work, "Morte e Vida Severina," was translated into English in part by 1976 Neustadt laureate Elizabeth Bishop and reprinted in *Selected Poetry, 1937–1990* (1994), ed. Djelal Kadir. In addition to the Neustadt Prize, Cabral was honored with the 1990 Camões Prize.

It has made possible too the exercise of poetry as emotive exploration of the world of things and as rigorous construction of lucid formal structures, lucid objects of language.

—João Cabral de Melo Neto

The Rigors of Necessity
Djelal Kadir

Your Excellency Dom Austregésilo de Athayde, President of the Brazilian Academy of Letters, who has received us so warmly in this House, Distinguished Speakers who have preceded us at the podium, Esteemed Members of the Academy, Ladies and Gentlemen.

It is an incomparable privilege to have the opportunity in this solemn session of the Brazilian Academy of Letters to address to you words of praise in honor of one of your most illustrious poets, His Excellency Ambassador João Cabral de Melo Neto, twelfth laureate of the Neustadt International Prize for Literature.

With the recent and deserved recognition of the universal value of his work, the Brazilian poet João Cabral de Melo Neto takes his indisputable place in what is being defined as the literary pantheon of our century. The eleven great writers who preceded him already figure among those who have defined our literary canon in the second half of the twentieth century.

To arrive at the final outcome, our newest laureate, so ably advocated by the Brazilian writer and our admired friend and colleague Silviano Santiago, had to compete with the significant qualifications of such eminent writers as the Russian poet Bella Akhmadulina, the English novelist John Berger, the Italian poet Andrea Zanzotto, the Turkish novelist Orhan Pamuk, the Uruguayan writer Eduardo Galeano, and the Japanese novelist Kenzaburō Ōe, to mention a few of the candidates who were presented to the 1992 jury. What proved most impressive for the international jury of writers in the Cabral oeuvre was its rigorous honesty and profound humanity. Despite the scant quantity of his poetry available in English—a scarcity we shall ameliorate shortly with the publication of a collection of his poetry in translation—the quality of his work stood out, eliciting the admiration of the jurors, whose international and linguistic diversity converged upon the felicitous consensus that brings us together today in this historic place to celebrate this historic occasion.

Scarcity is one of the fundamental principles of João Cabral's poetics. In an interview with Selden Rodman in 1974, Cabral affirmed that poetry originates either in abundance or in insufficiency. As exemplary poets of overflow, he cites Walt Whitman, Paul Claudel, Pablo Neruda, Vinícius de Moraes, Allen Ginsberg. For his part, João Cabral de Melo Neto identifies himself with poets who write from a basis of dearth, citing as examples George Herbert, Stéphane Mallarmé, T. S. Eliot, Paul Valéry, Richard Wilbur, Marianne Moore, and Elizabeth Bishop—poets who write in order to compensate for a profoundly felt necessity or insufficiency.

Beginning with his earliest works, João Cabral has sought a form of writing that corresponds to what Ralph Waldo Emerson in the last century called pleonastically "our necessary poverty." For Emerson, that necessity is the very insufficiency that incites creative impetus, an impetus that is as strong as it is invisible, that is mysteriously sparse but tenaciously powerful. In this economy of sparseness, João Cabral has fashioned a poetic world, a world so spare that it excludes the very figure of the poet himself, or at least that figure as subject with the voice of a personal pronoun. When the inevitability of the lyrical subject becomes indispensable, our poet laureate turns apocryphal, as in the unforgettable poem "Dúvidas Apócrifas de Marianne Moore" (Apocryphal Doubts of Marianne Moore), where the Anglo-American poet serves the reticent Luso-American laureate as screen and even as pretext:

I have always avoided speaking of me,
speaking to me. I wanted to speak of things.
But, in the selection of those things,
might there not be a speaking of me?

Might that modesty of speaking me
not contain a confession,
an oblique confession,
in reverse, and ever immodest?

How pure or impure is
the thing spoken of?

Or does it always impose itself, im-
purely even, on anyone wishing to speak of it?

How is one to know, with so many things
to speak or not to speak of?
And if avoiding it altogether, is
not speaking a way of speaking of things? (trans. Kadir)

So much reticence! Nevertheless, João Cabral de Melo Neto characterizes himself as a social poet. And he is, in the strict sense of the word, since his poetry is founded in the social and human context of the geographic region that engendered him, that arid region of his native Pernambuco, which is as dry as Cabral has sought to be in the economy of his poetic language. His is a needful geography whose necessity he converts into the felt need of a poetic principle that demands of the poet a lapidary genius and the ingenuity of a stonemason and an engineer.

Shunning the rhetorical flourish and the ideological megaphone, Cabral has labored at his wordsmith's bench with quiet diligence and eloquent concision. In his remarkable terseness, he has endeavored to show rather than tell, and to show without being seen, an achievement best characterized by his own words as "song without guitar," "unceremoniously" wrought in "civil geometry." His trademark thus has been a visual poetry as opposed to a musical fanfare. And he has often reflected on the relationship between painting and the language of poetry, a language that aspires ceaselessly to become lapidary and constructivist. A number of his verse collections reflect this preoccupation with stonemasonry and engineering even in their titles. And like the builder at his task who fashions his edifice stone by stone, João Cabral has always labored with the painstaking awareness that poetry is made word for word, often letter by letter. In this sense, his poetry carries the unmistakable mark of a sculptor's chisel or a painter's brush, metaphorical instruments wielded by the poet with deliberate and measured reserve. And his decorum carries the mark of the humble rather than the haughty, deliberately linking itself with the modest but vital endeavors of the folk that engendered his poetic calling. Chores like fishing or culling beans, for example.

And this, ladies and gentlemen, is where my path happened upon João Cabral's poetic vocation a quarter of a century ago, when, having fallen fortuitously through the crevices of time and space, I found myself transported from the life of a young shepherd in the mountains of my native Cyprus to the halls of Yale University studying philosophy and literature. I discovered then in the Portuguese of this Brazilian poet that it was alright to be there, even for those who come from a life of such modest endeavors. Cabral's poetry taught me that there is a viable continuity between the most humble occupations and the loftiest preoccupations of philosophy and poetry. That was in 1966, when my second-year Portugueselanguage class allowed me the temerity to pick up a recently published volume of poems, a 111-page volume titled *A Educação pela Pedra* (Education by Stone) which had just been released in Rio de Janeiro in July of that year. That temerity and the fates would lead me to the even greater and more terrific impertinence of the moment, delivering an encomium for this great poet in his own House, directing myself to you, esteemed Academicians, in the language of my poor apprenticeship, here in the most august House of this language. I beg your most merciful indulgence for such audacity. And though it be the work of destiny, I do accept fully my responsibility in this predicament, and I do so in the spirit of the Stoic's philosophy that has its origins in the island of my birth.

Cutting my Portuguese teeth on Cabral's poetic stones, I came across something a bit more malleable in that pedagogic quarry. It was a poem entitled "Catar Feijão" (Culling Beans), and it evoked most vividly for me the gnarled hands of my grandmother culling beans, hands whose agility and uncanny intelligence I have yet to learn how to imitate. Being as instructive as any statement I know on the art of poetry, and as illustrative as any of our laureate's lessons in the poet's masonry, "Catar Feijão" could well be a manual, a vade mecum of any poet and student of poetry:

1

Culling beans is not unlike writing:
you toss the kernels into the water of the clay pot
and the words into that of a sheet of paper;

then, you toss out whatever floats.
Indeed, all words will float on the paper, ice-cold water,
its verb small and green and commonsensical:
in order to cull that bean, blow on it,
and toss out the frivolous and hollow, the chaff and the echo.

2
Now, there is a risk in that bean-culling:
the risk that among those heavy seeds any-old
kernel may enter, of stone or study-matter,
an unchewable grain, a tooth-breaker.
Not so, for culling words:
the stone gives the phrase its most vivid seed:
it obstructs flowing, floating reading,
it incites attention, luring it with risk. (trans. Kadir)

Not knowing, for lack of precedent, how well the voice of a Pernambucan poet and the inflection of a Cypriot might harmonize, the present exercise is fraught with great risk indeed. In the face of such risks, let us call these beans the pebbles of Demosthenes, those stones the stammering father of our rhetorical tradition put into his mouth when he went to declaim phrases to the sea. These are the hard-rock impediments the poet must perpetually overcome, as does the reader. For João Cabral teaches us not only how his kind of poetry is written, but also how it is to be read. And lest our reading facility ebb into the facile, we are waylaid, forced into the rigors of having to negotiate stone-hard obstructions and to absorb the necessary lesson of their difficulty. Language, of course, is poetry's greatest difficulty and also its greatest danger. And language becomes most perilous when it would yield with ease to one's facility.

João Cabral's poetic career consists in shunning the temptation to succumb to the facile and the gratuitous. That is why, I suspect, he has been averse to the musicality of poetry, preferring, instead, the sparsely pictorial and the assonantal rhyme to the jangle of consonantal sonority or the bombast of the declamatory. His is another sort of eloquence. And being a self-declared poet of need and insufficiency, Cabral has labored diligently to pare down the magnitude of need's necessity for fulfillment, not out of parsimony, but from an unmistakable sense of generosity. This is the poetic generosity that endeavors to allow the human subjects of his poetry to show forth on their own terms. In this sense, the geometrical and mathematical rigors of self-curtailment in Cabral's poetry, far from being the cold and mechanical acts of a formalism, represent the rigors of a poetry that is profoundly human and socially connected. And, as his wife, the poet Marly de Oliveira, has noted in her foreword to the second volume of his collected verse, Cabral's is an emotive poetry, a poetry laden with lucid emotion, the lucidity inherited from Paul Valéry's mathematical verse.

Our laureate is an artfully subtractive poet engaged in the labors of winnowing, culling, paring down. A poet who opts for the economy of the minimal with maximum effect. He practices a laconic art of deference in a poetry that curtails its own voice, as well as the ego of its author, yielding to the human context that links poetic vocation with daily life and worldly experience. In this self-circumscription, the poetry of João Cabral has transcended its own conscientious and deliberate limits, emerging as a universal cultural phenomenon that is admired by poets and lay readers all over the world. Because of his diligent labors and self-effacing devotion, João Cabral has been adopted by the Brazilian people as their reigning national poet, a status reconfirmed most recently by the São Paulo Prize conferred upon him by the government of that Brazilian state. For all these reasons, in March 1992 an international jury of his peers selected João Cabral de Melo Neto as the laureate of the 1992 Neustadt International Prize for Literature.

I am truly honored by this opportunity and the privilege of addressing you on the merits of João Cabral de Melo Neto's poetry, and doing so in this solemn session of the Brazilian Academy of Letters in the House of the great Machado de Assis. Thank you.

Rio de Janeiro
August 31, 1992

Translation from the Portuguese by Djelal Kadir

Djelal Kadir *(b. 1946, Cyprus) is Edwin Erle Sparks Professor (emeritus) of Comparative Literature at Penn State University and served as the seventh editor (1991–1996) in the history of* Books Abroad / World Literature Today.

Lucid Objects of Language
João Cabral de Melo Neto

Mr. President of the Brazilian Academy of Letters, Professor Djelal Kadir, Mr. Walter Neustadt Jr., my fellow members of the Academy, Ladies and Gentlemen,

On the occasion of being the recipient of so prestigious a prize, conferred upon a writer of the Portuguese language for the first time, I ought to explain one thing before all else: you have rewarded a Brazilian writer who, practically, has only written poetry—that is, a poet.

I do not know how it is in your northerly country, but in mine, in its colloquial usage, the word *poet* has a certain connotation between bohemian and irresponsible, contemplative and inspired, all things that have nothing to do with my way of conceiving poetry and with what I have managed to accomplish.

I regret that Miss Marianne Moore, who died, unfortunately, before receiving the laurels of your prize, cannot, like Francis Ponge and Elizabeth Bishop, laureates both of the Neustadt Prize, comfort me with her poet's counsel today upon receiving this prize as a poet. In truth, these were poets whose vision of poetry has nothing to do with that confessional lyricism that nowadays, since Romanticism, passes for everything that is considered poetry. In a way (and upon saying so I cannot help the feeling of a certain *mauvaise conscience*), what I have written until today has nothing to do with the "lyricism" that has come to be not only the quality of certain poets, but synonymous with what is expected of all poets.

In reality, starting with Romanticism, and in the name of individual expression, poets have left by the wayside the greater part of the kinds of material that previously could be treated in poetry. Historical poetry, didactic poetry, epic poetry, dramatic poetry, narrative poetry, confrontational poetry, all abandoned in favor of poetry of personal expression of states of mind. Everything has been sacrificed to lyricism, and this has been generalized and called poetry. Now, lyricism was merely one of the aspects in which poetry manifested itself. Thus, I do not know why today's critics and historians, though they find it strange, admit that poetry is a literary genre that survives in small circles. Meanwhile, those same critics and historians of today's literature do not keep from dedicating to that genre that is so minoritarian the best of their studies, even while they systematically begin with this genre their manuals and histories of literature, and this not just here but in any country. We know that lyricism was originally a genre to be sung, and thus it is not surprising that the current lyricism, postromantic, not sung, should be restricted to a small circle. The question is, wouldn't the true lyricism of our time be in what is called the popular song, produced and consumed all over the world, beyond geographic borders and language differences, in incomparably greater quantities than any other literary genre, however popular? Might not this natural necessity for lyricism that human beings feel be tended to today by that incalculable volume of works at which the very refined turn up their noses and which the erudite exclude from their studies? That is, might not that needed lyricism be today in the lyrics of popular songs? In those songs that, by virtue of the new technologies of communication, are produced and consumed in our time in quantities enormously larger than those of literatures ever reached in all countries and in all epochs?

Ladies and gentlemen, it is not because of simple aversion that I refuse to inscribe myself into that exclusive club of "lyrics" that today constitutes almost entirely the poetry written in our world. Nor is there any disdain on my part for that lyricism manifested in popular music—I think, on the contrary, that those new techniques have given lyricism a possibility of expression and communication never known before. I am merely offering a possible topic of meditation to the theoreticians of literature, and appealing to them not to seek in not-sung (or unsingable) poetry written today a quality, that of lyricism, that was never the intention of the authors to achieve or even to explore.

Poetry seems to me something much broader: it is the exploration of the materiality of words and of the possibilities of organization of verbal structures, things that have nothing to do with what is romantically called inspiration, or even intuition. In this respect, I believe that lyricism, upon finding in popular music the element that fulfills it and gives it its prestige, has liberated written and not-sung poetry and has allowed it to return to operate in territory that once belonged to it. It has made possible too the exercise of poetry as emotive exploration of the world of things and as rigorous construction of lucid formal structures, lucid objects of language. Thank you.

Rio de Janeiro
August 31, 1992

Translation from the Portuguese by Djelal Kadir

KAMAU BRATHWAITE
THE 1994 LAUREATE

Kamau Brathwaite (1930–2020), a poet, historian, literary critic, and essayist, was born in Bridgetown, the capital city of Barbados. Brathwaite spent his childhood in Barbados but would spend his adult life traveling, learning, and teaching all over the globe. He attended Harrison University in Barbados and Pembroke College in Cambridge, England, where he graduated with honors in 1953. After graduation, Brathwaite embarked on a journey to Ghana where he worked in Ghana's Ministry of Education for more than ten years. During that time, he familiarized himself with Ghanaian traditional verse and precolonial African myths, which would be influential in his own writing. He earned his PhD in philosophy from the University of Sussex in 1968, and taught at Harvard University, the University of the West Indies, and New York University. His works include the *Rights of Passage* trilogy (1967–69), *Days & Nights* (1975), *Mother*

Poem (1977), *History of the Voice: The Development of Nation Language in Anglophone Caribbean Poetry* (1984), *Sun Poem* (1982), *Middle Passages* (1992), *Dream Stories* (1994), *Born to Slow Horses* (2005), and, most recently, *The Lazarus Poems* (2017).

The constant i wd even say consistent fabric & praxis of my work has been to connect broken islands, cracked, broken words, worlds, friendships, ancestories.

—Kamau Brathwaite

The Voice of African Presence
Ngũgĩ wa Thiong'o

In May this year [1994] my wife and I called a few friends to our house in Orange, New Jersey, to celebrate the arrival of our daughter, born at the end of April. Among them was Kamau Brathwaite, who later rose to read a poem to honor the new arrival. The poem had lines that repeated the name of our daughter, Mũmbi, Mũmbi, Mũmbi, Mũmbi, almost like a religious chant. Now *Mũmbi* means "creator," and we gave our daughter the name because she is in fact my mother, Wanjik, who died in 1989 but is now reborn in Mũmbi. Her full name, then, is Mũmbi Wanjikũ, creator of my mother. Mũmbi is also the name of the original mother of all Gĩkũyũ people. In thinking about the evening afterwards, I was struck anew by Kamau Brathwaite's invocation of the name.

My thoughts took me back to 1972, when Kamau, then Edward Brathwaite, came to the Department of Literature at Nairobi University, Kenya, on a City of Nairobi Fellowship. The department was undergoing tremendous changes. We were trying to break away from the old colonial tradition that emphasized our colonial connections to Europe as primary but not our natural connections to Africa and the rest of the world. We are all familiar with the often-told stories of African children having to learn all about daffodils and snow long before they are able to name the flowers of their own lands. Rebellion against this was the basis of the 1969 Nairobi declaration calling for the abolition of the English Department as then constituted and for its restructuring along entirely new lines. By 1972 we had started breaking away from the centrality of English literature in our syllabus to a new dispensation that emphasized the centrality of the African experience at home on the continent and abroad in the Caribbean, Afro-America, and other parts of the world. We wanted a dialogue among all the literatures of the entire pan-African universe and between them and those of South America, Asia, and Europe in that order. Central to the enterprise was orature, the long tradition of verbal arts passed from mouth to ear in both their classical and contemporary expressions. Other needs arose from the new centrality. For instance, instead of inviting Shakespearean scholars from England, we now wanted scholars from the rest of Africa, from the Caribbean, and from Afro-America. That kind of academic exchange and communication would be more useful to us in cementing the new foundation of our literary and cultural studies. We were also rebelling against a tradition that taught literature as if it was divorced from its social and historical milieu. We wanted to see, explore connections between phenomena. So we hoped that we would get scholars with a sensitive awareness of the connections between literature and life. Who was going to be our first visitor? This was a crucial question, particularly in our new beginnings: suppose we brought a scholar who would come to reinforce the very traditions we were now fighting against?

I had met Edward Brathwaite in London in 1966 when I was doing research on Caribbean literature at Leeds University. It was a gathering which in fact was the formal beginning of the Caribbean Arts Movement. I did not know then that Brathwaite was its founding spirit. Even less did I know that at different but crucial moments in our literary lives we had both been influenced in a fundamental way by one of the classics of Barabajan and Caribbean literature, George Lamming's *In the Castle of My Skin*. For me, Kamau's brilliant poems in *Rights of Passage*, out in 1967 and followed by *Masks* in 1968 and *Islands* in 1969, had added to that sense of self-discovery. In this I was not alone. Those collections became part of the new syllabus. There was in fact something about their content and form that made everybody feel that they fit the historical moment, our search for a connection. And so there was really little doubt as to whom we wanted as our first scholar of what we saw as the beginnings of a new era. Brathwaite was then teaching history at the University of the West Indies' Mona Campus in Jamaica. We were very excited when he accepted our invitation, although the fellowship did not really amount to much in terms of money. As a lecturer, he proved a great teacher. He saw no barriers between geography, history, and literature. What formed the African and Caribbean sensibility could not be divorced from the landscape and the historical experience.

This to me is still one of the most remarkable elements in the life and work of Kamau Brathwaite. He is a connecting spirit. Europe, Africa, the Caribbean, and now America, all important landmarks in his life and thought, find expression in his work in their impact on one another. He explores the African presence in Africa, the Caribbean, and the world, not in its staticness but in its movement, in its changingness, in its interactions. In these interactions the African presence is not a passive element. Whether across the Sahara deserts, through the savannas and tropical forests, across the Atlantic, say, in all its continental and diasporic dimensions, it is a resisting spirit, refusing to succumb, ready to rebuild anew from the ashes of natural disasters and human degradation. In his work, taken as a whole, the physical cannot be divorced from the metaphysical or the material from the religious. In his capacity to move freely from geography to history to literature to cultural criticism, Brathwaite exemplifies a great tradition of the Caribbean intellectual, the tradition of C. L. R. James, Frantz Fanon, Walter Rodney, Aimé Césaire, George Lamming, to mention just a few who readily come to mind. What connects these names, apart from their intellectual versatility, is also their unapologetic claim to Africa as their roots. These islands have given so much to twentieth-century Africa and the world, and our students in Nairobi could now see that for themselves in the presence of the lecturer before them. It was remarkable, and Brathwaite was the talk among the students and faculty.

But it was when Edward Brathwaite performed sections from his poems that we truly appreciated what we had been sensing. The voice. We were being mesmerized by the voice of orature. We were captives of a heritage we knew so well but from which our education had been alienating us. His voice was returning us to our formative roots in *orature.* This was what had been created by our mothers and fathers, and it was there in his performance for us all to see. This orality runs through Brathwaite's entire work and is what gives it its very distinctive quality. This comes out powerfully through performance and makes us realize that, in his literary output, Brathwaite gropes for the word in its oral purity. In doing so, he is groping for the voice of the peasant, the submerged voice of the many who toil and endure.

But alas, our enthusiasm was not necessarily shared by the establishment, who thought they had already given in too much by agreeing to have a scholar who came from places other than England itself, the real home of real literature. Tension was in fact developing between, on the one hand, the students and the faculty, who understood, and on the other the administrative establishment, who could not realize whom we had in our midst and treat him accordingly.

Then something happened that I will never forget. I invited Brathwaite to my rented home in Tigoni, Limuru. The land around Tigoni and Limuru is truly beautiful. Not surprisingly, Tigoni was fairly central to Kenya's history, because it was one of the earliest bones of contention between the British colonial settlers and Kenyans. The demand for the return of the stolen lands of Tigoni to their original owners was one of the key elements in the anticolonial militancy which in the fifties erupted into the Mau Mau armed struggle. The fact that now in the seventies Tigoni was occupied by African landlords, though not the actual original owners, symbolized that Kenya was no longer exclusively a white man's country. Brathwaite was coming into an area hallowed with memories of intense struggles.

I should add that the invitations to meet Brathwaite were sent solely through word of mouth. It turned out to be a big welcome party, with the faculty and some students driving thirty kilometers from Nairobi to attend the gathering. Women led by my mother came from all the villages around. So the peasants from the villages and the men and women of letters from Nairobi, the big city, now gathered in this rural outpost to celebrate Brathwaite's presence. Ceremonial goats were slaughtered in his honor. The women performed. The voice of orality from rural Kenya. It was during the ceremony, with the women singing Gĩtiiro, a kind of dialogue in song and dance, that Edward Brathwaite was given the name of Kamau, the name of a generation that long ago had struggled with the elements to tame the land and make us into what we now were. Edward, the name of the British king under whose brief reign in the 1920s some of the Tigoni lands had been appropriated by blue-blooded aristocrats who wanted to turn Kenya into a white man's country, had now been replaced by Kamau. Naming Brathwaite became the heart of the ceremony, which was also symbolically appropriate.

The right to name ourselves, our landscape; the struggle for the means with which to name ourselves; the search, in other words, for the true voice of our collective being—is this not at the heart of Kamau Brathwaite's work from *Rights of Passage* in 1967 to the *Barabajan Poems* in 1994 and elaborated in his critical works, now collected under the suggestive title *Roots?* The right, the process, and the means to name our world are behind his notion of the Nation Language, that submerged language of the enslaved which, through evolutionary and at times revolutionary subversion of the dominating, asserts itself, often changing the character of what was supposed to be the mainstream.

It was this ceremony way back in 1972 that I was remembering when going over Kamau's invocations on Mūmbi's name in May this year. Little did Kamau know that he was actually invoking the name of my mother and that of all the peasants who welcomed him in 1972 and gave him his name, asserting through song and dance that he was being welcomed in the lands where his ancestral umbilical cord had been buried. Didn't know? That is not even true, because all his work is really an invocation of the power of the African peasantry in all its struggles in Africa, the Caribbean, and the world. He is saying that if we are to claim the twentieth and twenty-first century properly and creatively, we have to connect ourselves to that power. Acknowledgment of the past becomes the basis of strengthening the present and opening out to the future.

Kamau and I are now in the same Department of Comparative Literature at New York University, for reasons that well go back to what we were trying to do at Nairobi in the seventies and therefore what had made possible that invitation; but that is another story. Tonight, my wife and I are very touched at being asked to be part of this truly great occasion in honor of one of the most remarkable voices of the twentieth century. For we are celebrating thirty years of a continuous creative output in theater, poetry, criticism, and history, from his plays published in 1964 to his most recent production, *Barabajan Poems,* in 1994. We are celebrating a producer who through journals like *Savacou* has created forums for others. We are celebrating a teacher who has drawn from, and given back to, Africa, the Caribbean, Europe, and the US. We are celebrating a gifted individual who believes in the collective spirit as seen in his work as the founding spirit of efforts like the Caribbean Arts Movement. We are celebrating the voice of connections, because what is so remarkable about him is not that he is a great poet, historian, critic, and teacher, but that these are not separate entities in himself. They are rather expressions of a searching spirit, searching for the connective link in human life and struggles. We are also celebrating a most courageous man who has gone through personal adversities without succumbing to the death of the spirit. In congratulating Kamau for the 1994 Neustadt Prize, we wish him all the best as we eagerly wait for his many future productions. We hope he will continue to inspire us to join hands so that individually and collectively, we, to paraphrase him, can make here, on these broken grounds . . . something torn and new . . . , a communal future of wholeness.

Norman, Oklahoma
September 30, 1994

Renowned Kenyan writer, editor, and academic **Ngũgĩ wa Thiong'o** *(b. 1938) was himself a finalist for the 2008 Neustadt Prize and also successfully championed Nuruddin Farah for the prize in 1998. He is currently a distinguished professor of English and comparative literature at the University of California, Irvine.*

Newstead to Neustadt
Kamau Brathwaite

Professor Kadir, Editor of *World Literature Today* & Coordinator of this
Moment

Yr Excellencies: The Hon David Walters, Governor of Oklahoma; Yr
Excellency Rudi Webster, Ambassador of Barbados to the United States;
Yr Excellency Richard Leiton Bernal, Ambassador of Jamaica to the United
States and Mrs. Bernal (even though you are not here)

Professor Morris, Interim President of the University of Oklahoma; Jahruba,
divine musicians; Professor Harclyde Walcott, Artistic Director, the Philip
Sherlock Arts Centre, University of the West Indies, Mona, Jamaica; Mary
Brathwaite Morgan, my sister & Assistant Registrar, University of the West
Indies, Mona, Jamaica; Ngũgĩ wa Thiong'o & Njerri Ndungu

Walter Neustadt Jr. and Mrs. Neustadt and members of the Neustadt Family—

First I must acknowledge the totem honour you accord me in bringing
me here for this most prestigious of literary awards. As I keep on saying,
I had *no idea* this kind of thing was going on behind my back. You meet
in camera and unexpectedly publish me the picture you have so darkly
selected. The names of my colleague previous winners, the names of those
in consideration with me this year—the whole thing is so awesome it has me
walking, like a certain musician, on eggshells

What all this says is that there are still some places in the world where
writers & their writing are taken seriously, our work focussed and treated
w/respect—and at the end of the evening we're even handsomely *paid*
for it; presented w/this silver feather as a reminder of responsibility—

somewhere one senses also an arrow pointed at the heart of any personal
presumption—& there will be later even a subtle kind of festschrift erected
in our honour

Is ALTOGETHER TOO MUCH! But I not complainin. We complain enough about
'neglect'. Here at least & at last are dedicated people putting our poems
where their hearts are: Neustadt, *WLT*, Oklahoma!

And all this, haltering as it is, is to sincerely thank you on behalf of my muse,
my muses & on behalf of the Caribbean—for here is a person from these
small islands far south of here who has been brought all these prairie miles
of North American heartland to this crossroads of the 'Trail of Tears' for this
honour by an African brother a further 10,000 miles away (I refer to Kofi
Awoonor, my colleague-fellow poet & Neustadt advocat who unfortunately
cd not be here w/us this evening) and who now that he is here, recognizes, as
he hopes to show in the second part of this thanks-tune, that he was always
on the way here—that the Prize is the occasion, almost the xcuse—but not
the DNA of the business; that there is time & spaces shared by our three
landscapes—

Antillean, OklaHOMEan, African—
in which he recognize his poem

I'll speak about this in the second part of this Acknowledgement

What I want to end w/here is a plea for continued conversation among
ourselves. In a world of increase & increasing materialism—trailer-loads of
it along the information superhighway—we, as livicators of this special art
of vision/writing, dreamer/saying, are much reduced; in danger, some of us,
of becoming petitioners not practitioners—dependent upon grants; upon,
as Tennessee Williams long ago warned, the generosity &/or kindness of
strangers; estranged as many of us are from our villages, our oumforts, from
our own zodiacs

And almost as a desperate response of counter-insurrection, it wd seem,
instead of SHARING more w/each other, we pull apart into our own script/
ure, into the precise particular bleeding of our own individual tick-hearts,
into our own deconstructions, for goodness sake; so that the possible Global
Village (Ogotemmellian as this may be) is on its way towards the Global
Ghetto; and even as

artists (assuming that you will agree w/ me that there is a special grief,
a special GIFT, a special plomb in being this) we allow Ourselves to be
divided—or worse, to remain divided—by race by age by class by colour by
gender by preoccupation of the stampen ground; producing therefore more
heat than light, more artifice than art beat & far more argument than Sphinx

And I'm not saying this because I'm xpected to
SAY SOMETHING
on an august day in September such as this, but because the constant i wd
even say consistent fabric & praxis of my work has been to connect broken
islands, cracked, broken words, worlds, friendships, ancestories & I have
seen the sea outside our yard bring grain by gentle grain out of its granary,
cost upon coast, & then in one long sweep of light or night, take all away
again A poem tree of tidalectics. A strange 12-branching history of it which I
leave you wit

from Newstead to Neustadt
*
haltering the landscapes of the wind

The place i grow in—the underside of the leaf of my childhood—like the
other & inner slide of the sea into which I am born—is call Newstead,
the hoom & heart of that miracle village you must know by now as Mile
& Quarter (MyLann Quarter) [*Barabajan Poems* 1994]. Here is open
canefield caneland snuggled by the darker colour of trees, time, green waters
of vegetation flowing around the islands of hills, Brevitor caves, windmills,

Great white houses (yr horses) on the horizon among more lime, more trees
& our warm sleepy cooking-smoke villages in the shallow valleys of sound.
And at the centre of this is this house of the ancestors, Newstead, which is
quietly preparing itself for the Neustadt Prize in a similar landscape of spirit
& spirits sixty years later on, on the other side of the wall

I bring you therefore a very special greeting of the most intimate recognition.
I in a sense am sent to return to myself what you both give me: speech, shafts
of canelight, a green silver feather, my ancestories coming to be born here
again: planter & slave, Ogoun & buffalo, Newstead & Neustadt spiritdances
of the native crossroads

And because this is such a special something in such an awesome silence
of such sound in which to rise this evening & celebration THANK YOU for
these thousand years brought to this brief account of visibility in this time &
in this town & w/this tongue, I wish w/yr permission & w/as much aplomb
& care as i can limp & limbo up to & pour a brief libation at the foot of the
several trees of me/mory I growing see here in these beautiful landscapes
where the umbilical chords of my voice, I suppose we will have to call it
that—book, bell, trigger, treasure of metaphor—have been placed all along
the curved tale & tails of my journey by my mother & father & sisters &
my ancestor brother & Bob'ob the Ogoun carpenter & Grannpa & Esse
& Fillmore and 'all the aunts & uncles' & Queen Victoria & the Sistine
Chapel & Oshogbo & Hounsi Twenefor & Stephen Daedalus & Stephen
Agyemann & Boukman & W B Yeats & Sycorax & Oya & Agamemnon
dead [. . .]

Norman, Oklahoma
September 30, 1994

ASSIA DJEBAR
THE 1996 LAUREATE

Assia Djebar (1936–2015) was the pen name of Fatima-Zohra Imalayen. She was born in a small coastal town in Algeria, where her father taught French. In 1955 she became the first woman to be accepted into the École Normale Supérieure in Paris, where she published her first novel in 1957. Her pen name originated with this novel, a work she feared would anger her father. Her first collection of verse was published in 1969, the same year that she would also publish her first work of drama. In 1978 she became a film director, and her work on *La nouba des femmes du Mont Chenoua* earned her the prestigious Grand Prize at the Venice Film Festival in 1979. In 2005, based on her superior body of work, Djebar was accepted into the Académie Française as its first member from the Maghreb. Djebar's body of prose includes the titles *Le Soif* (1957; Eng. *The Mischief*, 1958), *Les Alouettes Naïves* (1967), *Femmes d'Alger dans leur appartement* (1980; Eng. *The Women of Algiers in Their Apartment*, 1992), and *Vaste est la prison* (1995; Eng. *So Vast the Prison,*

1999). Her director's credits include the films *La Nouba des femmes du Mont Chenoua* (1977) and *La Zerda ou les chants de l'oubli* (1992). In addition to the Neustadt Prize, Djebar was honored with the 1998 International Prize of Palmi and the 2000 Peace Prize of the German Book Trade.

Perhaps my books can prolong the echo of the voices of so many other women . . . those who keep as their hope the power of their dreams, the tenacity of their memory, and especially the unshaken force of their revolt.

—Assia Djebar

A Letter to Assia Djebar
Barbara Frischmuth

Altaussee [Austria], 4 July 1996

Dear Assia,

Time and again I have been asked why I nominated *you* for the Neustadt Prize, but the answer to that question, considering your complex manner of writing, can only be a complex, multilayered one. I first came across you—actually I was pushed into you—when a representative of your Swiss publisher who recalled my earlier studies in Oriental languages and literatures sent me your book *Fantasia*. I leafed through it attempting to recognize Arabic expressions despite their francophone formulation. (Although my Arabic, which was always only "beginning-level," has long since trickled away in the flow of the years, I still like to play this little game.) Then I began to read, and with the very first page I fell under the spell of your "multiple fractured" language. I was greatly moved at how you constructed a monument to your father as "the giver of the language" in which you write. As indicated in the texts, he was a strict parent yet also one who took you by the hand and led you to school. My own father "fell" in Russia in 1943 (to use one of those euphemistic expressions for the various ways of dying in a war). I was two years old at the time and have no memory of him at all. But therefore I have never missed him either. Still, the way in which you speak of your Muslim father, who so lovingly planned your education, caused me to think about the father I never knew, just as if he had actually been lost to me.

And you, you who have received an inheritance from your father—namely, the French language and thereby a certain freedom—you had the courage, above all in your book *Loin de Médine* (Eng. *Far from Medina*, 1994), to speak of a very important subject, the daughters of Muslims and their rights to claim their inheritance, and for that alone you deserve every prize in the world. The clarity with which you diagnose the early splitting of Islam into the Sunni and Shi'a camps as a consequence of the denial of that inheritance should be the envy of many a Muslim theologian. They all speak of Ali; you speak of Fatima. It was a stroke of genius to give voice to the women around Mohammed and in Mohammed's day, to show who they were: warriors, poets, queens, noblewomen, and slaves, not merely Arab women from Mecca and Medina. In letting them speak, you rewrite the history of the origins of Muslim civilization and you quite rightly emphasize the fact that for young girls and women the Islamic revolution consisted in assuring them an inheritance, assuring them that they might receive from their fathers what was due them. But then Fatima, Mohammed's daughter, was robbed of this inheritance when she was not permitted to be "the scribe at his death"—that is, to serve as trustee of his spiritual inheritance. The consequences are well known, but I have never heard the cause (or at least one of the principal causes) called by name so clearly. For that you deserve full credit, Assia.

You appear not only to have examined your own inheritance in a critical light but also to have analyzed it precisely. "Thus the language that my father had been at such pains for me to learn [the French of your French-teacher father] serves as a go-between, and from now a double, contradictory sign reigns over my initiation," you state in *Fantasia,* and thus you make language itself the theme of your literature—namely, that "multiple fractured" language which you say in *Le blanc de l'Algérie* (1995; Eng. *Algerian White*, 2000) "has inscribed itself incessantly in a linguistic triangle" consisting of Berber, Arabic, and French. You speak of the "language of power" which seeks to marginalize anything considered to be "other," as French did to Arabic at first, then Arabic did in turn to French when it became the narrowly construed "national language." You add two more "languages of power": Latin, which was an obligatory course of study at my *gymnasium;* and Turkish, which I later studied voluntarily and at several universities. But I would not wish to read your books in any of these "languages of power," Assia. Perhaps the German translations—which are all quite good—are for precisely that reason the most suitable means of conveying to me, line by line, the unsettling content of your works: that fundamental conflict which I know from early on, since I too write in an "elevated or literary language" quite different from the dialect of my childhood and from the colloquial speech of my native land.

The sentence in which you so aptly define this constellation demands to be quoted: "To attempt an autobiography using French words alone is to lend oneself to the vivisector's scalpel, revealing what lies beneath the skin. The flesh flakes off and with it, seemingly, the last shreds of the unwritten language of my childhood." And in your books the scabs fall away as well, along with the hastily applied bandages meant more to cover than to heal the wounds inflicted upon your land in the course of its history.

Therefore I can only marvel that you have taken it upon yourself to deal with history, with raw and unhealed history. For your incorruptible eye, which has enabled even me, who knows Algeria only through television, to understand something of what has occurred and is occurring in that country, is also scientifically trained. One notices that, and I find that one may take note of it. But by itself that still would not yield a portrait in which I as an outsider can recognize not only Algeria but rather the entire horrifying course of the world. Likely, the fact that your account—so full of love and passion but also of revulsion—sounds so completely unpartisan or unbiased has to do with that distance which French accords to you in respect to your country and its history. From the very beginning, that account inspired trust in me, trust as a reader, which means that one may submit oneself unreservedly to your view of things without later feeling one has been deceived or misled concerning the facts of the matter.

The fact that the language of your childhood, the language in which you feel, shines forth time and again between the lines of your text, not in the form of individual words but rather in the form of perceptions which must first be "translated" or transcribed, opens up an entirely new dimension for French. I notice a similar phenomenon among Turks who write in German, the offspring of the first generation of guest workers, most of whom were very young when they first came to our country. Their German is as good as that of anyone who has spent thirteen years in a German-language school, but there is more to it than that: a barely perceptible shift or displacement, which, when it is handled in masterly fashion, endows German with a completely new charm. Your art—forgive me for tossing you into a single pot with others in this regard, but the connection is very important to me—and also the art of many of your Turkish, Persian, and Arab colleagues, whether they now write in French or in German, lies in that evocation of the inexhaustible resources of a world not narrated in the language in which it is spoken, a world in which feelings are deeply rooted and from which one must escape in order to be able to recognize it. Just how narrow the connection to this original world still is can be seen in the empty spaces it leaves behind, spaces which stand out in the written language like large gleaming specks against a background of cultural and sociohistorical networks. In somewhat more concrete terms, this touching human warmth, the all-permeating sympathy, the precise and detailed depiction of all the violence, crime, and perfidy which, despite everything, never posits hatred as the unavoidable counterpole—that is what, it seems to me, shines forth from your early language.

The astonishment which erupts from the young girl for the first time in speech persists in more restrained form, permeates all your books, and infects me too as a reader. And not only the astonishment but also the affection, an affection that demands time, time to expose everything that has been buried, to inspect it, as you have done with the countless stories and faces of the women of your land, the mothers and grandmothers who "were already dead long before the grave." You have made their voices audible and stripped away their multiple veils, directed our attention to their humanity and let them narrate their fate from their own point of view. And for all the clarity with which you have recorded this scandalous history of confinement, masking, and imposed silence, you have always retained a certain tenderness for the "others" (contrary to tradition, let me for once designate men as the "others"), as your latest book, *Le blanc de l'Algérie,* proves, for there you urge upon us, your readers, all the Algerian writers who have been killed or have died from illnesses. Instead of polemicizing, you recount how things happened, you attempt to follow your friends down to their final moments, in loving sympathy and with the intention of turning them into objects of affection transcending their deaths. At the same time, you succeed so well in capturing the sheer monstrousness of this war which re-erupts daily in your country that our eyes grow wide with horror. You also do not shy away from stealing into the minds of those who commit these atrocities, conveying their supposed arguments, rationales, and justifications, and showing the chain of violent acts that has made criminals of victims (and sometimes vice versa) to be a chain which binds the combatants to each other. I marvel at you for this as well.

In your works those young warriors who have strangled, stabbed, or shot to death your Algerian writer-colleagues and have considered themselves in the right in doing so talk among themselves in such a manner that one can imagine what goes on in their minds, even as one's outrage mounts, however senseless the deeds may appear and however perverted the logic of the arguments may be. They call themselves "God's Fools," an expression for madmen and mystics in early Islam, for those "from whom the pen had been taken away. Whose words and deeds the angel-scribes did not record, because the fools were not subject to the law and for them the duty of adhering to the law's precepts did not apply. (Go mad and let reason forsake you, said Leila to Madshnun. Then no one will harm you when you enter my village .)" Lokman Sarrakhsi was one of those fools of our Dear Lord, as were many others of whom the legends tell. But never executioners, who carried out judgments rendered by others.

That, then, is the list of themes which caused my interest in your work to become so strong; but it was not merely a matter of themes, as you yourself know only too well, not even when language itself is the theme. What attracted me to you most was your manner of treating those themes in your "fragmented language." (Incidentally, your narrative art is extremely refined, bathed in all the waters of the prose writer's art.) And I readily admit that this manner of yours stirs in me a delight that is not at all easy to allay— which means simply that I do not wish to stop reading you. I say *you* intentionally, for we are our books and ultimately write ourselves in an almost corporeal fashion, just as our language is always a physical, bodily thing, even in those moments when it appears most infused by the spirit or the intellect. It made me extremely happy, Assia, that I was at last able to make your personal acquaintance in Norman, and that we all danced together, and that Hanan al-Shaykh was present, and all the others as well. I hope that this prize makes you even more well known, and—what is likely more important—that it will afford you time, time "for the retreat of writing, in search of a language outside the languages," as you wished yourself at the end of *Le blanc de l'Algérie.*

I embrace you,

Barbara

Translation from the German by William Riggan

Barbara Frischmuth *(b. 1941) is an Austrian writer of novels, short stories,
and plays as well as a translator. Two of her novels and a selection of short stories have appeared in English translation by Ariadne Press.*

Assia Djebar's Lyrical Longing and Pitiless Pen
William H. Gass

The lyricism which comes through the French to us is indeed like a painter's
light and falls softly through a curtain on Assia Djebar's affecting scenes, as
if we were supposed to see a woman bathing in a Pierre Bonnard or a dancer
in a Degas and not a woman weeping in her kitchen, calling out to Allah for
relief, the light letting us wonder what her trouble is since she has a shower
and a sink—a porcelain sink and a pink marble tub, built-in cabinets to boot—
good fortune could not have a broader smile—and a husband with the easy
name of "he" whose feet at least come and go, go, god be praised, into the
masculine monitored streets on masculine business concerning masculine
affairs, into those vast spaces a male god made.

Assia Djebar makes it clear to us, who have a different history and live
in a different time, what, for an Algerian woman, her apartment is—her whole
small world—because even when she leaves it, she is not allowed to touch that
great outdoors, ideally not even with her eyes.

In Afghanistan unveiled women have been beaten with radio anten-
nas ripped from parked cars; adulterers will be stoned as in the good old
days; surgeons are forbidden to operate upon female bodies, bodies which
have been turned into sheeted ghosts more menacing than lepers; women's
schools are closed; and in Iran, bicycle seats, since they resemble saddles, are
denied a woman's weight. And why are saddles denied them? They may not
rise so high or ride astride a stallion. The gradient of oppression is long and

steep; the climb, in those layered gowns, is difficult. In every country, some-one no longer a child is swaddled, another injustice is suffered, varied tyran-nies are endured.

In their apartments, even those women whose senses have been awak-ened by love can only carry them like bedclothes into the courtyard to be aired. How many paces from one room to another? How many days will pass before, at night, the cool air comes? Here escape is measured by degrees, as though digging a tunnel: how far shall she walk before removing her veil? It is a world where women watch women, where mothers try to tie their daugh-ters to custom as much as the men do. A curse, a prayer, jostle for the same breath, and both are useless. Was it better when there was no alternative to be dreamt, to be glimpsed on television, to be encountered in some city square?

Assia Djebar, compelled by circumstances to write about the daily life of Algerian women (her inherited subject) in a tongue which is not theirs, has, nevertheless, with her novels and stories, her poetry, a play, and her films, exposed the plight of her countrywomen to the wide world. With her percep-tive, sensual, and resourceful French, which reaches us now hidden under one more layer of foreign language, she has drawn open this curtained cul-ture and spoken of it without shrillness, without endangering the modesty of her models, without the pleasures of righteous indignation, but with a pen so pitiless it spares us nothing of this massive crime, a condition which faces its future by walking backward into the past, as Assia Djebar, a trained historian and teacher, knows well, so that her characters include women living at the dawn of Islam as well as those suffering from its nightfall.

To expose . . . to lay bare . . . What an extraordinary and daring accom-plishment. How many layers of concealment had to be removed—seven veils? And each one symbolic, through and through, of political, sexual, and edu-cational enstiflement. Algerian women, their feelings held out of sight in their veiled heads, their ears allowed to hear prayers, their eyes given them to weep with, fists to beat upon their chests, their mouths for ritual wailing, their Arabic softened as when women speak to women; kept in closed compounds, weighed upon by husbands who have been arranged for them, so they may then be fondled like a pipe stem; their entire life and outlook surrounded by the plans of men and the cruel and stupid tyrannies of male "isms," by a land, for women, empty of openness or opportunity; followed always by death, as though they were a bone to a starved dog, by a death which will claim them when they become worn and ill and thin from bearing the children they will see sicken and die before they see their own death in the doorway.

It is difficult to know whether it would have been better for the Algerian women Assia Djebar has written of to be able to read her themselves and realize that one of them has portrayed, even celebrated, their plight, although to meager consequence; or to have their story sent into distant comers, so far away as Oklahoma, into an America where the awareness her work brings may only add to our despair at mankind's management of man, or perhaps encourage a sympathy which dresses up a sense of superiority and inherent indifference the way wind reddens a cold cheek.

When men hide their women away, they are also hiding something of themselves, and the cruelties they practice are cruel to them too. If I strike a tree stump often enough with an axe, I shall make muscle, not merely firewood; and if I am a jailer, I grow bars, and my heart is hard as pavement, and I soon see only stone, the air is stale, and my food tastes of tin. How beautifully Assia Djebar presents these sour consequences, like a shining coin pressed painfully into a suppliant palm.

My copy of *A Sister to Scheherazade* (that wonderful double-threaded story of two women who have been quite different wives to the same man, finding the same man as different as two men, though hung from his history like wash on a line) is described on its cover as Fiction/Women's Literature. Heinemann does not mean to say simply that this book is about women, for *Madame Bovary* is about them, *Anna Karenina* is about them, *Sister Carrie* is about them, as is *The Wings of the Dove*. So does this label mean that Assia Djebar's work is by a woman, and can safely be ignored, or that it is a book written for women the way garter belts are fabricated? I do hate such sections of the bookstore—those of "special interest," where literary importance is lowered to the level of the economics of politics and women's subjects are sanitized while women are insulted.

Penetration, pregnancy, pain, a new life delivered to an old death. The womb is not a prison for the child; the womb imprisons the woman. Assia Djebar's work should be placed in that section of the store most frequented by men: among books on horses, hunting, sport. Look there . . . a Delacroix depicting three women sitting at the edge of a darkness, waiting like saucers for their cups, like clothing in a dresser drawer. Ah . . . a volume about harems. Perhaps the man will put his curious nose in it like the fabled camel's into the tent.

Assia Djebar's work deserves to receive this distinguished prize because of the importance of her subject, certainly, and on account of the moral horrors it so vividly and fearlessly depicts. But let us for a moment wildly suppose that women have been liberated all over the world, and that men are being stoned for adultery, and circumcised when caught uncovered in the street, kept out of college but allowed to drink tea. Is *Women of Algiers,* in such a circumstance, now of only historical interest?

I remember a moment—it is in the story "The Woman Who Weeps"— when a woman whose husband has beaten her describes how her face felt as if it were going to fall into her hands, and that image took me to the poor creature, her head in hers, whom Malte Laurids Brigge encounters in a Paris street, and who, startled by his approach, pulls herself so sharply away that she leaves her torn face in her palms where it can be seen now from the inside; then, within a page length of "The Woman Who Weeps," the sultry weather is said to be subsiding like an overripe fruit will drop, and I'm sent off to recall Mahfouz's description of the Cairo sun setting in the middle of the afternoon into the city's smog, a sunset I've seen, passing from lemon to orange to plum. That is to say: Assia Djebar has entered the whole of this head's literature, so I shall remember her words when I turn to Mahfouz and her image when I reread Rilke. The sun, dunked in dust, but always a fruit. Feeding the soil its seed.

The Neustadt Prize, the most important international award we have, stands for this priceless connection which literature can make between distantly separated places and far-off times, between a ceremony in Oklahoma and a city in Algeria, between men who will worship women despite the damage they've done them and the guilt they bear, and the women whom the men hope will not one day feed them to the hogs.

This brief salute to a long career is being given by another writer and not an ambassador, not a politician, and did not begin therefore with the custom-ary invocation of distinguished names and positions (undoubtedly deserv-ing of everyone's gratitude), because that absence was meant by me to be another sign of our prizewinner's success (and the jury's good sense), for she has realized one of our deepest dreams: to write beautifully while still both-ering people.

Assia Djebar is not being celebrated here because she has brought us more bad news, or exotic treats, or even her eloquent indignation, worthy as much of that may be; we are lauding her here because she has given weeping its words and longing its lyrics.

International Writers Center
Washington University, St. Louis

William H. Gass *(1924–2017) was the author of seven works of fiction, nine books of essays, and a book of conversations. A professor of philosophy and the humanities at Washington University in St. Louis, his many prizes included an American Book Award, three National Book Critics Circle Awards, and the Truman Capote Award for Literary Criticism. Knopf published* The William H. Gass Reader *in 2018.*

The Power of Solidarity in the Solitude of Exile
Assia Djebar

In Louisiana, on the 29th of March 1996, when I heard that I had been awarded the Neustadt Prize, I received the news with both joy and sadness. "I am happy, I am unhappy," I told Djelal Kadir over the telephone. "Happy for myself, unhappy for my country in the present time." I was both unhappy and happy for all my friends and colleagues who had died, for all those who had fallen: foreign priests, young women teachers and journalists, and the many anonymous dead in Algeria today. Happy that they have come with me, for as I present myself today before you, they are all around me; unhappy each time I speak of them, each time that I write of their absence . . .

The Arab poet Adonis has written: "Joy has wings but no body / Sadness has a body, but no wings!" Unlike my poet friend, I would like to thank you by offering a response that would have the wings—or the energy—of sadness, and that would give a body, a solidity, to the joy of our encounter here today.

I present myself as the fourteenth laureate of the Neustadt International Prize for Literature. Allow me to say a word about two of my most prestigious forerunners: Elizabeth Bishop, the great American poet, and Francis Ponge, the great French poet—"the master of still life in poetry," as Michel Butor described him. Following these two predecessors, I am the second woman and the second French-speaking writer to receive the Neustadt Prize. But in relation to them, my difference is double: on the one hand, I am a writer of fiction, a novelist; on the other hand, I come from a world where women are traditionally kept "in the shadows" and have been excluded from writing for much too long. For myself, I come from a South presently in tumult and in transition.

"Women in the shadows?" I, however, am not in the shadows. Far from it. I am an exception. Let us remember the names of other celebrated women writers: I think of the Senegalese author Mariama Bâ, who died too young, leaving us two poignant novels; I think of the great Iranian poet Forough Farrokhzad, who died in an accident at an even younger age, in the late 1960s; I also think of an Egyptian woman, the novelist Latifa el Zayyat, who passed away this past September 12 at the age of seventy-three and whose first novel, *La porte ouverte* (1960), opened the door for a new literature created by women of the Arabic language.

I inscribe my name in the celebrated list of Neustadt laureates, surrounded by my African sisters and those of Muslim origin: they could have been here, honored in my place tonight. I feel them at my side, now as I stand here before you: though they are invisible, they are very much present.

I mentioned that I am a writer of fiction. The Peruvian novelist Mario

Vargas Llosa has defined fiction in one of his essays as "truth through lying." He adds a remark that I would like to have written myself: "In the heart of all fiction, the flame of protest burns brightly." During the years of 1995 and 1996, not only in Algeria, where women are victimized because they embody images of modernity in movement, and in Iran, where silence weighs down on those women who resist, but also in Afghanistan these past few months, where the women who flee do so under the veils of ghosts which we find so strange, my own protest, born from this Islamic culture (a culture, however, where in Turkey, in Pakistan, and in Bangladesh, political women are often in command), my protest develops within fictions which I hope might become an "open door" for those women who live under the threat of an atavistic fundamentalism. I remain doubtful as to the "utility" or the impact of writings of the imagination in circumstances such as these.... I think, rather, that, in spite of me and in spite of my writings, perhaps my books can prolong the echo of the voices of so many other women—not all of whom are necessarily intellectuals or artists—those who keep as their hope the power of their dreams, the tenacity of their memory, and especially the unshaken force of their revolt.

Ladies and gentlemen, by honoring me here today, you give strength to my vulnerability, as you give the power of solidarity to the solitude of my exile. This Neustadt Prize will allow me to continue to write, to create, and to breathe, still in the grip of anxiety, but now assured of a public who listens.

"The stone sings while sleeping," the Arab poet writes. So does sadness, the sadness that literature must transform into luminescence. Ladies and gentlemen, I thank you.

Norman, Oklahoma
October 18, 1996

Translation from the French by Pamela A. Genova

NURUDDIN FARAH
THE 1998 LAUREATE

Nuruddin Farah was born in Baidoa, Somalia, in 1945 and now lives in
Cape Town, South Africa. He is the author of twelve novels, which have won
numerous awards and have been translated into more than twenty languages.
His mother was a traditional storyteller, and his father was a merchant who
later worked for the British government as an interpreter. Farah grew up in
a multilingual environment and learned to speak Somali, Amharic, English,
Italian, and Arabic. When he began to write, Farah chose English as the
language of his works. His first novel, *From a Crooked Rib* (1970), depicts
the authoritarian role of patriarchy in African society and earned him praise
as a "male feminist." The publication of his second novel, *A Naked Needle*
(1976), angered the dictatorial Somali regime and finally forced Farah
into exile following several death threats. Farah would not return to live
in Somalia again, but his lifelong pursuit has been to preserve his country
through his writing. His other publications include *Gifts* (1993), *Secrets*

(1997, which won the Prix de l'Astrolabe 2000), *Crossbones* (2011), *Hiding in Plain Sight* (2014), and *North of Dawn* (2018).

Reading these books helped me to reach out, as though I was meant to touch the frontiers of this immense world.

—Nuruddin Farah

Nuruddin Farah's Crucible of the Imagination
Kwame Anthony Appiah

I know exactly why I remember so very well the first time I met Nuruddin Farah: it is because he made me laugh. Not just a wry smile or two, or a modest guffaw. He made me laugh so much that my abdominal muscles ached for days; so much, that I had to beg him to stop talking for a while, because I was doubled up, about to fall to the ground. I remember, too, what it was that he was so funny about. He was telling stories about a meeting with another great African writer, the South African author Bessie Head, whose eccentricities he was delineating with a mixture of gentleness, puzzlement, and profound respect. He was not telling stories *against* her: I remember thinking that if Bessie Head was listening somewhere, from beyond the grave, she would have understood at once that Nuruddin's stories and my laughter were a celebration of her; there was no mockery. What I *don't* remember is where we were—it must have been a conference about African writing—or when it was.

Though I remember my laughter, I don't remember the stories. But even if I did, I know I couldn't tell them as he did, catching each ebbing wave of laughter with another tale slipped in to return me to convulsions. So Nuruddin was locked away in my mind and heart forever not just as the marvelous writer I had read and heard of before I met him, but as this wonderful teller of stories.

I think of this anecdote as emblematic: for this was, as I say, a story about a woman—a crazy woman, but also a great writer. And anyone who has read any of Nuruddin's novels knows that he is always telling stories that have women at their center, and that his women are not the passive objects of his writing but central, vital subjects in the brilliantly imagined, fully realized, magical world of Nuruddin Farah. Indeed, his first novel, *From a Crooked Rib,* depicts the life of Somali women so compellingly that the Nigerian novelist Buchi Emecheta once wondered out loud if it could really

have been written by a man. She must have been kept wondering ever since
by so many Farah women.

In *Maps,* his 1986 novel, there is Misra, the Ethiopian maid who raises
Askar, the Somali protagonist, a refugee from the 1977–78 war between
Ethiopia and Somalia in his native Ogaden. Misra is not Askar's kinswoman,
not even his countrywoman, and, as a foster parent to an orphan, she is and
is not his mother: but her life is tied up with this young man whom she has
raised, her love for him running against the loyalties to people and nation
which are the source of so much bloodshed and division, but which are also at
the heart of Askar's identity. In the first chapter, addressed to Askar (but perhaps, the novel's ending suggests, in a voice Askar himself is ventriloquising),
Nuruddin Farah writes: "The point of you was that, in small and large ways,
you determined what Misra's life would be like the moment you took it over."

What follows is a wonderful portrait of a bond between a mother and
a child, told with enormous respect for her love, and for her own insistence
that, despite all that is done to her because she is woman, she is glad to be a
woman. We know she is glad to be a woman because she says so. When young
Askar wakes one day with blood on his sheets, he responds to Misra's suggestion that he has begun to menstruate with an angry "But I am a man." Maybe,
he suggests later, he is sick, should see a doctor.

> She didn't like his explanation. "It means you prefer being sick to
> being a woman."
> "Naturally," he said. "Who wouldn't?"
> She said, "*I* wouldn't."

But, as I say, Misra is one among a multitude. Throughout the extraordinary
trilogy that he called *Variations on the Theme of an African Dictatorship*—in
Sweet and Sour Milk (1979), which won the 1980 English-Speaking Union
Literary Award, *Sardines* (1981), and *Close Sesame* (1983)—there are so many
uncommon women: Margaritta, in *Sweet and Sour Milk,* who leads us into the
world of clandestine resistance to Somalia's dictator, the Generalissimo (who
is not named in the novel by his real-world name, Siyad Barre); or Medina, in

Sardines, "as strong-minded," Nuruddin says, "as she was unbending in her decisions," who leaves her husband, a minister in the government, to raise their child, Ubax, alone. Medina is protecting her daughter from the insistence of her mother-in-law, Idil, that Ubax be circumcised. She is a cosmopolitan, who amuses her daughter by reading her Chinua Achebe and the *Arabian Nights* in her own translations, a member of what Nuruddin calls "the privilegentsia," who speaks "four European languages quite well" and writes "in two." But she is also secretly working to end the dictatorship.

Medina is joined in *Variations on the Theme of an African Dictatorship* not only by her precocious, demanding daughter, Ubax, but also by such splendid creations as her mother Fatima bint Thabit, a Yemeni traditionalist; by Idil, her authoritarian mother-in-law; by Sagal, athlete and revolutionary; by Amina and Ebia, Sagal's friends. The trilogy of *Sweet and Sour Milk, Sardines,* and *Close Sesame* is a powerful assault on dictatorship *and* a powerful indictment of the oppression of women, and the particular forms it takes in Somalia: but it is also a celebration of women's agency.

If I seem to be belaboring a point, it is not because I find it surprising that a man should write convincingly about the lives and interests and concerns of women. Writing is always more about identification than identity: the work of the imagination is never simply to express our selves. Nor, despite what many would assume, is a man's preoccupation with the situation of women especially surprising in Africa: *Things Fall Apart,* the novel by Chinua Achebe that thrust modern African writing in English onto the world stage, is, in part, a novel about the tragedy of men who do not respect the feminine in nature, in their wives and mothers and daughters, and in themselves. Nuruddin Farah's treatment of women's lives is not remarkable because he is a man; it is remarkable because of the power of its moral and literary achievement. And the obvious centrality, in his work, of the suffering of women and their agency is, I think, a reflection of what is deepest in his political argument, which is his recognition of the intimate connection between the dynamics of power in the family—in relations between husbands and wives, brothers and sisters, parents and children, uncles and aunts and cousins, one generation and another—and the broader politics of states and nations. A society that is filled with contempt for women or children or the old, he suggests again and again, cannot have a healthy politics: and the poisonous, murderous struggles that have overtaken his own Somalia have their beginning, he seems to argue, in the struggles of family life. Farah is not the first feminist to have grasped that the personal is political; but he is, in my view, the African writer who has given this thesis its most persuasive imaginative demonstration.

It is important, therefore, that Nuruddin Farah's world is also full of intensely realized representations of love and loyalty: in *Secrets,* the most recent of his novels, there is the long love affair between Damac and Yaqat, mother and father to Kalaman, the novel's central figure, two people held together in a horrifying fatal secret that is both the tie between them and the greatest threat to their happiness. And there is the extraordinary relationship between Kalaman and his grandfather, Nonno, each of whom has named the other; theirs is a relationship that survives from the child's birth to the grandfather's death despite the same secret, which also stands between and binds them.

Equally memorable for me is the wonderful love of father, son, and grandson in *Close Sesame:* with Deeriye the grandfather, Mursal the son, and Samawade the grandson, locked together in a bond between the generations that is cruelly destroyed by the moral demands of life under dictatorship. Not only is *Close Sesame* a powerfully moving celebration of family across the generations; it has also given us, in Deeriye, the most fully realized picture that I am aware of in English of the interior life of a devout Moslem—indeed, one of the richest representations of a prayerfully devout human being I have ever read. Most Somalis are raised, as Nuruddin Farah was, as Moslems; as a result, the act of imagination here will probably not receive the same attention as the manner in which he has found his way into the minds of so many imaginary women. So, in celebrating the powers of his imagination, we should perhaps notice, too, that Nuruddin Farah, though raised as a Moslem, is not himself devout: he does not claim, even when it would advance his interests, to be so. One of Farah's many literary admirers is Salman Rushdie, who must, I suspect, be especially admiring of Nuruddin's capacity to represent respectfully an Islam that is no longer fully his own.

*

Nuruddin Farah, whom we honor today, was born in Baidoa in 1945, but moved at the age of one to what was then the British-administered Ogaden, where his father was a translator. When the British departed from the Ogaden, they left its many Somali inhabitants to the Ethiopians, creating a region of conflict that was to smolder always and burst, from time to time, into the flames of Somali-Ethiopian warfare over the next four decades. In 1963 his family moved to Mogadiscio during one of these wars, one family among a million refugees over the years driven by these conflicts from the Ogaden. He went to university in Chandigarh in India (choosing it over an offer from Wisconsin), and published that first novel, *From a Crooked Rib,* in London in 1970, at the age of twenty-five, becoming, with that work, the first Somali novelist—though, of course, by no means her first great literary figure, since he was raised within a tradition of oral literature that is among the richest in the world. The Mogadiscio in which he grew up was a densely cosmopolitan product of waves of political and cultural colonizers: Italianate architecture, Islam and Arabic civilization, the English language, all embedded within a Somali culture. Nuruddin speaks not only Somali but also Italian, Arabic, Amharic (the language of Ethiopian rule, from the days in the Ogaden), and, of course, the wonderful English in which he has written his eight novels and almost all his work.

In 1974 he left Somalia to begin a period of nomadic peregrination of a sort that would have made sense to his Somali ancestors, even if he has carried it out on a larger scale, living in Europe, North America, and Africa. In 1976 he published *A Naked Needle,* a novel that caught the unfriendly eye of Mohamed Siyad Barre, Somalia's dictator. He was planning to return home from Rome, and had called his brother to arrange to be collected at the airport, when he learned, from his brother, that Siyad Barre was angry with him. What began as a weeklong postponement of his return, to give the Generalissimo time to cool down, turned into a twenty-twoyear exile, which ended in 1996, five years after Siyad Barre's departure had plunged Somalia into the crisis from which it has still not emerged.

In the meanwhile Nuruddin has lived in Italy, Germany, Britain, the United States, Uganda, Sudan, Ethiopia, and Gambia; his latest place of residence is Kaduna, in northern Nigeria, the home of Amina, his wife. But next year they will be packing their tent again and moving to Cape Town. In 1986 he was kicked out of Gambia for accusing President Sir Dawda Jawara of being more interested in golf than governing. ("Stupid of me," was his laconic comment to an Associated Press journalist.) In Uganda, in 1990, he got on the wrong side of President Yoweri Museveni, then chairman of the Organization of African Unity, accusing him of failing to mediate the war in Somalia. "Museveni was inept," Nuruddin said with the special tact he reserves for presidents. After Museveni denounced him at a news conference, Nuruddin took the hint and moved to Ethiopia. Nuruddin Farah has been thrown out by more African countries than most people have visited; he has visited more than most people could name.

I wish I had time to tell you more about his writing: about the thoroughly original way his characters live as much in their dreams as in their waking lives; to describe how his novels are morally serious without being preachy, or how he teases you by writing of events that seem magical but also always have possible unmagical explanations; to show you the richness and power of his prose. I wish I could explain to you how a man who was deprived by exile of his people and his family has kept his people and his family—and the idea of family and people—alive in the crucible of the imagination. But these, fortunately, are things I don't have to tell you about, because you can read him for yourselves: all of them are there in *Secrets,* a work which proves that a master of the novel is still growing in his craft. Read it. I promise it will reward your reading: but I also have to warn you that you will end up having to read the rest of his work.

I know I am keeping you from the man himself, but I should like to say one more thing in closing: Nuruddin is a man with an extraordinary gift for friendship, and friendship is something that we should honor more than we do and give thanks for when we can. But Nuruddin is also, as I have been telling you, a magnificent novelist, and we should honor and be grateful for that, too. I have been struggling as to which of these gratitudes I should express in closing. But I realized today that I do not have to choose between thanking him for his novels and for his friendship. For his novels are a friend's gift: and he has given them, as a gift of friendship, to the great company of men and women now reading his novels around the world.

Norman, Oklahoma
October 29, 1998

Kwame Anthony Appiah *(b. 1954, London) is a philosopher, novelist, cultural theorist, and scholar of African and African American studies who teaches in New York University's Department of Philosophy and School of Law. Among his many awards and honors, he was elected a Fellow of the Royal Society of Literature in 2017.*

Wordsmith with a Difference
Nuruddin Farah

I was born into a difference at a time in my continent's history when the power of speech lay elsewhere, in other people's tongues. In those days, we, as colonials and as Somalia, existed more in reference to whom we were made into as colonial subjects than whom we presumed ourselves to be, or who we ought to have been. Ours was a language divested of authority. Moreover, I was born into a difference with its own specificity: of a mother and a father who were not wholly literate in Somali. I say "not wholly literate," because even though my father had mastered the rudimentaries of reading and writing in at least three languages and my mother was an oral poet, the truth is they were seldom engaged in activities I would associate with the fully literate.

At the age of four and a half, my three elder brothers and I were sent to school by our parents. I doubt that my parents could articulate what must have been a disturbing ambivalence in their minds; I doubt that they meant to pay hefty fees they could ill afford with a view to imposing philosophical discontinuities between their worldview and ours. We became literate in the foreign tongues in which we received our formal education. It would dawn on me before my tenth year, once I became aware of my potential, that there were immense benefits to being literate in foreign tongues. For not only could I read the Koran as a professional reciter might—by then I had earned the honorific "Haafizul Qur'an," a title given to those who have obtained the formidable distinction of committing the entire Scripture to memory—but I could read Dostoevsky and Victor Hugo in Arabic, or struggle my way through Bertrand Russell's *History of Western Philosophy* in English. Not that I understood much of what I read. But one thing was very obvious: I had gained access to a larger and more varied world than the one my parents ever anticipated, a world more dangerous but at the same time more rewarding than that which my age mates had known. And what a different world it was, with some of the distances made smaller, no bigger than a book, and new distances amplified. Reading these books helped me to reach out, as though I was meant to touch the frontiers of this immense world. I was touched by what I read, I was moved, I was changed too. In those faraway days, a particular piece of wisdom from the Prophet Mohammed was frequently on everyone's lips: "To acquire knowledge, one must travel very, very far, even to China, if need be." I had no idea where China was. However, I sensed it as if I were more than prepared to travel there or even beyond it. We valued knowledge for what it was worth, and were ready to seek it wherever we might. Because of our peculiar circumstances as colonial subjects and especially as Somalis, it mattered little where we found it, in foreign tongues or in books written by others and published in other lands. We got used to the inconveniences with which we associated these alien languages. We might have been the proverbial hunchback who makes do with his daily discomforts, but who continues to live his life most fully regardless.

Out of love, and because they wanted the best for us, our parents did not stand in the way of our acquisition of knowledge, well aware of the fact that we were growing into alien children, not wholly of their making. My father was instrumental in the establishment of a community school in our town. He travelled far in his search for a teacher willing to come and live in Kallafo. Of the many whom he interviewed, the one whom he liked best proved to be demanding, insisting that he be given free lodging in addition to his monthly salary, conditions which my father ultimately accepted. Once he arrived, the teacher lived in our own compound, and until he got married he was fed out of the same kitchen as ourselves, his guests more ours than his, as we had more space in our part of the compound.

Later, when a Christian missionary group established its own school, my brothers and I were all sent there. The school was run by evangelists, eager to win converts to their faith. But not if you paid a school fee, because then you were treated differently. As it turned out, it was not obligatory for us to attend the special Bible classes in the after-school hours, since our parents had the wherewithal to foot the bills. Not so the boys from poorer families, a handful of whom converted to Christianity out of convenience. We all knew who these were. One of them used to lend me his Bible, which boasted the marked passages thought to be relevant to one's redemption. From our perspective, it was as though we were doing a course in comparative religion, something I am sure our parents were aware of. As Somalis, we all had an extremely robust confidence in our faith then, and were convinced that we were equal to any challenges posed by other religions. We had no qualms in quoting to the missionaries the verse from the Koran, "To each his religion, you [keep to] yours and we to our own!" Our society was so self-confidently tolerant in those days, so accepting of the differences in character and mental acumen between ourselves and the Christian missionaries, whom we accused of taking advantage of those with no means to fight them off.

As residents of Kallafo, a town with a population of fifteen to twenty thousand, we were accommodating of others who were different from ourselves. The Lord knows there was a wide variety of other peoples from different parts of the world for a town in the backwaters of the Shebelle River in the Somali-speaking Ogaden. We had Yemeni Arabs in our midst, we had a small community of farmers originally from East Africa, a wide array of Somalis from other corners of the peninsula, plus a couple of Palestinian families, refugees really, who were on their way elsewhere for resettlement. Ours was a tolerant Islam. You lived your life as you saw fit, not according to self-appointed Mullahs threatening you with fire and brimstone if, in their opinion, you strayed from the righteousness of the faith, as they decreed it. We were who we were, self-confidently proud of who we perceived ourselves to be, in spite of our status as colonial subjects. With our minds open, our hearts likewise, we received the world, and along with it the knowledge that made the world larger and more varied too.

There is something forward-looking about knowing other languages, something outward-looking about studying the cultures of other peoples: not only do you enrich your understanding of your own culture, but it makes you appreciate yours all the more. I remember my first encounter with *A Thousand and One Nights* and how, reading it in the original, I felt suddenly whole. In fact, the more I read and got to know about other people's cultures, even if cursorily, the more confident I became about my own. I became more convinced than ever that I needed to create a universe familiar enough to Somalis, and which might inspire a sense of mission in themselves. Not that I could do much about the language in which I ought to write. When I started writing, no standardised system of spelling or of writing existed in Somali; none was established until October of 1972.

Despite this, writing in foreign tongues was as much fun as reading had been entertaining and edifying too. I felt encouraged by what I read, stories whose cunning and sophistication enabled me to get in touch with the narrative genius that is the African folktale. Literature of the written and oral variety became a mansion in which I moved with self-edifying ease, reading books in foreign tongues and listening to the oral wisdom transmitted in Somali. Meanwhile I enjoyed going from *Kalila and Dimna* to Ernest Hemingway, to Mark Twain, to Agatha Christie, to a Somali poem recited under the shade of a tree. I was elated by this multicultural encounter, the world now unitary, and now boasting of a wealth of differences, each expressive of a human need: the need to gain more knowledge about myself and about the lives of others, in order to be fulfilled.

It was easy for me to make the journey from the Arabic culture of *A Thousand and One Nights* to the translation of *Kalila and Dimna* from Sanskrit. With a bit of help from my eldest brother, who encouraged me, I was able to tackle Dostoevsky and Hugo in Arabic too. The quirkiness of my reading could be explained in part by the fact that, because of the oral nature of our society, books in any tongue were seldom available. But what a pleasure they were to me when I had them, and what a delight to lose my bearings in the multistoried mansion of a writer's imagined universe. Sadly, I admit to having become more fascinated by the written variety of literature, perhaps because, as with all new converts, I was attracted to the barely familiar in preference to the oral tradition which was everywhere around me. There was a freshness to the stories in the books every time I read them. I was a child apart, my parents two wordsmiths, in their different ways, each forging out of the smithy of their souls a creative reckoning of an oral universe. It was in deference to their efforts that I lent a new lease on life later to the tales told to me orally, tales that I worked into my own, all the more to appreciate them.

In addition to the powers associated with being literate in foreign tongues, there were economic benefits too. As a child, I lived in a part of the world where a large segment of the population do not read and write. So whenever I was short of cash, I hired out my services to an illiterate adult in need of a letter to be written. It occurred to me too that perhaps I had more power than did my father as an interpreter, whose oral rendering of what the Englishman said in Swahili had something short-lived about it. As a scribe, I had more power, giving flesh to ideas orally delivered and therefore transient, and which, by dint of being written down in another language, became more real. In written form, the letter could be read and reread, and its message could travel farther than an oral one, travel through space and time, unaltered.

There was something else. I had at my mercy grown men, my father's age, some humouring me so I might write a letter for them without pay, or at a discount. On occasion, my parents interceded on behalf of some of our relations. I was always paid the compliment of being a very lucky boy, some providing me with a chair and a table, some with a drink. Deferent silence attended my every intervention, respect for my status accompanied the order of the moment. I was lavishly pampered. I was so adept at what I set out to do that, in my eleventh year, I delivered a speech I helped write to the visiting emperor, Haile Selassie, an honour accorded to me after two grown men, both of them my teachers, felt too intimidated by the prospect of standing before His Majesty. My photographs decorated many a royal wall in Addis Ababa for a while as a result of delivering it.

I grew more confident the more I read. The more I got to know about the injustices perpetrated by men against the womenfolk, the more conscious I grew of my powers. I had not yet completed my twelfth year when an elderly man, a friend of my father's, required that I write a letter for him to his estranged wife—estranged, because he had the frequent habit of beating her. Apparently the woman had gone to another town where she had taken refuge amongst her kin, refusing to return in spite of their pleas and despite the assurances the husband had given to her elder brother, now sitting close by. The elder brother kept nodding his head, as if in agreement with the wife-beater, who was adamantly insistent that he had done no wrong. I also gathered that, in a message orally delivered to the husband and her elder brother, the woman had filed for divorce, a request neither the husband nor her elder brother was prepared to consider. "I will not divorce you," he instructed me to write, "and if you do not come back within a couple of days of receiving this letter, I will have you brought back forcibly and will beat you until all your bones are broken."

Unbeknownst to him, I did what was within my power to do: I sabotaged the intent of the man's message by a deliberate omission, supported by an intentional mishearing of his statements. In the letter I made him say that if she did not come back within a few days of receiving this letter, or if she continued raising objections against her being beaten by her legal husband, then there was nothing left for him but to divorce her, as she had requested. It was perhaps with a view to giving myself legal cover that I demanded the husband put the authority of his thumb to the bottom right-hand side of the letter.

Six months later I learnt of what had inevitably come to pass: the estranged wife, assuming that she was divorced, remarried another man of her choice, a man who was more tender toward her. The case went to court, and the letter I had written for the husband was produced. The Islamic Qadi decreed that the woman was now legally the wife of her current husband, by whom she had a son. I could not determine from the expression on my father's face if he were proud of me or ashamed. But he was clearly disturbed by "my wily ways," as he put it, forbidding me henceforth to write letters on behalf of others.

A question I've often asked myself is: are my parents continued in me? One was a translator communicating in Swahili to the Englishman and then transmitting the response in Somali. My father learnt Swahili as a child because he was brought up in Nairobi, in the very city—then a small town—in which the Englishman came to acquire the language, perhaps with the assistance of a native instructor. It is safe to assume that the colonialist's register of Swahili was different from my father's. Even so, almost all the transactions being oral, my father, and his boss the Governor, spoke as if in twinship with each other, the one employing Swahili, the other rendering it into Somali. I wonder if there was a point when my father ceased to be the Englishman's sidekick and became an agent in his own right, with a new authority to his agency?

Was there a point when my father's relationship to the truth of the Englishman's authority took on its own energy, through the agency generated by his own truth and authority as a colonial? No doubt there was a world's distance between the moment my father heard the Englishman say something in Swahili and the moment he interpreted this into Somali. Did my father, by interpreting, insinuate himself into the ideas he worked with, ideas to which he gave a new lease of life? How much, if any, did he transform these ideas? And did he take vengeance on the colonial master who originated the ideas? In short, was my father ever an anticolonialist?

Being a poet, my mother helped me gain access to hidden, creative energies within me, even in so young a child. I remember the placidity of her moods, as she paced back and forth in a bedroom with the door locked from inside. A family poet, she composed *buraanbur* lyrics in praise of the bride or bridegroom, or made up a special lullaby for one of her many children. Unlike my father, she had the self-confident vitality to reinvent the world daily by singing about it. There was a self-assuredness to all her doings. I thought she was more articulate than my father, who, patriarch that he was, talked in certainties, never doubting that he might be wrong. She was a great one to help one confront one's quotidian uncertainties.

Born into a difference: I lived in a world different from that of my parents. Not that I always had their permission to be different from them. All the same, we met, my parents and I, as though we were travellers meeting in a transit lounge. As children raised apart, we were, in essentials, journeymen of the future, hybrids of a new sort. In an effort to get closer to my mother, or perhaps to bridge a chasm, I learnt as much of the oral tradition as I possibly could. It was maybe in imitation of the poet in her that I tried my hand at making up my own lyrics in Somali to tunes borrowed from the songs that were popular in those days.

As a youth, I was as inventive as children who speak the correct language to the correct parent, to each parent his or her own, in a world with its own value systems, where the calendars are not the same, where people do not worship the same deities. For me, as a child, the most prominent distances were those between temperaments, my mother's and my father's. I am alluding to the fact that language, and what uses we make of it, is the longest distance between two persons, the one a poet, sensitive, committed to ideas larger than herself, the other despondently despotic, a patriarch willing to submit the world to the authority of his whim. My mother once described another man who was equally deficient in sensibilities as rather like a three-legged stool with one leg missing. She demonstrated what she meant, her head exaggeratedly tilted to one side, one of her arms bent at the elbow, hanging down as though broken.

She was interested in what I wrote, my mother was, often requesting that I tell her the stories as I developed them in my head. Generous to me, she accommodated my eccentricities and provided me with as much space as I required. (We spoke once of how she might have become a major poet if she hadn't spent all her time looking after her numerous children.) Interested in where the story was headed, she put me right when I got the spirit of the tale wrong. Not my father. He would've been happier, he told me, if I had become a clerk at the bank and brought home all my earnings. And yet it was he who had sought out "knowledge" in the shape of teachers, he who had helped establish the first school in our town. My mother died sixteen years after we last met, whilst I was still in exile. But my father and I met more recently in a hospital in Mombasa, Kenya, where he was recovering from an injury to his head. I found him intolerant of my views. We had a set-to about my choice of dress, of habits, of friends. He was at his friendliest when showing me off to his cronies, when he chose to be praiseful of my achievements as a writer.

On my way to the airport, I called on him to make peace with him, and to say my farewell. The two of us alone, I reminded him of how I had been impressed with his contributions in terms of our secular education, which hadn't until then been available in our town; how, in fact, it was he who had made it possible for me to become a writer. He looked restless, a man wanting to get something off his chest. And he spoke regretfully about "knowledge." Pronouncing the Somali word for knowledge, *aqoon*, as though it were synonymous with venom, he accused me of betraying all his aspirations, and of being treacherous to his and everyone's expectations of me. I do not know why, but I reminded him of the dialogue between Knowledge and Everyman in the English morality play *Everyman*, when Knowledge says, "Everyman, I will go with thee and be thy guide, In thy most need to go by thy side." Maybe I hoped he would be supportive of my efforts as a writer the way my mother had been. Would he not agree, I wondered, that I had continued where he and my mother left off as a professional interpreter, and a poet, considering that I turned out to be a wordsmith with a difference.

He said, "No one trusts subversives."

I said I was not sure what he meant.

In his reply he quoted a Somali folktale in which a boy, born to a single mother, reaches the mature age of nine before uttering a word. The woman prays daily, appealing to God to make her son speak. At the age of ten, he does so. To his mother, he says, "Shall we fornicate, Mother, you and I?" Shocked, the mother then prays to the Almighty to make him mute once again.

I asked myself if, in the opinion of my father, I was subversive, because I wrote in foreign tongues, or because, in my writings, I challenged the authoritarian tendencies of Somali tradition? I could say, in self-defence (but did not), that writing in cosmopolitan settings, in foreign tongues, is, to my mind, more forward-looking, ultimately more outward-looking, than much of the writing done in the indigenous languages in Africa and elsewhere; that a great body of these literatures is remarkable for its nationalistic bent, and its jingoism too; and that much of Somali oral poetry and prose is reactionary, inward-looking in a clannish sort of way.

Instead I said, "I was born into a difference, born into a world not of my own making. I wish the two of us would be sufficiently tolerant of each other so as to celebrate our differences. It is time we got to know ourselves better, time we celebrated the differences in our worldviews."

Norman, Oklahoma
October 29, 1998

DAVID MALOUF
THE 2000 LAUREATE

David Malouf was born in Queensland, Australia, in 1934 and became a
full-time writer in 1978. He has published poetry, novels, short stories,
essays, opera librettos, and a play and has been widely translated. His first
two published books were collections of poetry. His first novel, *Johnno*
(1975), is the semi-autobiographical tale of a young man growing up in
Brisbane during the Second World War. His second novel, *An Imaginary
Life* (1978), is a fictional account of the exiled Roman poet Ovid. Later
novels include *Child's Play with Eustace & The Prowler* (1982), *Fly Away
Peter* (1982), *Harland's Half Acre* (1985), *The Great World* (1990)—
which won the Commonwealth Writers Prize (overall winner, best book)
and the Prix Femina Étranger (France)—and the acclaimed *Remembering
Babylon* (1993), which was shortlisted for the Booker Prize for Fiction,
won the first International IMPAC Dublin Literary Award in 1996, and the
Commonwealth Writers Prize (South East Asia and South Pacific Region,

best book). *The Conversations at Curlow Creek* (1996) followed. His collections of short stories include *Antipodes* (1985), *Dream Stuff* (2000), and *Every Move You Make* (2006). Recent publications are *Ransom* (2009), a novel inspired by a part of Homer's *Iliad,* and *Earth Hour* (2014), a poetry collection. He was shortlisted for the Man Booker International Prize in 2011. His most recent volume of poetry is *An Open Book* (2018).

It's a tribute to all forms of making, from the grandest to the most domestic and humble, as the sign of our human need to come home to the world we live in, to make a home of whatever things, small or large, that we have added to it.

—David Malouf

David Malouf's Music of Human Loss and Love
Ihab Hassan

In the finest writers, the evidence may overflow the work. It moves in a gesture, fills a pause. Or it may guide you on a walk, such as David Malouf invited us— Sally Hassan and me—to take around Cremorne Point, in Sydney. Think of a winter day, the sky blue, strung with pale clouds, barely a chill in the air. The path wound through trees, shrubs, flowers, rocks tumbling down toward the waters of Jackson Harbour on one side, the creamy houses of Cremorne rising on the other. And as we walked, we talked of Australian history, Aboriginal misery, the new immigrants, the fabulous wines of Oz. But David Malouf kept noticing, stopping, pointing: here was a ghost gum, here an angophora, there some primitive ferns, and look at that little yellow wattle. Then he stooped, touching with tenderness a tiny pink flower, pink shading into magenta, flickering in the grass. "I don't know the name of this one," he said sadly.

And right there I saw a glimmer of his gift: wakefulness and precision of feeling, blended in wonder, and a delicacy that can surprise the mystery of creation itself. It was this elusive quality, inward with his poetic sensibility, a quality akin to love, that first drew me to the work of David Malouf. It was the same quality that prompted me to nominate him for the Neustadt International Prize for Literature before I had ever met the man. There may have been some extrinsic factor in my beguilement, which I am certain owed nothing to our common Arab background—his, Lebanese Christian; mine, Egyptian Moslem. That extrinsic factor may have been the Antipodes, crying for just recognition.

Consider this: English, the world's largest second language, has become many dialects, many Englishes, expressing now diverse cultures, creeds, climes. Australian English, like Indian or Nigerian or American English, has its own tang and timbre—a sound full of wry coloratura. Modern Australian writers, from Patrick White and Les Murray to David Malouf, convince us how live that language is, and how it promises to fill the ears of the world with new cadences, fresh feelings.

The language rises from the continent Down Under, and from its now polyglot throat. Home of the most ancient, continuous culture, dating back some fifty thousand years, Australia enters the world's awareness through two bloody gates: the genocide of Aborigines and the incarceration of the Anglo-Irish poor. From this dreadful origin has come one of the most vital, decent, and humorous multicultural societies. Immigrants from Southern Europe, the Middle East, and above all Asia have deeply enriched the old Anglo-Celtic and Aboriginal strains. Australia, which Malouf once described as a "raft," "a new float of lives in busy interaction," is dreaming its future, as it once dreamt its primordial past, with zest and only a modicum of turbulence.

But the revival of a continent—a strange continent at that, full of wombats, bandicoots, emus, wallabies, where swans are black, Christmas comes in heat waves, and trees shed their bark instead of their leaves—that revival is not a function of history or politics or even myth alone. The revival draws on the roots of that obscure energy we call, in dumb amazement, the human spirit. It is this energy that David Malouf taps in his oeuvre, comprising some twenty prizewinning volumes of fiction, poetry, drama, essays, memoirs, and libretti.

The work, compellingly universal in appeal, carries the signature of a truly original temperament. Its master themes are easy enough to discern: history, nature, love, art, memory, the frailties of identity, and, above all, the spirit's unappeased quest, on the highways and darker byways of existence, for reconciliation in the heart of being. Far more difficult to convey here are the sensuous splendor, technical ingenuity, aching insight, and luminous wisdom of that work.

Luminous, indeed, in its delicacy, like that little pink and magenta flower, but musical too, in another fold of mind. The music issues, of course, from Malouf's personal voice. But it rises also, farther away, from the center of compassion, a music of human loss in a universe wherein nothing is ever lost, a counterpoint of forms, drawn to dissolution, yet ever re-creating their patterns in the imagination. "I have always felt," Malouf wrote in the preface to his libretto for *Jane Eyre*, "that in any action that presents itself as a subject

of opera there should be an element that for its fullest expression demands
music rather than simply tolerating it." That demand for music, music of
different and sometimes inaudible kinds, is what the work of David Malouf
makes on us, makes and supremely satisfies.

University of Wisconsin–Milwaukee

Ihab Hassan *(1925–2015) was an Egyptian-born literary theorist and writer.
The recipient of two Guggenheim Fellowships and three Senior Fulbright
Lectureships, he was Vilas Research Professor (emeritus) at the University of
Wisconsin–Milwaukee.*

A Writing Life
David Malouf

An award like the Neustadt, which is given for a body of work, is bound to
draw attention to just that, to the sort of whole a writer's work makes. It's a
question that can scarcely arise of course till the body of work is actually there,
till one after another, novel, story, poem, has been added to the rest, relates
itself to the rest, and subtly changes it; what emerges then is likely to be as surprising to the writer as it is obvious to his readers and commentators, since
he never consciously planned it—how could he, following his instincts and
working piecemeal in the dark? How could he know, beginning tentatively
as we all do, what would lie up ahead? What is revealed at last, if the writer
has been working at any depth and exploring to the full all that is in him, all
that he knows and does not know that he knows till it appears on the page
before him, is nothing less than his own consciousness, soaked through with
the experience of a particular temperament in a particular place and time. I

want to say something here of how the books that make up my body of work got themselves written; something too of the extent to which they are, like all things created in this way, the expression of an idiosyncratic reading of the world, of nature, of men and women, of life's events and accidents, and at the same time products of the particular world I came out of, mid- to late twentieth-century Australia.

I began as a poet and had already published three collections of verse, and got myself some reputation as a poet, before I produced a piece of fiction I felt in any way pleased with. In fact, I had been trying my hand at fiction from the start, stories, a novel, but a convincing prose voice, a narrative tone that might be as rich and straightforward as the one I had struck in poetry, eluded me. So, for a long time I published only poems. Later, when the works of fiction did come, and followed one another quickly, I found that ideas—a phrase, an image—this might, if followed up and allowed to develop, have become a poem, tended to be absorbed in whatever fiction I was engaged on, though I continued to write poetry and still do. Novels are voracious. They demand the whole of your attention. There's a hard little voice in them that insists *Don't go away, this is for me.* Part of the joy of novel writing is this sense you have, for the "duration" so to speak, that the whole universe has turned in the direction of what you are writing, that every stray thought that comes to you, everything you read in the newspaper or see in the street, every conversation you overhear, is a message from the book, which has, by a kind of magnetism, drawn the whole world into its sphere.

My first novel was called *Johnno*. When I wrote it, in 1972, after nearly ten years of failed beginnings, I was already in my late thirties. It wasn't published—I still wasn't sure that I wanted it to be seen—till three years later.

It was about growing up in my hometown, Brisbane, a place that for some reason had never till then got itself into a book—or not anyway in a form that had brought it alive in people's minds and stuck. I wanted to put it on the map; to make it, in all its particularity, a place that would exist powerfully in the lives of readers in the same way that Dickens's London does, or Dostoevsky's Petersburg. That is, as a place fully imagined, since I had already grasped something paradoxical, which is that places become real in a

reader's mind not as embodiments of observation and fact but through invention, as imaginary places that bear the names of real ones, and if they are created with sufficient immediacy and glow, will in the end replace the real one;
or perhaps I should say live as its more lively and convincing double. What
I wanted to do was to create a fictional Brisbane that the reader, wherever
he happened to be from, would enter as if he were returning to the place he
had grown up in, and whose weather, light, architecture, and verbal habits
and social tensions had shaped him as they had my two central characters.
Of those two characters, one was destroyed by the place, the other saved by
his need, his writer's need, to re-create and objectify it to the point where he
could at last see what it was, then wrestle with it and understand or forgive.

That first novel was in the first person, though I should add—I had
learned a thing or two from all those failed drafts—that the narrator was not
myself. For one thing, he knew more than I had ever done, or than I knew,
in fact, till the half-autobiographical experience I was dealing with had been
shaped by the needs of fiction and set down. What I mean to stress, in saying this, is that everything in the book, characters, events, places, even what
remained of my own experience, had been, as they must be of course, relived
in imagination: imagined. Even the most realistic books—and *Johnno* is
meant to at least *look* realistic—books that are set in real verifiable places and
deal with actual events, can live in the reader's mind only to the extent that
they are works of imagination and engage the reader's imagination.

Second novels, as most writers will tell you, are the real test. It is with the
second novel that a writer begins to stake out his territory, establish that he is
there for the long haul, and begins to perceive in the first outlines of an emerging body of work the obsessive preoccupations and odd ways of thinking and
feeling that he must follow if his writing is to be coherent and whole.

I solved this problem of the second novel, without quite knowing as yet
that it was a problem, by leaping as far from *Johnno* as possible, to the very limits of my imagination. The book I wrote, *An Imaginary Life*, part prose poem,
part speculative essay, part dramatic monologue, was about the Roman poet
Ovid in exile and made the fairly outrageous claim for an Australian book in
the 1970s that an Australian writer could take up a non-Australian subject and

write about a non-Australian place without ceasing to be either Australian or himself. But how, if the work sprang from any deep place in him, could it not express what he was and what had shaped him? Early Australian commentators tended to see *An Imaginary Life* as what they called a European book. It was European readers who pointed out that so many of the subjects it took up, all the anxieties it expressed, the optimism it breathed, spoke to them at least of the new world and of a sensibility that was unmistakably antipodean.

But the point I want to make here is this: that what I had done in these two very different books, and without as yet quite seeing it, was to map out the limits of my world as a writer. I tend to see my work at this distance in spatial rather than chronological terms, and for me the interesting thing about *An Imaginary Life* is that it seems to have got itself written out of sequence. It ought to have been my last book, an old man's summing up, a late meditation on death, on continuity and change, the possibility of transformation, along with all those other topics that come up in a book that is open enough, lyrical enough, to be discursively rich in topics: the power of language as a means of structuring, interpreting, remaking experience; the need to remap the world so that wherever you happen to be is the centre; the interplay of civilisation and wildness, animal and human, body and soul; the moves by which we embrace accident and reread it as fate—all topics I would return to and deal with in new ways later. So, as I say, a last book that in my case happened to come second, and, in appearing so early, opened up the whole view backward, or rather ahead. My succeeding books, *Fly Away Peter, Harland's Half Acre, The Great World, Remembering Babylon,* have in some ways been a matter of "filling in" the ground between the realism of my first book and the distant but, as it has appeared, connected *non*realism of the second.

Two comments about being a writer whose immediate world and material happen to be Australian.

The first has to do with nature; not that grand category of creation we all belong to, and whose chain of connectedness has been an important element in my writing, but nature as it embodies itself, in a particular place, as land, landscape, weather, space, light, and which not only forms a background to the dramas and occasions we call history but also significantly shapes them, and shapes as well the psyche of those who live with the opportunities and limitations they present.

We tend to forget that in most places what we call nature is something *made*, a landscape shaped by centuries of industry and use that deeply humanises it and gives back, by reflection, a happy sense of human presence and power, of an idealised vision made real. In Australia what we mostly have before us is *un*made nature, a landscape that gives back no comfortable and reassuring vision of the centrality of humans and their works. This makes Australian attitudes to nature, and Australian writing about it, very different from the ones that appear in other forms of English. Nature in Australian poetry and fiction is seldom the source of moral reflections on order and industry. It does not offer itself as an emblematic language of feeling, or, as the Duke in *As You Like It* suggests, as material for sermons. What the vastness of Australian spaces evokes is anxiety. This is a landscape that has no need of human presence or a shaping mind or hand to complete it. It is already complete—which seems to be how the aboriginal world has always seen it; the land, for them, is something to be known, protected, revered, but not, as is our way, to be changed and "improved." For those of us who come to it with a European culture behind us, of making, of making use, it is a challenging and forbidding presence, and its beauty, its resistance, its hostility as some have seen it, raises questions about man's place in the scheme of things that do not arise, or not so sharply, elsewhere.

This leads me to the second point I want to make about the world as the Australian writer encounters it.

That largely unmade landscape is also, from our non-aboriginal point of view, very largely uninterpreted. It has not yet had laid down over it, as in England or France or other places with a long history of settlement and culture, that network of myths and legends and folk stories that make a landscape glow in the mind, that fund of associations and references which gives it meaning and depth. The work has begun, of course, but the network is still open. It is still full of interesting spaces and gaps. The meanings are not yet definitive. This puts the Australian writer in a position that is unusual, maybe at this point unique.

In one way we stand, like other contemporary writers, at the end of a tradition, the tradition that goes back, through the language we work in, English, to the Greeks and beyond; we live within that tradition with the same sense of "lateness" as Thomas Bernhard, or Thomas Pynchon, or Italo Calvino, or Georges Perec. But when it comes to the world that immediately surrounds us, we also stand, in a curious telescoping of time, at the beginning—in the position, say, of Hesiod, with the real making still to do.

Not all Australian writers feel this: daily life in Australia is varied and complex enough for a writer to ignore the sort of things I have been speaking of and write urban novels of the immediate present, just as in London or New York. That I *have* felt it, and in the sort of personal way that shapes all of one's thinking and feeling, is clear from the books themselves, which would be very different if I had not. In these matters we all do what we need to do, what our particular sort of writing demands.

A good many of my novels deal with verifiable moments in Australian history, not with known events but with that underside of events which is where most of us experience them, and in many cases go on experiencing them as pain or loss. I would want to call this an interior history, and what interests me is that in the ordinary way of things, so much of this, in Australia, goes unexpressed: unwritten about but also unspoken.

When Australia was still a small nation of just under four million, at the time of the First World War, we lost sixty-two thousand men at Gallipoli and in the trenches in France. I grew up in the shadow of that loss, which struck every small town and virtually every family in Australia, but did not produce, as it did in England, say, or in Germany and France, a reparative literature—poems, novels, plays—through which the deep horrors of that experience could be remade and taken in and come to terms with. The men who had directly suffered did not write about it, and, except in an offhand way, did not speak about it either. But until such things *are* spoken about, and, most of all, have been taken inside and lived through in the imagination, reexperienced as meaning rather than muddle, individual lives, and the larger life of the community, cannot recover and be healed. When a significant body of writing about the First World War did appear at last in Australia, it was in poems and fiction produced nearly forty years after the event by my generation; I did it myself in *Fly Away Peter*. It's a matter, as always, of the writer's dealing with what touches him personally—these things cannot be taken up coldly or out of duty—but by doing so, he also provides a kind of healing for the world he comes out of, whose sorrows and losses he shares with the rest.

One other thing I would like to add, which is where the two aspects of the Australian scene that I have been outlining, the land and the history, come together. This is the process by which, as settlers and latecomers, we have begun to come into full possession of the place.

Of course we already possess it in fact, through occupation or conquest, and that possession is legitimised by law. But there is only one way that we can truly possess the land (I wrote a novel, *Harland's Half Acre*, about this): that is by taking it into ourselves, interiorising and reimagining it as native people have done. This too is a work for poetry, and for the kind of fiction that dares to take on what it is too often left for poetry alone to do.

I want to end with a short poem that speaks of the business of making in all its forms; of what it means to us; what we are seeking when we set out there in the world some artefact, some made thing, that was not previously part of nature but is now, so that nature is changed, enlarged by its presence. It's a tribute to all forms of making, from the grandest to the most domestic and humble, as the sign of our human need to come home to the world we live in, to make a home of whatever things, small or large, that we have added to it.

Making

That a man should wonder
what he might find
at day's end beyond darkness:
something made
that was not there till he made it,

a thing unique
as all that our eyes

are schooled to. At its hour
at the masthead, Canopus,
a moon if it is writ

in the calendar, and this,
which nature had not thought
to add but once
there cannot do without
and whether of breath

made, or stone, egg-white,
earth, old sticks, odd clippings,
to be as the child lost
in his own story seeks it,
a home, another home.

Norman, Oklahoma
October 20, 2000

ÁLVARO MUTIS
THE 2002 LAUREATE

Álvaro Mutis (1923–2013) was a Colombian poet, novelist, and essayist. Though he was born in Colombia, he lived in Brussels until he was eleven years old. His first collection of poetry was published in 1948, and his first short stories appeared in 1978. Mutis is best known for his award-winning novellas, published in the United States in two collections, *Maqroll* and *The Adventures of Maqroll*. His body of work includes *La Nieve del Almirante* (1986; Eng. *The Snow of the Admiral*, 1995), *Ilona llega con la lluvia* (1987; Eng. *Ilona Comes with the Rain*, 1995), *La última escala del Tramp Steamer* (1989; Eng. *The Tramp Steamer's Last Port of Call*, 1995), and *Abdul Bashur, soñador de navíos* (1991; Eng. *Abdul Bashur, Dreamer of Ships*, 1995). His most famous book is *Empresas y Tribulaciones de Maqroll el Gaviero* (Eng. *The Adventures and Misadventures of Maqroll*), consisting of seven novellas.

All that I have written is destined to celebrate and perpetuate that corner of the *tierra caliente* from which emanates the very substance of my dreams, my nostalgias, my terrors, and my fortunes.

—Álvaro Mutis

The Passionate Fire of Álvaro Mutis
Juan Gustavo Cobo Borda

Who among today's Spanish-language writers is capable of engaging in dialogue, with poised enthusiasm, with authors as diverse as the Italian Giuseppe Ungaretti, the Frenchman Francis Ponge, the Pole Czesław Miłosz, or the Brazilian João Cabral de Melo Neto, as well as with those who have been or are presently the author's close friends, such as Octavio Paz and Gabriel García Márquez?

The Colombian Álvaro Mutis (b. 1923) is, without doubt, a contemporary writer who possesses a cultural background sufficiently broad and universal to transcend languages and borders. This cosmopolitanism allows him to moderate a compelling debate where poetry and its interplay with the destiny of humankind in this tenuous world succeed in bringing together participants from all walks of life. His work has been translated into approximately twenty languages, including English, French, German, Italian, Portuguese, Japanese, Greek, Hebrew, Turkish, Polish, Dutch, Swedish, and Danish. Such international acclaim fits seamlessly within the ideal of a world community of literature that the Neustadt Prize endeavors to foster and recognize.

Mutis's poetry, short stories, novels, and essays reflect a convergence of historical influences, beginning with the Bible, extending to the cultures of Islam and Byzantium, and finally arriving at such seminal figures in Latin American history as Simón Bolívar—all of which embody and illuminate the complex relationship between Europe and America. A universal dialogue of cultures that comes alive in Mutis's essays and commentary reflects his intimate understanding of Russian literature, French history, and the development of the novel in the United States, without ever distorting or underestimating the pivotal role of Spain in the formation of Latin America.

Mutis represents a rare combination of the cosmopolitan and the universal on the one hand and Latin America's unique local flavor on the other. Like

Jorge Luis Borges, Mutis is capable of appreciating, understanding, and evaluating through his literary creations the various nations that a broad world offers us as readers.

There is yet another argument for championing Mutis's work for the Neustadt Prize: the central figure who brings everything together, endowing it with unique character, is a protagonist named Maqroll el Gaviero (Maqroll the Lookout). Marginalized, out of place, adrift on the rough seas of an indifferent world, his adventures are both pilgrimages and farces, undertaken with lucid and penetrating fatalism.

Such despair, intuitive and stripped of all self-delusion, goes hand in hand with a sober and sublime respect for the illusions to which human beings cling so fiercely, giving rise to one of the most perfect creations of twentieth-century Latin American literature. Maqroll becomes, for readers the world over, a compelling and indispensable being.

Mutis's fiction takes place within the evocative framework of the tropics, a burning landscape where splendor commingles with the limits of human endurance and where the fragility of memory and the devastating force of untamed nature devour both the creations and the cherished beliefs of humankind. Along with violence and desire, these elements combine to produce a passionate search for those traits that lead to the stubborn obsession of individuals to make their lives—in the midst of precarious and conflicting societies—more secure and enduring. Here, too, a most ancient awareness confronts a world in perpetual crisis and renewal. From this backdrop have sprung the vibrant pages of *La Nieve del Almirante* (1986), *Ilona llega con la lluvia* (1987), *Un bel morir* (1989), *La última escala del Tramp Steamer* (1989), *Amirbar* (1990), and *Abdul Bashur, soñador de navíos* (1991), and also the stories and testimonials found in *La mansión de Araucaíma* (1973) and *Diario de Lecumberri* (1959).

With refined literary acumen, Mutis succeeds in creating a saga deeply rooted in verse, as found in the *Summa de Maqroll el Gaviero*, where the plot never departs from the epic and universal aspects of poetry. On the contrary, his fiction offers a sagacious parable not only of the Colombia and the coffee-growing lands of the author's childhood, but also of a land that resonates throughout all Latin America. He shows to what extent his country has been changed and how its passionately held core values have been destroyed by harsh and painful realities. Nevertheless, Mutis always penetrates beyond those tragedies in an unambiguous attempt to pose vital questions that force his protagonists to confront their own transcendental existence. From his exile in Mexico he has succeeded in crafting tangible and compelling images of his homeland and of Latin American reality in general. Mutis uses these images as a foundation for the construction of a unique world that manages to subsist due to its internal consistency and its faithfulness to the obsessions that have haunted the author since 1948, when he published his first collection of poetry, *La Balanza* (The scales). His characters are forged from a passionate fire originating in a long coexistence with the author himself.

Although his protagonists create a stage where European and Western influences contend with the hybridization and metamorphosis they undergo upon arriving in the New World, Mutis's work is never a simple essay about identity. It is a literary journey in which the reader discovers and confronts his- or herself.

The utopia that Mutis ultimately proposes is that of an infinite and open reading process similar to the one Joseph Conrad defined when referring to Marcel Proust: one in which analysis has become the creator. A literary journey where a single, definitive reading of a work is all but impossible, thus allowing the text to accompany us through the successive changes in our own lives without becoming irrelevant. By honoring and recognizing Álvaro Mutis, the jurors of the Neustadt International Prize for Literature will be honoring one of the great creative literary minds of our time and, consequently, reaffirming the Neustadt Prize's own criteria for literary excellence.

Bogotá, Colombia

Translation from the Spanish by David Draper Clark

Juan Gustavo Cobo Borda *(b. 1948, Bogotá), a distinguished poet and critic, was elected to permanent membership in the Academia Colombiana de la*

Lengua in 1993, pursued a career in government service beginning in the mid-1970s, and has been a member of WLT's editorial board since 2001.

Álvaro Mutis on Himself
Álvaro Mutis

I was born in Bogotá on August 25, 1923, the feast day of Saint Louis, king of France. I cannot deny the influence of my patron saint on my devotion to monarchies. I completed early studies in Brussels, then returned to Colombia for periods that were at first vacations, and, later—as they became more and more extended—I lived on a coffee and sugar plantation that my maternal grandfather had founded. It was called "Coello" and was located in the foothills of the Central Highlands. All that I have written is destined to celebrate and perpetuate that corner of the *tierra caliente* from which emanates the very substance of my dreams, my nostalgias, my terrors, and my fortunes. There is not a single line of my work that is not connected, in a secret or explicit way, to the limitless world that for me is that corner of the region of Tolima in Colombia.

In a final attempt to earn my high school diploma, I enrolled in the Colegio Mayor de Nuestra Señora del Rosario in Bogotá. My professor of Spanish literature was the noted Colombian poet Eduardo Carranza, and two blocks from the school were the pool halls of the Café Europa and the Café Paris. Carranza's classes were for me an unforgettable and passionate initiation to poetry. Billiards and poetry took precedence over my acquiring that much-sought-after diploma.

Alternating his poems with my own, Carlos Patiño and I published a chapbook titled *La Balanza* (The scales), which we distributed ourselves among our bookseller friends on April 8, 1948. The following day, our publication went out of print as the result of a fire. On April 9 the "Bogotazo" occurred when the downtown of the city was set ablaze by the enraged supporters of presidential candidate Jorge Eliécer Gaitán, who was assassinated that day in the capital. In 1953—after publishing some poems, the first in the journal *La Razón* at the hands of Alberto Zalamea, and others in the Sunday supplement to *El Espectador*, thanks to Eduardo Zalamea Borda—my verse collection *Los elementos del desastre* (The elements of the disaster) appeared in the collection "Poets of Spain and America" published by Losada, directed by Rafael Alberti and Guillermo de la Torre in Buenos Aires.

In 1956 I traveled to Mexico, where I reside today. Octavio Paz, who had written some laudatory reviews of my poetry, opened doors for me in literary supplements and magazines. Paz himself presented my work in a generous essay on my book *Reseña de los Hospitales de Ultramar* (A report on the overseas hospitals), published in 1958 as a supplement to number 56 of the magazine *Mito*, directed in Colombia by Jorge Gaitán Durán. In 1959 *Diario de Lecumberri* (Diary of Lecumberri) came out, published by the Universidad Veracruzana in its Fiction series. In 1964 Ediciones Era, also in Mexico, published a collection of poems, all written in Mexico, entitled *Los trabajos perdidos* (Wasted efforts). Two works appearing simultaneously in 1973 were *Summa de Maqroll el Gaviero*, which brought together all my poetry up to that date, published by Barral Editores of Barcelona, and *La Mansión de Araucaíma* (The mansion of Araucaíma), released by Sudamericana in Buenos Aires, which collected all my short stories. In 1978 Seix Barral of Barcelona produced a new expanded edition of the collection that included the short story "El último rostro" (The last face seen).

In 1982 Mexico's Fondo de Cultura Económica brought out a book of poems entitled *Caravansary* in its Tierra Firme collection. In 1984 the same publisher produced another volume of poetry, *Los emisarios* (The emissaries), in the same series, and in 1985 Cátedra of Madrid released *Crónica Regia y Alabanza del Reino* (Royal account and praise of the realm), poems dedicated to King Phillip II, his family, and court. In these last works I explore—not without difficulties, vacillations, and flashes of doubt—a new way of telling the same old thing, that which will remain the same and which, for

me, is the only thing worth telling: that the ghosts from my avid and scat-
tered readings during childhood at the Coello plantation visit me with invari-
able frequency—ghosts born in large part in the corners of the history of the
Western world and in the golden decadence of Byzantium, engulfed, always,
by the warm mists of the coffee plantations.

In 1987, and with the same purpose of recapturing vast periods from my
past, I published *Un Homenaje y siete Nocturnos* (An homage and seven noc-
turnes), brought out by El Equilibrista of Mexico and Pamiela of Pamplona.
Subsequently, I resolved to try my hand at the short story by expanding
some of the prose pieces I had written on Maqroll el Gaviero (Maqroll the
Lookout), a character who, beginning with the first poems I wrote, has visited me sporadically. Out of this enterprise was born *Empresas y tribulaciones
de Maqroll el Gaviero*, which includes the following novellas: *La Nieve del
Almirante* (1986; Eng. *The Snow of the Admiral*, 1995), *Ilona llega con la
lluvia* (1987; Eng. *Ilona Comes with the Rain*, 1995), *Un bel morir* (1989;
Eng. *Un Bel Morir*, 1995), *La última escala del Tramp Steamer* (1989; Eng.
The Tramp Steamer's Last Port of Call, 1995), *Amirbar* (1990; Eng. *Amirbar*,
1995), *Abdul Bashur, soñador de navíos* (1991; Eng. *Abdul Bashur, Dreamer
of Ships*, 1995), and *Tríptico de mar y tierra* (1993; Eng. *Triptych on Sea and
Land*, 1995). After being published separately, in Spain as well as in Latin
America, the works were released as two volumes with the publishing house
Siruela in 1993 and in a single volume with Alfaguara in 1995.[1]

In 1988 Mexico's Fondo de Cultura Económica published short stories
and essays under the title *La muerte del Estratega* (The death of the strate-
gist), and in 1990 it brought out *Summa de Maqroll el Gaviero*, which collected all my poetry up to that time. The volume was reprinted in Spain by
Visor in 1992.

Of my prose works, there are translations into English, French, German,
Italian, Portuguese, Danish, Swedish, Polish, Greek, Dutch, and Turkish.
Of my poetry, complete translations exist in French, Italian, and Romanian,
and there are anthologized versions in Chinese, Russian, English, Greek, and
German.

I have never taken part in politics; I have never voted, and the last event in the political realm that truly concerned me or had anything to do with me in a clear and honest way was the fall of Constantinople at the hands of the Turks on May 29, 1453, nor have I failed to recognize that I still have not gotten over the trip to Canossa by the Salic King Henry IV in January 1077 to pay homage to the Sovereign Pontiff Gregory VII—a trip of such ill-fated consequences for the Christian West. Hence, I am a defender of the Holy Roman Empire, monarchic, and legitimist.

Norman, Oklahoma
October 18, 2002

Translation from the Spanish by David Draper Clark

Editorial note: First published as "Mutis por Mutis," in *Caminos y encuentros de Maqroll el Gaviero: Escritos sobre Álvaro Mutis*, ed. Javier Ruíz Portella (Barcelona: Áltera, 2001), 19–23.

1. In English, all seven novellas are available in *The Adventures and Misadventures of Maqroll*, trans. Edith Grossman (New York Review Books, 2002).

ADAM ZAGAJEWSKI
THE 2004 LAUREATE

Adam Zagajewski (b. 1945) was born in the city of Lwów (now Lvov, Ukraine) but was forced to leave almost immediately thereafter when the Red Army occupied the area. After studying philosophy at Jagiellonian University in Kraków, Zagajewski emigrated to Paris, where he would remain until 2002. He began writing poetry in the 1970s and helped lead the movement that would come to be known as the Polish New Wave. He built his career around teaching at various universities throughout the world, including the University of Houston and the University of Chicago in the United States. Much of Zagajewski's body of work has been translated into English, including the poetry collections *Tremor* (1985), *Canvas* (1991), *Mysticism for Beginners* (1997), *World Without End: New and Selected Poems* (2002), *A Defense of Ardor* (2004), *Eternal Enemies* (2008), *Unseen Hand* (2011), *Slight Exaggeration* (2017), and *Asymmetry*

(2018). He also wrote a memoir, published in 2000, entitled *Another Beauty*. In addition to his Neustadt honor, Zagajewski was also named a Guggenheim Fellow in 1992.

Poetry must be written, continued, risked, tried, revised, erased, and tried again as long as we breathe and love, doubt and believe.

—Adam Zagajewski

Enchantment and Despair in the
Poetry of Adam Zagajewski
Bogdana Carpenter

The leading poet of his generation, Adam Zagajewski continues the best tradition of Polish postwar poetry—established by such writers as Czesław Miłosz, Zbigniew Herbert, and Wisława Szymborska—in verse marked by intellectuality, historical awareness, a strong ethical stance, and formal sophistication. At the same time, Zagajewski has found his own distinct voice, not to be confused with any of his illustrious predecessors. In his poetry, he manages to combine tradition and innovation, participation in a poetic community, and staunch individualism. The fabric of Zagajewski's poetry is made of disparate elements: reality and dreams, the keen observation of reality and imagination, artistry and spirituality, erudition and spontaneity of emotions. In his poetry culture and nature share equal space.

Zagajewski's biography, as well as his poetry, are marked by polarities: allegiance to his native city and a sense of displacement caused by exile; solidarity with his generation and a sense of solitude; a dark vision of the world and tender sensitivity to its beauty, despair, and joy. These geographic, historical, and philosophical polarities define the space within which he moves as a poet. They explain his acute awareness of twentieth-century history, combined with a willingness to forget it in favor of an ahistorical, existential dimension.

Born in Lwów in 1945, Adam Zagajewski left his native city as an infant after its occupation by the victorious Red Army and subsequent integration into the Soviet Union. He lived first in Gliwice, a depressing Silesian city that before World War II belonged to Germany, but as a result of shifting frontiers became part of Poland after 1945. At the age of eighteen he moved to Kraków, where he studied philosophy at the Jagiellonian University. In the 1980s and 1990s he lived in Paris, but he returned to Kraków in July 2002. Each winter he teaches creative writing at the University of Houston. Zagajewski's life follows a twentieth-century paradigm of exile—a life lived outside the place to which we belong by birth and culture. As in so many other writers, exile resulted in a sense of displacement: "If people are divided into the settled, the emigrants and the homeless, then I certainly belong to the third category," he confesses.

Zagajewski's poetic career started in the 1970s when he formed part of a movement known as the New Wave or the Generation '68; this group called for poetry of social and political commitment. The principal target was the language of official communist propaganda, cleverly paraphrased in poetry to reveal its vacuity and falseness. From the beginning, the group was united more by its political goals than by its poetics. Zagajewski was one of the first to break away. He wrote an essay entitled "Solidarity and Solitude"; its title summarizes well his position, midway between commitment to collective causes and self-introspection. Or, as he puts it in a poem, "I take a seat in between.... I am alone but not lonely."

Philosophically, Zagajewski's poetry moves between two worlds, "one serene, the other insane." The world experienced by the senses is one of beauty and splendor, but the world known from history is one of suffering, death, and destruction. Although Zagajewski did not experience war directly, "the iron grip" of the twentieth century is the source of his pessimism and dark vision. By temperament, Zagajewski is a *homo aestheticus*, sensitive to beauty in all its manifestations—people, nature, art, music: "Only in the beauty created / by others is there consolation." The dark specter of history remains in the background and is rarely mentioned by name. In one of the poems, for example, its destructive power is evoked by such sharp objects as scissors, penknives, pruning shears, and razor blades. The foreground of Zagajewski's poetry is luminous, filled with buckets of raspberries and gentle hills; it is the world at peace where one can hear birds grow quiet and listen with rapture to Gregorian chants.

Behind soft air, wet leaves, and scarlet sunsets, however, lurk crematoria and razed cities: "Where starlings sing now, a branch / of Auschwitz had been built." A generation younger than Tadeusz Różewicz, Zbigniew Herbert, and Wisława Szymborska—the pleiad of Polish poets referred to by Miłosz as "poets of ruins"—Zagajewski's historical awareness stems less from memory than knowledge and imagination. This is why in his poetry enchantment and despair, a glimmering surface and dark interior, honey and soot walk hand in hand, and it is from the clash of these opposite emotions that the spark comes in his lines. "A poem grows on contradictions but it can't cover it," he writes in one of his poems.

Nevertheless, Zagajewski never turns to cynicism or nihilism; despite everything, he is a poet of affirmation who believes that "not every thunderbolt kills" and that "incidental dreams vanish at dawn / and the great ones keep growing." Art transforms pain into beauty. It is Zagajewski's great gift to know how to translate both ugliness and splendor into the brilliance of a poetic word: "I was in that strait where / suffering changes into song." His is a poetry of striking metaphors: beautiful, intricate, but at the same time apt and precise. They become instruments of cognition as well as moments of epiphany, when passive contemplation is transformed into the creative act of forging a new reality: "shining moments plucked from my imagination like a thorn drawn from an athlete's narrow foot."

This Neustadt ceremony carries with it a special poignancy and symbolism: Adam Zagajewski is the second Polish poet to win the Neustadt Prize. The first—and until today the only other Polish writer to receive it— was Czesław Miłosz in 1978. Miłosz who, according to Joseph Brodsky, was one of the greatest poets of the twentieth century, died on August 14, 2004. Awarding the prestigious Neustadt International Prize for Literature to Adam Zagajewski, the most gifted poetic heir of Miłosz, is like passing on a baton, providing reassurance that Polish poetry is alive and doing well.

Norman, Oklahoma
October 1, 2004

Bogdana Carpenter *is emeritus professor of Polish and comparative literature at the University of Michigan and an esteemed translator of Polish literature. A native of Poland, she grew up, as did Adam Zagajewski, in the city of Gliwice. She was a student of Czesław Miłosz at the University of California at Berkeley, where she earned a PhD in comparative literature.*

Poetry for Beginners
Adam Zagajewski

Let me express my gratitude for this prize, the Neustadt International Prize for Literature, which I've known about since 1978, when Czesław Miłosz received it. I remember regarding with awe his Neustadt photograph representing a handsome poet in a tuxedo, smiling and proud. Miłosz was in the 1970s a poet for the happy few, a secret and—within the Soviet-dominated part of Europe—prohibited poet whom we in Kraków read avidly, the way one studies a sacred text. We read his work in informal seminars, in private apartments, for he was banned from the university then.

Norman, Oklahoma, may not be Paris, and yet you display here a generosity that is mostly lacking in the old, traditional centers. It seems also—I've learned all this after the news about the prize reached me in Kraków—that you've invented an ingenious and completely transparent system for your international jury's debate and vote.

Thank you for this beautiful prize; when I look at the list of its winners I can't believe my eyes. I find on this list the great names of contemporary literature, starting with Giuseppe Ungaretti. Then comes Gabriel García Márquez, Elizabeth Bishop, Octavio Paz, and many others. Could you imagine a room filled with all these giants? The roar of laughter, friendly exchanges, but also brilliant, malicious remarks? Norman, Oklahoma, has established itself as one of the undeclared capitals of modernity.

I want to thank the Neustadt family for their kindness and for their interest in the art of writing, and *World Literature Today* for its zeal and tenacity in covering so many different linguistic realms of fiction and poetry. My gratitude goes also to Bogdana Carpenter who, unbeknownst to me, championed my work in front of the other jurors. Given the time difference between Oklahoma and Poland, I can easily claim that she fought for me as I was sleeping in Kraków under the gray October sky. Thank you, Clare Cavanagh, the magic translator of my poems and essays. And, last but not least, thank you, Maya—for everything.

Standing here in front of you, I'm thinking of Joseph Brodsky, who came to Norman to present and praise Miłosz's work for the Neustadt. I'm also thinking of my great compatriot, my mentor and friend, Zbigniew Herbert, whose name appeared several times during the Neustadt Prize deliberations and who, almost always unlucky in the external circumstances of his existence, was never chosen the winner of the prize—of course, he would have deserved this award in such an obvious way that even saying this seems to me futile.

I look at you, dear audience; I see many juvenile faces, and I realize that some young, very young poets, poet-candidates, so far unknown to the world and yet great in their daydreams and potential promises, have gathered in this room. This makes me think of poetry itself, poetry that is greater than any of us can comprehend.

Here we are, in this beautiful modern hall within the Sam Noble Oklahoma Museum of Natural History; we find ourselves in the company of dinosaurs and other dignified beasts, illiterate yet intriguing, once dangerous, now posthumously domesticated. And yet there's a different, silent, and invisible company that doesn't need any special building to be permanently present in our lives (well, a good library is a useful thing)—the dead poets' society: Homer and Sappho, Virgil and Keats, Emily Dickinson and Adam Mickiewicz, Antonio Machado and Anna Swir. The fact that we, the living ones, still write poems verges on impudence. After all these masterpieces! After all this perfection! After all these dramatic events, after Shelley's drowning death, after Keats's agony in Rome, after Goethe's long and laborious life, after Mickiewicz's expedition to Turkey, after Georg Trakl's anguish in a military hospital in Kraków! Can we match the legendary realm, can we fancy ourselves poets in a way comparable to theirs?

We respond to this question through our deeds, through the action of writing. We know that to answer it directly would be impertinent, not necessary, but we also recognize that imagination has to struggle with the dragon of time afresh each day. Time brings about new things, good and bad; we must ascertain them. Time kills people and civilizations; we must save them, to remember them in poetry. We understand that the ongoing war between imagination and time (alas, a war that will never be won) cannot end, that we cannot turn, all of us, into historians of poetry and content ourselves with reading old poets. Poetry must be written, continued, risked, tried, revised, erased, and tried again as long as we breathe and love, doubt and believe. We always remember, of course, that we write our poems in the gigantic shadow of the dead and that we should be humble, at least in those long hours when we do not compose. (Being too humble in the very moment of creation would not be very wise.)

We need to go on, paying the price, sometimes, of being not only imperfect but even, who knows, arrogant and ridiculous.

An award like yours, the Neustadt Prize, with its silver feather lost by a silver eagle somewhere in the silver imaginary mountains, helps a lot. It helps to forget, if only for a brief moment of a ceremony like this one, the immense risk involved in writing poetry today. Poetry, according to Friedrich Hölderlin, this bard of loneliness, is the most innocent of all occupations. That is very true, and yet innocence is perhaps the most daring thing in the entire world.

Norman, Oklahoma
October 1, 2004

CLARIBEL ALEGRÍA
THE 2006 LAUREATE

Claribel Alegría (1924–2018) is often considered the most important contemporary Central American writer. She was born in Estelí, Nicaragua, but spent most of her youth in the Santa Ana region of western El Salvador because of her father's political exile. In 1943 she came to the United States to study at George Washington University, where she received her bachelor's degree in philosophy and letters. She would not return to her country of origin until 1979, after the Sandinista National Liberation Front took control of the government. Influenced by the political climate of Central America, Alegría's poetry focused on the human condition in the region. Alegría's numerous books of poetry include *Anillo de silencio* (1948), *Acuario* (1956), *Huésped de mi tiempo* (1961), *Sobrevivo* (1978), *Mujer del río /Woman of the River* (1989), *Saudade* (1999; Eng. *Sorrow*, 1999), and *Soltando amarras* (2002; Eng. *Casting Off*, 2003). Her two major poetry anthologies in Spanish include *Una vida en poemas*, ed.

Conny Villafranca F. (2003), and *Esto soy: Antología poética de Claribel Alegría*, ed. Luis Alvarenga (2004). Posthumously, her work was included in *Ghost Fishing: An Eco-Justice Poetry Anthology* (2018).

> Quite often I have used my poetry as a sword, and I have brandished it against my internal and external demons.
>
> —Claribel Alegría

Knowing Claribel Alegría
Daisy Zamora

Which Claribel Alegría should I speak of today? The fiction writer, the chronicler of history, the storyteller, the political activist, the translator, or the poet? After years of reading her work (a vast literary landscape that includes poetry, fiction, historical testimony, translations, and anthologies) and having the privilege of knowing her personally for many years, I can say with some authority that a rare, extraordinary symbiosis exists between Claribel Alegría and her writing—that is, between her life and her words.

Nicaraguan poet José Coronel Urtecho once said that either to read her work and get to know her afterward, or to know her first and then read her work, is like being a witness to a miracle. One realizes in either case that Claribel and her writing are one and the same, and that unusual, miraculous fact provokes a sense of bewilderment, a feeling that such a range of accomplishment should be impossible, at the very least an illusion, and that is because the quality of a writer being one with his or her own writing is rare indeed. But for Claribel Alegría, the ethics of her work, the energy and beauty of her words, stand for herself, for her acts as a person, for the way her life matches her words. That being the case, I will center my remarks on the particular symbiosis between Claribel Alegría and her poetry.

At first glance, her poetry can be superficially judged as being simple because of its brief lines and language, which give it a fast, pulsating quality, a mercurial rhythm (even when the poet herself reads it aloud) that sounds almost like the singing of a nightingale. But such apparent simplicity is a mirage. On closer examination, an attentive reading reveals a powerful, accurate distillation of language, line by line, until it achieves, like a nightingale, a maximum capacity of complex expression. The exact weight that the poet extracts from the apparent simplicity of each word, and the complexity it really contains and expresses, gives the work perfect balance. Each poem has within itself a compass that guides it on the right path, in such a way that it never digresses, never gets lost, or misses its own route toward harmony and lucidity.

The same may be said of Claribel as a person, as a human being. Whoever reads her poetry can easily imagine how she is, and in the event that the reader happens to meet her, he or she becomes a witness to the miracle I mentioned before, amazed by the evidence of how similar the poet and her poetry are, how both share the same substance.

In 1989 José Coronel Urtecho, whom I mentioned before and who is one of our most important Nicaraguan poets (founder of the Vanguardia movement, one of its main leaders, whose seminal work has influenced several generations of writers in Nicaragua), wrote an extraordinary book called *Líneas para un boceto de Claribel Alegría* (Lines for a sketch of Claribel Alegría). In that book, he writes that Claribel's poetry is like something "sifted" through her being, after having gone completely "through" her. One never knows where the borders between herself and her words converge, the zone or line where light and shadow meet or melt, because the poet and her imagination and her words blend into one reality. Word by word, line by line, poem by poem, Claribel is her poetry, and her poetry is her. Coronel Urtecho also wrote that every time he read Claribel's poems, he was amazed all over again by how she can be such a great poet even in her shortest poems, because each of her words is loaded with so much life and meaning. He said that all her poems are miraculous.

Claribel's unusual and extraordinary ability to be one and the same with her poetry springs from an authentic and profound sense of humanity. She has the capacity to imagine, to visualize the "other," to move toward the other, toward the human. She has within herself a deep sense of her own dignity as a human being as well as of the dignity of others, which also includes a compassionate understanding for the world as a whole. This is the basic and authentic quality of a true humanist, and one finds this quality present throughout her entire body of work.

Sergio Ramírez, a most important Nicaraguan writer and former vice president of Nicaragua, has called her "the mythical Claribel Alegría" who was surrounded from early childhood by many great figures of Latin American literature, like Salvador Salazar Arrué (Salarrué), José Vasconcelos, and Joaquín García Monge. Later on, she studied with the Spanish poet Juan Ramon Jiménez, who took her to meet Ezra Pound, by then locked up in St. Elizabeth's Hospital. Still later, Miguel Ángel Asturias visited her in Santa Ana in El Salvador. In Santiago, Chile, she met Augusto Monterroso, and went with Asturias to Isla Negra to meet Pablo Neruda. There are also the long friendships she and her husband, Darwin J. (Bud) Flakoll, had with Robert Graves, Juan Rulfo, Julio Cortázar, and many writers of the Latin American "boom," of whom Claribel and Bud were the early editors and translators, years before many of them became famous. Together, they edited the anthology *New Voices of Hispanic America* published by Beacon Press in Boston, in 1962, which included Julio Cortázar, Augusto Monterroso, Juan Rulfo, Blanca Varela, Juan José Arreola, Ernesto Cardenal, Augusto Roa Bastos, and others. Therefore, says Sergio Ramírez, Claribel was born for literature, which is a substantial part of her existence, of her life.

I could talk almost endlessly of Claribel Alegría's impressive body of work, but she never speaks of herself because she is always and forever too curious about others and of the world that surrounds her. She is so interested and engaged in learning more about life and about all of us, her fellow human beings, that she forgets to talk about herself. But when she enters a room, or wherever she goes, her presence is felt immediately. I can only explain it in this way: When she appears, it is as if a rose is placed in a room. If I brought a rose to this room and put it on this table, its presence, even though quiet and silent, would change the whole mood of the room. Even if we wanted to ignore it, we wouldn't be able to, because that rose, with its beauty, its form, its color, and its fragrance, would make us all pay attention to it, although it would not be saying: Hey, here I am, look at me!

Claribel Alegría is that rose.

Norman, Oklahoma
September 29, 2006

Daisy Zamora (b. 1950, Managua) is a prominent Nicaraguan poet, essayist, translator, and advocate for human rights and feminist issues. Her bilingual collection The Violent Foam: New and Selected Poems *was published by Curbstone in 2002.*

The Sword of Poetry
Claribel Alegría

First and foremost, I would like to express my appreciation for this important and unexpected prize in the name of my husband, Darwin "Bud" Flakoll, who passed away some years ago. I am profoundly grateful for this award and to the Neustadt family; the prestigious magazine *World Literature Today*; its executive director, Robert Con Davis-Undiano; its editor in chief, David Draper Clark; to the members of the jury who bestowed upon me this prize; and—last but not least—to Nicaraguan poet Daisy Zamora, who nominated me for the award. It is a very great honor to be here, with you, to accept this prize. In all modesty, I confess that I never dreamed of receiving it, and I hope not to disillusion you.

Throughout my life, I have made incursions into many literary genres, but ever since my childhood, poetry has been and continues to be my passion. From before I knew how to read, my parents had me memorize poems by Rubén Darío, the great Nicaraguan poet who founded the modernist movement that transformed the Spanish language and whose work I recited with pleasure to whoever was naïve enough to ask me to do so. The rhythm of Darío's poems fascinated me. Often—and even alone—I would recite his work out loud. Understanding the meaning of his verse didn't matter, for the music of his poems was the most important thing. It was like the voice of the wind, the pounding of rain on windows, or the eternal roar of the ocean waves. As

I grew older, I became more and more enamored of words. I wanted to know the meaning of each one of them and to memorize the dictionary.

Words are sensual. They seduce us and spark our imagination, but they also express intelligence and logic in constructing towers of ideals and culture. The Bible tells us that "In the beginning was the Word, and the Word was with God, and the Word was God." The word is our sword, our strength, the magic force that is given to things in order to name them. Having already entered into adolescence, I wanted to express myself through words. I evoked them, was delighted by them, but at times I also came to hate them, to come to blows with them when they didn't respond to me. As a poet, I like to invent and conjure up words, watch them fly, remain in flight, and many times fall and rise again bruised and wounded. There are words that reveal and others that conceal and still others that steal our sleep. Words are often empty, and we know not what to do with them, and they make us want to throw them to the floor and stomp on them to see what might emerge.

From very early on, I was quite fond of reading poetry. It is a habit of mine. At night, whenever possible, I read at least one poem before going to sleep. There have been good and bad influences on me as a poet. I have written many imitations of whatever I might be reading at any given time. I learned numerous tricks, some of which are quite useful and still serve me well. The Bible has greatly influenced me: the Book of Job, the Psalms, Ecclesiastes, the Song of Solomon. And poetry, as Percy Shelley observed, is like a great river into which thousands of tributaries flow. In essence, all poets contribute to writing the great endless poem.

The poet celebrates humankind, the universe, and the creator of the universe. It is impossible for one to remain indifferent to the turbulence that our planet and its inhabitants suffer through: war, hunger, earthquakes, misery, racism, violence, xenophobia, deforestation, AIDS, and childhood affliction, among others. In the region from which I come, Central America, we love poetry, and at times we use it to denounce what is happening around us. There are many fine testimonial poems. The poet, especially where I'm from, cannot and should not remain in an ivory tower.

To be a female poet was very difficult for me as an adolescent. I began writing relatively early. At the age of fourteen, after reading *Letters to a Young Poet*, by Rainer Maria Rilke, I knew that this vocation was for me. My parents never voiced opposition to the idea, but I used to write virtually in hiding. Except for my parents, I showed my poetry only to my literature professor; to Salarrué (Salvador Salazar Arrué), a great Salvadoran short-story writer; and to Alberto Guerra, a Nicaraguan/Salvadoran poet. If my women friends had been aware that I was writing poetry, they would have made fun of me, and no young man would want to approach me, not even to dance. Among my generation in Central America, women of the leisure class had the option of marrying or controlling their husband's purse strings or of remaining chaste and virtuous, baking cakes for their nieces and nephews.

Just a few years ago, one could easily identify the women in all of Latin America who stood out in literature. Names like Gabriela Mistral, Alfonsina Storni, Juana de Ibarború, Delmira Agustini, Claudia Lars, not to mention the greatest of them all, Sor Juana Inés de la Cruz, who, five hundred years ago, took off her feminist gloves when she wrote, "Stupid men, who, without cause, accuse women," words proclaimed rather shockingly. I suspect that Sor Juana opted to become a nun in order to have the opportunity to receive an education, without which she would have been veiled in silence.

In my particular case, after finishing secondary school, I had to spend two years learning to sew, cook fine cuisine, and play "Für Elise" on the piano before I could rebel. My father in no way wanted me to travel abroad to study or to attend the university in El Salvador. He said that there were hardly any women there and that I would be the object of disrespect. Finally, with the complicity of my mother, along with threats of my own, I succeeded in convincing my parents to allow me to travel to the United States to continue my studies. In spite of the fact that my father was *machista*, he never opposed my pursuing a career as a poet. On the contrary, I believe deep down that he was pleased that I did, for he loved poetry.

Soon before traveling to the United States, my parents invited me and my younger sister to gather in the living room. There, my father showed an upright Steinway piano to my sister, who had great musical talent, and told her, "This is your instrument. Take advantage of it." In turn, he brought me a wooden case with a felt-lined interior that housed a Parker fountain pen: "This is your instrument. Use it as a sword," he instructed. My father was intuitive. I'm sure he feared his own words, but he had to speak them to me, nevertheless. Quite often I have used my poetry as a sword, and I have brandished it against my internal and external demons.

Norman, Oklahoma
September 29, 2006

Translation from the Spanish by David Draper Clark

PATRICIA GRACE
THE 2008 LAUREATE

Patricia Grace (b. 1937) is the author of seven novels, five short-story
collections, and several children's books. In 2006 she received the New
Zealand Prime Minister's Award for Literary Achievement. Awards for her
work include the Deutz Medal for Fiction for the novel *Tu* at the Montana
New Zealand Book Awards in 2005, the New Zealand Fiction Award for
Potiki in 1987, the Children's Picture Book of the Year for *The Kuia and the
Spider* in 1982, and the Hubert Church Prose Award for the Best First Book
for *Waiariki* in 1976. She was also awarded Frankfurt's LiBeraturpreis in
1994 for *Potiki*, which has been translated into several languages. *Dogside
Story* was longlisted for the Booker Prize and won the Kiriyama Pacific Rim
Fiction Prize in 2001. Her latest novel, *Chappy*, was a finalist in the Ockham
New Zealand Awards for fiction and winner of Nga Kupu Ora Award 2016.
Her children's book *Whiti Te Ra* was also a Nga Kupu Ora Award winner in
2015. Her novel *Cousins* is in the process of being made into a feature film.

Grace was a recipient of the Distinguished Companion of the New Zealand Order of Merit (DCNZM) in 2007. She has received honorary doctorates in literature from Victoria University of Wellington in 1989 and the World Indigenous Nations University in 2016.

It is what we know—the touchables, reachables, the experiences and thoughts that we have, that are central to the work of a writer—the things that surprise, excite, hurt, or move us in some way.

—Patricia Grace

Patricia Grace, Storyteller of the People
Joy Harjo

Oketv semvnvckosen pom pvlhoyes. Momen pom vlakeckat heretos.
A beautiful day has been loaned to us. Your arrival makes it great.

Hopiyen vlvkeckat mvto cekices. Cem vtotketv vcake tomekv,
   ecerakkueces.
From far you have come, and we say thank you. Your great work we
   value.

Ceme porakkuececkat, matvpomen ece rakkueces.
You honor us, and we honor you.

Vnokeckv sulken cemoces.
We have lots of love/respect for you.

E te rangatira, tena koe. Nga mihi aroha. Ka nui te aroha kei
   waenganui i a tatou.
Greetings to you, esteemed leader. Greetings of love. There is much
   love between us all [gathered here].

We were all created by a story. Each and every one of us walked, swam, flew, crawled, or otherwise emerged from the story. It is a terrible and magnificent being, this story. Each of us has a part. Each thought, dream, word, and action of every one of us continues to feed the story. We have to tend the story to encourage it. It will in turn take care of us as we spiral through the sky.

Every once in a while a storyteller emerges who brings forth provocative, compassionate, and beautiful tales, the exact story-food the people need to carry them through tough, transformative times. Patricia Grace of the

Māori people is one of these storytellers given to the people of Aotearoa, and now to the world as she is honored as the twentieth laureate of the Neustadt International Prize for Literature.

What distinguishes Grace's storytelling in the novel, short story, and children's book form is her ability to reach back to the ancestors and the oldest knowledge and to pull it forward and weave it together with forward-seeing vision, to create what is needed to bring the living story forward. She uses the tools of grace, humor, humbleness, and wisdom to make the design. The design is not extravagant or show-off; it is exactly cut and crafted to fit the shape of Māori culture and ideals. In Patricia Grace's stories everyone has a voice. In her stories, there is no separation between the land, the water, the sky, and the will of the people. Those relationships are honored.

If we have gathered the materials to make a structure with rapt attention and songs and have followed a protocol of respect, then as we construct the story it will want to come and fill that place; it will endure and inspire. And we will endure and be inspired. Grace's stories make a shining and enduring place formed of the brilliant weave of Māori oral storytelling and contained within the shape of contemporary Western forms. We are welcomed in, and when we get up to leave, we have been well fed, we have made friends and family, and we are bound to understanding and knowledge of one another. We become each other in the moment of the story. We understand that we have all been colonized, challenged by the immense story we struggle within. We are attempting to reconstruct ourselves with the broken parts. Patricia Grace's stories lead us back toward wholeness, to a renewal of integrity. This is the power of story. This is the power of Patricia Grace's gift to the Māori people, to indigenous people and the world.

Last year as I prepared to present Patricia Grace's legacy to an esteemed panel of jurors from all over the world, I called together an informal meeting of Pacific Islander writers in Hawai'i. We sat at a table in Manoa, over home-cooked food and refreshing drinks. I had researched everything I could through books and the Internet and wanted to know what Grace's own people, what other writers from the Pacific had to say about her and her writing. I heard many things that afternoon. I was told of her extensive help in mentoring young writers, that she writes from within a Māori community, that she always went beyond as she published a substantial and continual solid body of literature and raised her seven children. We talked about how there's a Māori level and an English literal level and how each story contains a storehouse of wisdom and knowing. "It's about time an indigenous person finds their way into these kinds of circles," said one. "She's an ambassador for Māori women. Her novel *Cousins* restored women to the story of history. "Her range of Māori voices is unparalleled. . . . She has exposed the Māori world to the rest of the world, showing that Māori people are as diverse as any other." All the stories at the table as we talked about Patricia Grace kept spiraling back to respect, love, and accomplishment in these times of immense difficulty in our indigenous communities.

Finally, as I got up to leave, everyone wished me well in the presentation but agreed that, with such competition of world-renowned writers, Grace wouldn't have much of a chance. "We know her and love her in the Pacific," they said. "She's one of our treasures. She isn't known far outside the Pacific. At least the jurors will come to read her and her work might find a way through them." We now know the ending to this story and are here to celebrate. I must acknowledge the panel of jurors who were enthusiastically supportive of Grace. I did not have to do much convincing at all.

Joining me in celebration here tonight with their words are a few of Grace's Māori colleagues:

Kia ora taatou.

I send my greetings and my family's *aroha* to Patricia Grace for her Neustadt laureateship. The distinguished jury chose eminently well. Patricia Grace has mentored and encouraged many younger writers through her work with the Maori writers' organization Te Ha (which means "the breath") and through the example she has set being an ambassador for Maori writing and culture internationally. I have always looked up to her with admiration for this generosity, given all that she has achieved in literature. Her children's books have represented to New Zealand children all their wonderful possibilities from a Ma‾ori perspective and have become classics in our nation's literature. Her novels similarly engage Ma‾ori artistic potential and bring us to the same literary table as New Zealand's most successful women writers, Janet Frame and Katherine Mansfield, and all of our brothers and sisters who are renowned for their literary prowess from our Pacific region and elsewhere. Patricia is our first Neustadt laureate, and also the first Ma‾ori woman to publish a literary collection. I thank you for choosing so wisely this author who is of our country's community of writers and of her tribal people. She is a national *taonga*, that is, highly prized by those who respect great writing. Patricia is our *rangatira*, our leader. She is an important, compassionate voice, an immensely patient and nuanced voice, who shares Ma‾ori values and thus furthers our community. *Arohanui* to you, Patricia. Your writing brings *Mauri Ora*, the well-being of life's energy, to us all.

Robert Sullivan, Poet
Nga Puhi, Ngati Raukawa,
Kai Tahu, Galway Irish

Pat's work is such an inspiration to all indigenous people, to indigenous women, and especially, to Māori. We are very proud of her and gratified to see her honored by this very distinguished organization for her considerable contribution to the world of literature. Without writers such as Patricia Grace the world would know little, or nothing, of the enormous struggle Māori and other indigenous people all over the world have had—and continue to have—to survive and, hopefully, to thrive. Patricia Grace gives us a voice, she tells our stories, she shows in very human and personal ways the damaging effects of colonization and how we continue to exist and to prosper in spite of those. Her stories remind us that we are connected—to our past from which we draw wisdom and courage, and to others in similar situations around the world. As a Māori woman and a teacher of literature, I am especially grateful that Patricia Grace continues to write us into the wider world picture, adding our experiences to those of human beings everywhere.

Reina Whaitiri
Kaitahu, Aotearoa / New Zealand

Mvto Mvto, Patricia Grace, for taking care of your gift and sharing with us.

Norman, Oklahoma
September 19, 2008

Joy Harjo *(Mvskoke) has published eight books of poetry, a memoir, and a play. The recipient of many awards and fellowships, she is a Chancellor of the Academy of American Poets and was named the twenty-third U.S. Poet Laureate in 2019. She lives in Tulsa, Oklahoma.*

The World Is Where You Are
Patricia Grace

By way of further introducing myself to you, I would like to tell you briefly about the place in New Zealand where I live, and from there to lead into some thoughts about the work of a fiction writer and a little of what the process may involve.

I come from a place in New Zealand called Hongoeka Bay, which is right by the sea and is situated thirty kilometers from the capital city of Wellington on the North Island. There are about twenty-seven houses in this small settlement, and because we are by the sea we like to spend our leisure time fishing—either from small boats or from the rocks on the shore. We can gather shellfish there when the weather is calm and the tide is low. Or even when the tides are not so good, if you're the owner of a wetsuit (and if you're much younger than what I am), you can go diving in much deeper water. When the weather's rough and the waves are high, the surfers among us pick up their boards and go surfing.

It's a stony, rocky, and quite rugged coastline but a good place for walking or for family picnics. There's always plenty of driftwood about that we can gather, make a fire, and cook our fish or shellfish or maybe a few sausages.

It's the beginning of spring in Aotearoa, New Zealand, at the moment, and after quite a harsh winter we're all looking forward to better weather so we can get to the water.

The land we live on, the settlement that I am speaking of, is on ancestral land that has been handed down to us through generations, from our ancestors. It is a remnant of land of three interrelated tribal or family groups. Because of it being ancestral land, it means that everyone in our community is related to me or is married to a relative of mine. Some are closely related. For example, we have a son and daughter and their families living there. My brother lives in front of me. Several of my first cousins are close by. Others are more distantly related through common ancestry.

So when I was a child staying there I was among grandparents and other elders as well as aunts, uncles, and cousins. And this was like having several grandparents, many mothers and fathers, and many brothers and sisters. Now living there as an older person I still have my same cousins around me, and our children and their children have grown up together. When Māori people speak of family we include extended family, those related through genealogy. Even those no longer living are considered to be still part of the family.

There are a range of occupations and professions in our community. Among us are builders, drivers, artists, office workers, public servants, health professionals, and teachers. My husband and I both trained as teachers. I left teaching in 1984 to become a full-time writer, and my husband, Waiariki, continued a career in education.

As part of our community we have a carved and decorated ancestral meeting house. Ours is not an old house. It is a house we built ourselves—raising finances, using our own voluntary labor and our own artists. It was a task that took about fifteen years. The house was dedicated and opened in 1997.

This is where we get together for meetings, for cultural and spiritual events, for teaching and learning, and for all sorts of social occasions such as birthday celebrations and weddings. This is where we carry out traditional rituals and ceremonies—especially so when someone dies. Along with the building of the meeting house has come the building and growing of our-selves, especially in the learning and use of the Māori language, our arts and traditions.

Adjacent to the meeting house is a kitchen and dining room facility, so when we welcome visitors, whether they have come to pay respects to the dead or for any of many reasons, they are able to be accommodated—to sleep in the meeting house and to have meals, which we prepare for them, in the dining room. Sometimes we host twenty people, sometimes a hundred or more. This can be a lot of work, but what I like about it is that all generations work together on all that needs doing to make our visitors feel welcome and comfortable.

Because I live a family / extended family / community life, I suppose it is not surprising that this is evident in the writing that I do. Exploring intergen-erational relationships interests me greatly. In the writing of my novel *Potiki* I have drawn very much on the place where I live, in its setting and the type of community it is. Although the characters are all created characters, the issues surrounding land, which give foundation to the story, are ones that Māori communities live with every day.

The issues faced by the family in *Baby No-Eyes* are firmly based in reality. The characters in the stories "Valley" and "It Used to Be Green Once" lived in communities similar to the one I have described.

What I am doing, then, is writing about what I know.

It is what we know—the touchables, reachables, the experiences and thoughts that we have, that are central to the work of a writer—the things that surprise, excite, hurt, or move us in some way.

I am often asked why I became a writer, and I don't really know the answer to that. But as a child I did like the written word. I loved to read though

I didn't have many books at all. I could read by the time I went to school. But I didn't have writer role models, didn't know anyone who wrote. Except that my mother wrote letters now and again, I didn't see anyone writing.

Sometimes when people ask me why I became a writer, I tell them that it is because my parents worked in a stationery factory. My father used to bring home paper for us to write and draw on. I sometimes think that may be the true reason I became a writer—that fact that we had the raw material.

My parents both left school during the depression of the 1930s to work in a stationery factory, and that is where they met. Although my parents were not role models as far as actual writing went, they did share stories with us. Quite often these were family anecdotes or snippets about their own childhoods. But sometimes they were even less than that. They were just little one-liners that they would leave us with, that were funny or amazing in some way, and memorable.

For example, my mother told us about a great-great-grandfather who had two sets of teeth—two rows top and two rows bottom—and that they were very useful to him when climbing ship's rigging. Or my father would say, "You know your Uncle Jack rode on a whale."

Now the imagination could do wonders with unexplained morsels like that. Less can be more. I realize now that the Uncle Jack who rode on a whale may have done so when the poor dead animal was being towed ashore by a whaling boat. But in those days, what I imagined was that this fabled uncle spent his days riding the oceans of the world on the back of a whale, having all kinds of adventures.

If I was wanting to give advice to young writers (and there are many of you here today—you are writers because you do write), for those who wish to develop the craft of writing, I would say: Write every day. Read every day. Write what you know and push the boundaries of what you know.

You will want to explore how words work—how words can be made to work. You will want to be aware of the job that words, sentences, and paragraphs can do.

It is important for a writer to understand who he/she is and to understand that she/he is unique with a unique set of experiences, and that it is the everyday experiences which are important.

In the past, when workshopping with young writers, I've had things said to me such as, "Oh, I don't have anything to write about, my life is too dull, too boring." I have to persuade them that writing is about everyday things.

I know that many of you have read my story called "Beans." It's a good illustration of what I'm talking about because it's simply the story of a young boy going to play rugby on a Saturday morning and going home again. He is a boy who loves life. He draws the world in around him through sights, sounds, smell, and taste. He stands on his own two feet and doesn't need to be entertained. When I wrote the story I was living in a place similar to the one in the story. The story was based on one of our sons. I was writing a familiar, everyday event.

You can write about eating breakfast, a good day, a bad day, a sad day, a broken shoe, an embarrassment, a relationship. There is something happening to us every moment of our lives. None of us lives on a little antiseptic spot with nothing happening to us, around us, or inside of us.

Everything is food for someone who wants to write. To each ordinary day we bring our own individuality, our own style, our own creativity. It is good to remember that even though there is a big wide, world out there, the whole world is not out there.

The world is where you are. *Your* world is where you are.

Norman, Oklahoma
September 19, 2008

DUO DUO
THE 2010 LAUREATE

Duo Duo 多多 (b. 1951) is the pen name of Li Shizheng. He started
writing poetry in the early 1970s as a youth during the isolated, midnight
hours of the Cultural Revolution, and many of his early poems critiqued
the Cultural Revolution from an insider's point of view in a highly
sophisticated, original style. Often considered part of the "Misty" school
of contemporary Chinese poetry, he nevertheless kept a cautious distance
from any literary trends or labeling. After witnessing the 1989 Tiananmen
Square massacre, Duo Duo left China and did not return for more than a
decade. Upon his return to China in 2004, the literary community received
him with honor and praise. Duo Duo currently resides on Hainan Island
and teaches at Hainan University in China. Collections of his English
translations include *Looking Out from Death: From the Cultural Revolution
to Tiananmen Square* (1989) and *The Boy Who Catches Wasps* (2002).
Snow Plain, published in 2010, is a collection of translated short stories.

Perhaps pondering words is also
a form of seeking justice. If a
monologue can invite a chorus,
then perhaps it can speak for others
as well. Poetry is self-sufficient in
its uselessness, and therefore it is
contemptuous of power.

—Duo Duo

Duo Duo: Master of Wishful Thinking
Mai Mang

Duo Duo is a great lone traveler crossing borders of nation, language, and history as well as a resolute seer of some of the most basic, universal human values that have often been shadowed in our troubled modern time: creativity, nature, love, dreams, and wishful thinking.

Born in 1951, Duo Duo's poetry career began in the early 1970s in Beijing during the isolated, midnight hours of the Cultural Revolution. As a lone, disillusioned Red Guard youth, he was inspired by his clandestine reading of Baudelaire and other Western authors. His very first poems immediately strike one with unusually intense and abstract yet vivid visions, such as in the beginning lines of the short poem "Untitled" (1972): "The sound of singing eclipses the blood stench of revolution / August is stretched like a cruel bow." Or, in "Untitled" (1974): "The blood of one class has drained away / The archers of another class are still loosing their arrows." Or, in "To the Sun" (1973), whereas the entire poem sounds like a reformulated ode to the omnipresence and omnipotence of the sun, an orthodox reference to the "great helmsman" Chairman Mao at that time, the last line underscores, or exposes, the paradoxical fate of the sun itself: "You create, rising in the East / You are unfree, like a universally circulating coin!" These powerful, bare-boned epiphanies all critiqued the Cultural Revolution from an insider's point of view and in a highly sophisticated, dialectical, and original style. In Duo Duo's 1976 poem "Instructions," he further summarizes his and his contemporaries' artistic deeds conducted in the underground of the Cultural Revolution and delivers a sober conclusion: "What they have experienced— is only the tragedy of birth."

Through such negative visions, Duo Duo gained his own historical subjectivity and individual agency. He paid a high price for these insights. An abandoned, bad-blooded bastard child of revolution and modernism, Duo

Duo from the very onset of his career foresees a life that is exiled from but also imprisoned by history: "From that superstitious moment on / The motherland was led away by another father" ("Blessings," 1973); "Ah moonlight, hinting at the clearly seen exile . . ." ("Night," 1973). In "Marguerite's Travels with Me" (1974), Duo Duo reveals the ultimate existential gap faced by the lyrical protagonist torn between a real China and an imaginary West. The poem's first part starts with lines "Like you promised the Sun / Get crazy, Marguerite," echoing Baudelaire's famous "Invitation to the Voyage," and inviting a certain Marguerite to a spontaneous, freewheeling rhapsody of cosmopolitan travel. But such a fantastic voyage only ends up, in the second part, in pledging this imaginary "Ah, noble Marguerite / Ignorant Marguerite" to take an alternate, heavyhearted, utterly sobering visit to the impoverished Chinese countryside that had been hopelessly stuck in the mire of a failed revolutionary utopia. The idealized, romantic bond between Marguerite and "me" thus has to be rendered as an impossible cul-de-sac. Duo Duo's early poetry hence generates meaningful and nuanced reflections on history and revolution as well as on modernity and modernism, sketching a Sisyphean fate imposed upon individuals from within and without the borders of nation and history.

Duo Duo's poems of the 1980s continued but also expanded on his poetic experimentation. In particular, Duo Duo proves himself to be a great innovator of linguistic forms and poetic craft whose liberating power is always inspiring and sublime. Constantly, Duo Duo bets on "wishful thinking": "If the making of language comes from the kitchen / The heart is the bedroom. They say: / If the heart is the bedroom / Wishful thinking is the bedroom's master" ("Language Is Made In the Kitchen," 1984). Meanwhile, Duo Duo increasingly focuses on the theme of the northern landscapes of China, intending to invoke and restore an abundant correspondence between nature and ancient human spirit against the ensnarement of modern history and its rigid, harsh noise that lacks any human or natural breath. This elemental tendency is shown in his poem "Northern Voices" (1985), whose ending lines remind one of Laozi, the ancient Taoist philosopher's teaching that "the greatest utterance is silence": "All languages / Shall be shattered by the wordless voice."

But it would be a grave mistake to say that Duo Duo is a poet who has renounced hope and the prospect of human communication. While cleansing and reforming a polluted, ossified language, Duo Duo seeks to speak, nevertheless, through a different medium, and pays tribute to its great power and awe. Another poem in this "North" sequence, "Northern Sea" (1984), depicts a vast, almost eschatological, panoramic scene of solitude, alienation, and desolateness. And yet the same poem closes with an ultimate affirmation of human love, even if such love may be merely a phantom evoked from the past: "But from a large basket lifted up high / I see all those who have loved me / Closely, closely, closely—huddled together . . ."

In a most dramatic fashion, Duo Duo left China on precisely June 4, 1989, after witnessing the incidents of Tiananmen Square at first hand. During the ensuing fifteen years, Duo Duo lived in exile and traveled throughout western Europe, North America, and many other parts of the world, seeming to literally fulfill the dark prophecies of his own early poetry written during the Cultural Revolution. In poems written shortly after he settled in the West, such as "Rivers of Amsterdam" (1989), "In England" (1989–90), and "Watching the Sea" (1989–90), Duo Duo conjures his lyrical power and wrestles most bravely and indigenously with that giant beast called "exile." While cursed with a nightmarish and claustrophobic history, Duo Duo, this lone, exiled traveler and one of the "Nails far removed from the motherland" ("Map," 1990), actually succeeds in opening up a great, alien expanse of space for his poetry and creating a post-exilic and post-historical universe of deprivation and ineffability. And, as in his 1993 poem "Just Like It Used to Be," he presents an utterly defiant, haughty, and insuppressible "burst of a furious growth" and "ubiquitous powers of persuasion" that "No arrangement whatsoever can reproduce." Against the gravity of nihilism and desert of exile, this shamanistic, steadfast reaffirmation of "like it used to be" crystallizes a positive, primitive, and badly needed universal message: a persistent, heroic reclamation of the possibility of human speech and power of memory rising above differences of human tongues.

Among the esteemed so-called Misty poets of his generation, Duo Duo was nearly the last to emerge aboveground. His only book of poetry officially published in China prior to his exile was a thin volume, *Salute* (1988). However, his stature was universally revered, as evidenced by the fact he was awarded the first (and, until this day, only) Today Poetry Prize in 1988. The prize was presented to him by none other than Bei Dao himself, the other leading Misty poet and co-founder of the legendary samizdat literary journal *Today*. The award statement reads: "Since the early 1970s, Duo Duo's solitary and tireless exploration of the art of poetry has always inspired and influenced many of his contemporaries." Between 1989 and 2004, while sojourning in the West, Duo Duo kept up a strong output of poetry and prose writing and was invited to numerous international poetry readings and literary events. Duo Duo returned to China in 2004 to assume a professorship at Hainan University. Since his return, he has been steadily "rediscovered" by a younger generation of Chinese writers and poets. Duo Duo is an extremely fastidious craftsman of poetry as well as dedicated servant of the Muse. He does not publish his work regularly or professionally, as do most of his Western counterparts. Instead, he prefers to date his finished poems and let them sit in manuscript for extended periods, sometimes more than a decade, before he is willing to allow them to come to light, a habit that may have been directly derived from his experience of writing clandestinely during the Cultural Revolution. Such inclination to marginality and anonymity, on the other hand, like a Cain's mark, has haunted Duo Duo and kept him, almost criminally, from the recognition he truly deserves.

Duo Duo is one of the most original, penetrating, inspiring, and unforgettable voices ever heard in contemporary Chinese poetry. He is also, as Eliot Weinberger put it, "one of the mountains in the topographical map of contemporary world poetry." Duo Duo's contribution to both contemporary Chinese and world poetry is astounding and will be, in a definitive term, everlasting. Duo Duo is not an easy poet, whose obsessive, sometimes schizophrenic pursuit "to preserve / That which orders the stripes on the tiger's back / His madness!" ("The Winter Night Woman," 1985) poses great intellectual and aesthetic challenges to both his readers and his translators in other languages, who may not be readily familiar with the gigantic scope and difficulty of his odyssey beyond borders. Even the most able translations available today may not always do adequate justice to the brilliance of his Chinese originals. But it is precisely in this sense that I believe the 2010 Neustadt Prize belongs to Duo Duo, this marvelous, bold, persistent, if underappreciated Chinese genius of poetry. The Neustadt Prize will provide a perfect venue and forum for the world to listen to Duo Duo's distinctive voice issued from the dark depths of an alternate, labyrinth-like world that we used to live in but often tend to leave in oblivion.

New London, Connecticut

Author note: Of the poems cited in this nomination statement, I would like to acknowledge translations from the following three pioneering books on Duo Duo in the English-speaking world: Gregory Lee and John Cayley's *Looking Out from Death: From the Cultural Revolution to Tiananmen Square* (1989), Maghiel van Crevel's *Language Shattered: Contemporary Chinese Poetry and Duoduo* (1996), and Gregory Lee's *The Boy Who Catches Wasps* (2002). At some places I have modified them or have used my own translations from *Contemporary Chinese Literature: From the Cultural Revolution to the Future* (2007).

Mai Mang *(Yibing Huang* 麦芒*), born in Changde, Hunan, in 1967, established himself as a poet in the 1980s and received his BA, MA, and PhD in Chinese literature from Beijing University and a second PhD in comparative literature from UCLA. He is currently an associate professor of Chinese at Connecticut College.*

This Is the Reason We Persevere
Duo Duo

Ladies and Gentlemen:

Tonight, in front of everyone here, I wish to keep my tone low, so that the word *gratitude* can be heard more clearly. This is a word that must be said, and should have been said a long time ago.

Upon hearing the verses of Baudelaire, Lorca, Tsvetaeva, and Ehrenburg for the first time, a generation of Chinese poets was already grateful—for the transmission of creativity from hand to hand during those stark years. Words, in the hands of their receivers, had directly become destiny.

Poetry hit us with its power of immediacy, and I believed that from that point of impact, the power would be transmitted back out from us.

Since then, my borders have been only two rows of trees.

Even as I speak, remnants of the 1970s still resound, and contain every echo of the reshaping of one's character. One country, one voice—the poet expels himself from all that. Thus begins writing, thus begins exile. A position approaches me on its own. I am only one man; I establish myself on that. I am only a man.

I am not speaking about history, but about man, whose appearance in this word *history* has long been debated. In this word, life is led away by poetry, to search for, as Sylvia Plath said, "a country far away as health."

I am speaking about writing, that difficult étude.

In the process, what must be spoken meets what cannot be said. Each word is a catalyst, requiring the writer to break out forcefully from another story, from the primitive camp where history, society, and politics converge, to touch upon that "what" and that "who." At that touch, one finds the unlimited boundaries of man, concealed by words.

At this point, half of each word has been written, the half that can be understood. Grammar is still pondering the other half. Each word is not only a sign. Inside each word there is an orphan's brain. No words can be younger, but inside the word *suffering* are all the secrets of being human.

Perhaps pondering words is also a form of seeking justice. If a monologue can invite a chorus, then perhaps it can speak for others as well. Poetry is self-sufficient in its uselessness, and therefore it is contemptuous of power.

At the very least, the ideal of poetry demands this: even as the poet is still catching up, it has already revealed its most dignified aspect. It allows light to be cast on the scales, which light must shine and move upon. Light therefore arrives where man himself can arrive, so as to recognize love anew.

What illuminates us is hesitancy, so action is always condemning; darkness becomes more complete, to the point that it has sealed up all its remaining cracks, without knowing that light in fact originates from within itself. And that is what words must penetrate through.

The present is thereby even more hidden, the hierarchy cannot speak this rule—a spell that has been written down.

When the road has already become an unstressed word, even when tracing its genealogy, what returns are only the echoes of this particular civilization. So we stop here, we stop at the place where we think we can go back and experience the whole journey, on a quest for that word which has been enclosed in ore along with a swooning, ancient past—a sealed-up riddle that is only testing its listener.

In a poet's listening, at the limits of his honesty, at the ends of logic, a "what" will be opened, that "what"—the present moment. From its deepest roots, a word will burst out from the riddle. Perhaps this word is what has been revealed by hints: an approaching, an encountering, a dialogue.

The road is only in the present, and we use the echoes as milestones.

What I am speaking about is how a poet's experience is brought into words.

After experiencing the cacophony of revolution, subversion, experimentation, and deconstruction, what can the poet still hear? Inside this word that has burst out from the riddle—*silence*—is our common condition: on the level of a completely material world, on a human physical level, we are allowing a dysfunctional intelligence to peck at and eat away the landscape; it is a continuation of slogans; a sustainable violence is using memory as fuel, and what has been replenished is the echo of our condition, because the exile of words begins here.

But from the discursive space created by the poetic canon, what constantly echoes is the speech that has never been separated from silence: there is only memory, no forgetting, because there are no mountains, only peaks....

The pantheon of classical Chinese poets is emerging, bringing mountain ranges, rivers, weight, and pressure along in their words and between their lines, to be with us not only where language breaks but also at geological fault lines, waiting for us to pick up where they left off—another season in this meadow of life. In another story, in the same allegory, the way we return to the sound of the fresco is the way the light creates our horizon.

At this point, we need the voice of an all-encompassing story to speak.

To speak of East–West, West–East, to speak of this common stage on which we all appear—the earth, the advancing starry skies and dwellings—our allies in writing, our readers—our grasslands under the sea ...

Nature already has no other water or ink, the danger has been found, poetry has fallen to the periphery, and this periphery comes close to home. Poetry takes this periphery as a blessing and continues to offer rituals for the sick rivers, to offer readable landscapes for the heart.

This is the reason we persevere.

Norman, Oklahoma
October 22, 2010

Translation from the Chinese by Mai Mang

ROHINTON MISTRY
THE 2012 LAUREATE

Born in Bombay, **Rohinton Mistry** (b. 1952) has lived in Canada since 1975. He is the author of three novels, all of which have been shortlisted for the Booker Prize, and a collection of short stories, *Tales from Firozsha Baag*. His first novel, *Such a Long Journey*, won the Governor General's Award, the Commonwealth Writers Prize for Best Book, and the SmithBooks / Books in Canada First Novel Award. It was made into an acclaimed feature film in 1998. *A Fine Balance* was winner of the Giller Prize, the Commonwealth Writers Prize for Best Book, the Los Angeles Times Fiction Prize, the Royal Society of Literature's Winifred Holtby Award, and Denmark's ALOA Prize. It was shortlisted for the International IMPAC Dublin Literary Award, the Irish Times International Fiction Prize, and the Prix Femina. In 2002 *A Fine Balance* was selected for Oprah's Book Club. *Family Matters* won the Kiriyama Pacific Rim Book Prize for Fiction and the Canadian Authors Association Fiction Award. It was shortlisted for the International IMPAC

Dublin Literary Award and the James Tait Black Memorial Prize. Mistry was awarded the Trudeau Fellows Prize in 2004 and a Guggenheim Fellowship in 2005. Elected Fellow of the Royal Society of Literature in 2009, he was a finalist for the 2011 Man Booker International Prize. At the 2014 Times of India Mumbai Literature Festival, he was presented with its Lifetime Achievement Award. In 2016 he was appointed to the Order of Canada. His work has been published in more than thirty-five languages.

Remembering is a benediction: in time, the answer began to crystallize. In the space between the two, where the paradox resides, the idea of home could be built, anew, with memory and imagination, scaffolded by language.

—Rohinton Mistry

Rohinton Mistry's Omniscient Gaze
Samrat Upadhyay

I was in graduate school at Ohio University in the late 1980s, an aspiring writer from Nepal, when I read Rohinton Mistry's *Swimming Lessons and Other Stories from Firozsha Baag*. Those years I didn't have authors in English from my own country I could turn to, so it was mostly Indian writers whose work I was devouring. I'd already felt the heady jolt of Salman Rushdie's *Midnight's Children*, as many writers of my generation had. There were also others I was reading: Anita Desai, Bharati Mukherjee, Amitav Ghosh. And now here was Rohinton Mistry, and I knew that I had encountered someone who could teach me a thing or two about, as Raja Rao (the 1988 Neustadt winner) put it decades ago, "how to convey in a language that is not one's own the spirit that is one's own."

In a story called "Squatter" in *Swimming Lessons*, a young Indian who has immigrated to Canada finds that he is able to adapt to the Western way of life in everything, except one: in the bathroom he finds himself unable to sit on the commode and has to squat, desi-style. Even after living in Toronto for ten years, this character is "depressed and miserable, perched on top of the toilet, crouching on his haunches, feet planted firmly for balance upon the white plastic oval of the toilet seat." But our hero doesn't give up trying. "Each morning he seated himself to push and grunt," Mistry writes, "grunt and push, squirming and writhing unavailingly on the white plastic oval. Exhausted, he then hopped up, expert at balancing now, and completed the movement quite effortlessly."

For days I couldn't stop laughing at the picture of this young man's predicament. Yet it was not only funny, it was also the truth. With that one image, Mistry had captured for me a perennial problem of the migrant: how to adapt to one's new culture without giving up one's fundamental identity— that of a squatter!

Mistry is not a writer of linguistic riffs, he is not enamored by language for its own sake—and thank god for that. He's a writer who's interested in telling stories . . . stories about the human heart and the human mind and of how we all struggle in this world, whether we are migrants or bank workers, beggars or college students, tailors or pavement artists. An old-fashioned storyteller, Mistry is adept at revealing not only our flaws but also our virtues, our ability for human connection and kindness. Who can forget, for example, the bond that Gustad Noble and Tehmul-lungra form in *Such a Long Journey*? And what about the troubled yet moving relationship that forms among the four main characters in *A Fine Balance*: the prim Dina, the hounded tailors Isvar and Omprakash, and the endearing Maneck?

Mistry is a connoisseur of small details. The description of Crawford Market in *Such a Long Journey*, for example, is a welcome assault on the senses: "It was a dirty, smelly, overcrowded place," Mistry writes, "where the floors were slippery with animal ooze and vegetable waste, where the cavernous hall of meat was dark and foreboding, with huge wicked-looking meat hooks hanging from the ceiling . . . and the butchers trying various tacks to snare a customer, now importuning or wheedling, then boasting of the excellence of their meat while issuing dire warnings about the taintedness of their rivals', and always at the top of the voices."

Yet the sum of the little details in Mistry's novels accrue to something larger, an omniscient gaze that recalls Dickens and Tolstoy. It's not only individual lives that Mistry paints with such meticulousness; it's how he stretches his canvas to embrace the wider world that makes his work comparable to the contemporary giants of literature. Gustad Noble's struggles in *Such a Long Journey* are inextricably tied to the headaches of the nation under Indira Gandhi. In *A Fine Balance*, not only the city of Bombay but the whole of India ripples outward from the cramped shop where our tailors and their friends toil all day.

This is a largeness of the spirit, a merging of the individual consciousness with that of the collective yearning for love and belonging, and, simply, a decent, dignified life. In Mistry's hands, the form of the novel itself expands, and it ends up making us, the readers and the participants of his journey, filled with wonder at the beauty and spaciousness of this world.

Bloomington, Indiana

Samrat Upadhyay *is the author of several award-winning novels and story collections. He is the Martha C. Kraft Professor of Humanities and teaches creative writing at Indiana University.*

The Road from There to Here
Rohinton Mistry

A few months before I was to leave Bombay for Toronto, a friend asked to borrow my copy of *A Hard Day's Night*. It was 1975, and the Beatles had long since recorded their last studio album, but my friend—I'll call him Harish—working his way backward, was now enthralled by their earlier work.

He was constantly trying to find hidden meanings in songs, parsing, analyzing the lyric as though it were Wittgenstein or Schopenhauer. When B. B. King moaned that his woman had done him wrong, Harish was happy to spend an afternoon in the St. Xavier's College canteen debating, over endless cups of tea, what it was that the bluesman and his guitar were actually saying. With his ever-present flicker of a smile, Harish was agreeable company; the mischief he sought to provoke, the arguments he instigated were always welcome, as was his readiness for laughter.

Borrowing and lending within our circle of friends was rampant, second nature to us, learned long ago in kindergarten with rubber balls and painted wooden toys. And later, books and records, too, were considered common property, more or less. We traded, bartered, borrowed, and lent with a reckless disregard for Polonius's advice; otherwise, childhood and youth would have been bleak places.

When I gave Harish the Beatles LP, his request had barely registered. In 1975, India, in grave turmoil, had gripped everyone's attention. People were filling the streets in the hundreds of thousands, marching daily against misrule and corruption. Newspapers wrote, before censorship silenced them, about goon squads and torture, police brutality and custodial deaths, the disappearance of dissidents and union leaders, and about bodies found, bloodied, and broken, beside suburban railway tracks. The prime minister's response to all this, the unleashing of a State of Emergency, was barely a month away.

Changes in my personal life, though less drastic, were no less unsettling. My Canadian immigration visa had arrived. The convulsions that racked the country I observed detachedly, as I got ready to go. After all, my lower-middle-class life, like countless others, had been spent preparing for this moment, with encouragement from parents, friends, teachers, and counselors. The picture painted could have been titled *India: The Sinking Ship*: no prospects, no future in this place of ignorance and disease and poverty, where, instead of the rule of law, there was the law of bribery, where government would forever remain in corrupt or incompetent hands, where the only solution was to settle in the West, to make a better life for oneself, and where one would actually fit in much better, thanks to one's upbringing.

It strikes me now as odd that in the endless talk about what would be gained by migration, no one ever wondered if something might be lost. The stark choice, between clinging to the sinking ship or booking passage on the luxurious ocean liner, left little room for hesitation and deliberation. These were the generations who had borrowed, or borrowed from, the culture of the colonizer, that imperial lender who had made the loan seem a gift: seductive, pain-free, tantalizing. And, in time, the borrowers came to believe it was their birthright, their own culture, flowery frocks and Enid Blyton and Marmite and all, vastly superior to the native one which had been quietly expunged from their lives.

And where did it begin for me, the journey from there to here? The question is difficult; and perhaps this is oversimplification, but my father's record collection is as good a place to start as any.

In many ways, my long and winding road from Bombay to Toronto was merely an extension of the one that had led me to the LP of *A Hard Day's Night* from my father's 78 rpms. His eclectic collection of shellac pressings included things such as Gilbert and Sullivan operettas, Mozart's *Jupiter* Symphony, Brahms's *Hungarian Dances*, George Formby's "Blackpool Prom," a medley of English pub songs like "Down at the Old Bull and Bush," and so on, with Tin Pan Alley and Broadway also represented in the stack of records.

And though I never heard Ravi Shankar's sitar till many years later, when I saw the documentary where he performs with George Harrison in the *Concert for Bangladesh*, as a child I could sing all the words to "Don't Fence Me In": "Oh give me land lots of land under starry skies above, don't fence me in, let me ride through the wide-open country that I love, don't fence me in . . ."

The Gene Autry record was a serviceable soundtrack and theme song for the westerns I was reading then, the comics and novels, including the Lone Ranger series by Francis Striker. Cowboy was the career I had settled on. Those books were my operations manuals, consulted to make a list of required equipment: spurs, chaps, saddle, a white Stetson, bowie knife, belt and holsters for six-shooters. The job description seemed irresistible: riding the range, fighting cattle-rustlers and Injuns, lassoing the two-legged varmints and presenting them bound and helpless to the sheriff, and then, after sunset, building a fire to sit around and sing what else but "Don't Fence Me In," before falling asleep under the starlit sky. In short, the perfect life. I had decided that as soon as I was old enough I would leave Bombay on an Air India flight bound for the Wild West, where I would team up with the cowboys, wear a white hat, and ride a white horse. It never occurred to me that one look at this skinny subcontinental Indian boy and the white hats would relegate me to the losing side.

From time to time, I still marvel at the reach of that mythology and propaganda, halfway around the world, and the inadequacy of an education which kept me from making even the most superficial connection with, or feeling the slightest empathy for, the misnomered Indians of the Americas—subjugated, exploited, dispossessed, annihilated. Ignorance was not only bliss, it had fenced me in completely.

The gramophone that spun my father's 78s was his proudest possession, made in England by the Garrard Engineering and Manufacturing Company. My brothers and I were discouraged from playing it. This seemed unfair to us, who were always taught to share. Aware of the contradiction, our father would explain that the records were fragile, easily broken; besides, gramophones were dangerous for children because of the risk of electric shocks; and mishandling might blow the main fuse, plunging our flat into darkness, or even the entire block of flats. This convinced me, for it was a period during my childhood when I was scared of the dark, and of shadows, especially the shadows of foliage that played on the windowpane beside my bed, monster claws trying to break through the glass.

Every now and again, a brittle 78 would indeed shatter, and we would mourn its shellac shards for days. Electricity, too, sometimes corroborated my father's explanations by making the tone-arm deliver a nasty jolt. And fuse boxes and connections did go faulty, the wiring under perpetual siege from rats. But there is no doubt that my father guarded the gramophone fiercely, the cherished symbol of things he had wanted in his life: art, theater, ballet, the symphony—wanted for his family, in abundance, and could afford in meager portions only. The supply was scant, the price of admission mostly beyond reach.

When the Bolshoi Ballet came to Bombay in the 1960s, though, my father managed to get tickets for us all at Shanmukhanda Hall, a huge cavern of a place. Our seats were in the last row of the balcony. The dancers, in a performance of *La Dame aux Camélias*, would have been specks on the stage were it not for the binoculars loaned to us by our gentle upstairs neighbor. A veterinary surgeon, he was the principal of the Bombay Veterinary College. His duties included officiating at the Bombay Turf Club. The binoculars were the ones he used on Sunday afternoons to observe thousands of pounds of horseflesh fly around the Mahalaxmi Racecourse. At the ballet his bulky glasses captured the pirouettes and *pas de deux* as efficiently as the gallop and the canter. And I was certain that the people around us, peering through their dainty little opera glasses, could not see half as much as I with my big binoculars.

The Bolshoi Ballet was one of the rare moments when my father must have felt like a bona fide consumer of culture. But, over the years, as I pieced things together, I understood more. My father had started violin lessons at a young age—four or five, I think; and he had become rather good at the instrument by the time he was in university. Then everything changed. His father's illness, which sent their large and prosperous bookshop into decline, led to bankruptcy and the seizure of the books and bricks and mortar by the creditors. He had to give up his violin lessons, give up university, and, armed only with his BA in history and economics, find work to support the family.

So, years later, my father continued to carry the burden of yearnings created by the imperial lender, while the gramophone shouldered the weight of his dreams. He treated it with the same reverence that he showed his bookcase. Everything he did concerning the Garrard—dusting the rosewood cabinet, cleaning the tone-arm, selecting a record, switching on the turntable—had an air of ritual, as though in a temple. If the needle went blunt, he would select a new one from a small, enamelled metal box lined with tinfoil, and, for a while, the music would sound brighter, clearer. Those were the best days, the new-needle days; they made the future seem more hopeful.

I liked sitting close to the gramophone. With my cheek against the cabinet I could breathe in the warm fragrance of polished wood, feel the hum and vibration of the turntable, and imagine the music becoming a part of me. And I loved to watch the record spin because the grooves in the shiny shellac appeared to create an endless spiral which almost induced a trance, almost made visible the passage of time; and suddenly, eternity was not an idea that evaded grasping, but music that played forever.

My earliest memory of the gramophone is connected with a set of nursery-rhyme records, from the time I started kindergarten at Villa Theresa School. Thanks to the gramophone, I was already familiar with much of the kindergarten syllabus the nuns taught us: "Here We Go Round the Mulberry Bush," "Jack Sprat," "Oranges and Lemons," "A Frog He Would a-Wooing Go."

Time passed, and other records in my father's collection began to inter-est me. All grown up in the second standard and tired of nursery rhymes, I would ask my father to play selections from *The Maid of the Mountains* or *No, No, Nanette*. But, as master of ceremonies, he had to give equal time to my younger siblings. My requests would have to wait in line. To show my impa-tience, or just to show off, I would start singing something else: "He's up each mornin' bright and early, to wake up all the neighborhood, to bring to every boy and girlie, his happy serenade on wood . . ."

Then I would be asked to shut up. But before long I would start again, with another song: "A boy from Texas, a girl from Tennessee, he was so lonely in New York and so was she. The boy said howdy, the girl said hi y'all, he could have kissed her when he heard that southern drawl . . ."

Sometimes, we divagated into the realm of Indian music. There was a Hindi record called *Haji Malang Baba*, about a Sufi saint, whose shrine, halfway up a mountain in a suburb of Bombay, was visited by pilgrims of all races and religions—by Hindus, Muslims, Sikhs, Christians, Parsis—because Haji Malang granted all prayers and boons, in all languages. As for Hindi film music, a song from the blockbuster *Mother India* was my mother's favorite: "Na mai bhagwan hoon, na mai shaitaan hoon, array duniya jo chaahey sam-jay, mai to insaan hoon" (Neither am I a god, nor am I a devil, the world may think what it wants to, I'm just plain human). My mother's childhood influ-ences had been of a more ecumenical nature; she endeavored to embrace everything, and encouraged us to do the same.

The nursery rhymes were on seven-inch records, the other songs on ten-inch. And every gramophone recital ended with something classical, like Rachmaninoff or Tchaikovsky, on twelve-inch shellac. This was fitting, I used to think, the increase in size as one moved from children's music to music for big people.

The consumption of gramophone needles also kept increasing. My father was constantly replenishing them, regarding them to be necessities like milk and bread. The years went by, inflation continued to climb, and the economy, as it always has, continued to baffle the economists without damp-ening their enthusiasm for pontificating. Prices rose, wages languished, and, for the middle- and lower-middle classes, turned necessities into luxuries that they could no longer afford.

My father took to using a dark, menacing file to resharpen the blunted gramophone needles. This, in my eyes, profaned the sacred ritual; I hated the rasping sound that tore things out of their happy sequence.

But at least the music played on. Bing Crosby would croon for us, "Darling, je vous aime beaucoup, je ne sais pas what to do, you know you've completely stolen my heart . . ." After that, Caruso might sing Schubert's "Ave Maria," followed, perhaps, by Nelson Eddy's paeans of love for Rose Marie ringing out across the Canadian wilderness, in the middle of Bombay: "Oh Rose Marie I love you, I'm always dreaming of you . . ." Then Jeanette MacDonald would respond in kind with the "Indian Love Call," and our run-down flat would fill with joy and yearning and confusion.

Though I adored the old Garrard, I longed, now, for a modern record player that could play LPs and 45 rpms. Now I wanted to listen to the latest hits, be able to borrow them from my friends at St. Xavier's so I could take part in all the vital discussions and debate the important questions of the day: was "Eleanor Rigby" superior to "Yesterday"? If you could be any one of the Beatles, which one would you be? And why?

To my envy, neighbors in an adjacent flat bought a hi-fi soon after *The Sound of Music* came to Bombay. They already had a dog, the other object of my envy, and it became too much to bear. The soundtrack would pour out their window every afternoon when their seven-year-old daughter came home from school. The song about the lonely goatherd was her favorite, receiving lots of extra play.

Everyone had seen the film, and we listened with pleasure, the first few times. But the LP continued to be played over and over. By the end of the week, it seemed that Maria and the Captain with seven children had moved into our little three-room flat, to yodel their way through the rest of our lives.

In the end, the Von Trapp family was an auspicious presence, for when the film had finished its year-long run at the Regal, things improved financially at home. My father found freelance work to supplement his full-time job, and the result was a modern multispeed turntable. Manufactured in India by HMV, it looked like a cheap little suitcase, but to us it was an elegant sufficiency, capable of miracles: if, once upon a time, the Word was made flesh, then here, in our humble flat, the Vinyl was, at long last, made music.

And the denizens of this creation, this new world spinning at 33⅓ or 45 revolutions per minute—Cliff Richard, Elvis Presley, Herman's Hermits, the Rolling Stones, and many more—we welcomed them all, and all of their music, the good, the mediocre, the appalling, as though it had sprung from the soil of our South Bombay neighborhood. We held this truth to be self-evident, that everything with a "Made Somewhere in the West" tag was automatically superior. Through the years of high school, there were pointy shoes, tight pants, Elvis's sideburns, and Cliff's white fishnet T-shirt from the movie *Summer Holiday*, making short work of anything Indian in our lives that had survived the onslaught of the 78s, and so skilfully, we were forever oblivious of that sleight of hand. By the time we discovered Jethro Tull, Pink Floyd, and Crosby, Stills, Nash, and Young, our fate was sealed.

Resistance was impossible when the generations, old and young, were fifth-columnists contributing to the success of the multipronged campaign of infiltration, occupation, and conquest of imagination and language, begun so long ago. Nursery rhymes and Enid Blyton's Noddy books in kindergarten were merely the first salvo. The libraries at St. Xavier's High School and College came next, the very heart of the battlefield. And the British Council, the United States Information Services, the Max Mueller Bhavan all championed the cause by bringing up the rear, where books, films, music descended in a blizzard which, the cynics among us claimed, was thick enough to conceal entire cells of MI6 and CIA agents. The spies and spooks maintained a suitable invisibility, while we, the recipients of international generosity, entertained our newfound scepticism about the loving, sharing ways of superpowers, even as we revelled in Edward Elgar, Aaron Copland, Vaughan Williams, Mahalia Jackson, Benjamin Britten, Pete Seeger, Bob Dylan, and much, much more.

These foreign libraries were always deliciously air-conditioned. To step inside, out of the Bombay heat and humidity, was like entering Scotty's transporter on *Star Trek*, to be beamed instantly to a fantastic new planet, whence we returned cooled and refreshed, cradling our treasures of books and records. My friend Harish used to joke that if the LPs were not returned on time, the US cavalry would ride in to rescue them from the clutches of the Indians.

But borrowing finally requires reimbursement: the lender always comes calling. And the original loan, the one masquerading as the colonizer's gift, would be repaid in emigrant sons and daughters who had been raised to believe their ancient country was futureless, its ways inferior, and the only solution was to settle abroad to make a better life.

So now it was time to leave the sinking ship and head for the promised land. But it was hard, for in that vessel were people and places and things one cared about. To cope, there was self-deception and inconsistency, best served up wrapped in platitudes: that some day, in the not-too-distant future, we would all reunite, in the land of milk and honey; or, that one's own sojourn in the foreign land would last a few years at best, till one returned home, redeemed by wealth and success.

Such were the tricks to thwart emotions, to sort twenty-three years of life to fit into one suitcase—maximum weight: twenty kilos. The most precious among things to be left behind were never even considered, impossible to convey in any case. Things like the fragrance in the air, every June, of the approaching monsoon; and before the rains, the flamboyant gulmohar trees, blooming across Bombay in a scarlet blaze; or the taste of sweet translucent targolay, fruit of the palmyra palm; and the evening breeze off the Arabian Sea, like silk upon the skin.

Instead, one fretted about the easily replaceable, such as the small collection of LPs. Not surprisingly, it was as absurdly eclectic as my father's 78s. Excluded by the baggage allowance was Rodgers and Hammerstein's *Oklahoma!* and Bizet's *Carmen*. There was no room for Harry Belafonte, Jim Reeves, James Taylor, or Richie Havens. Not even for *Mary Poppins*, Joni Mitchell, Joe Cocker, or Leon Russell.

And there was the Beatles album, still with my friend Harish. I wanted it in its slot, before I left Bombay. On the verge of exchanging my life, my country for one that I had never seen and knew almost nothing about, I was fixated on getting that record back.

With departure less than a week away, I finally reminded him. He was not done with it, he said. It would have been churlish to press harder, and we parted, as usual, with a joke, a laugh, he wishing me *bon voyage*, as though I were off on a short holiday.

Pursuit of the LP continued in my first letters from Toronto. Perhaps I should have taken a page from Harish's book and looked instead for the hidden meaning. But homesickness was an ailment of the less sophisticated, more suited to the emblematic peasant who leaves his drought-stricken village for work in the city, believing, season after season, that he will soon be home. I, of course, having read all the right books, knew I could not go home again. But at least my LP would return to where it belonged.

And so the long-playing album kept spinning, round and round in my head, like the 78s I used to watch as a child on the old gramophone. I remembered, again, how my father would stand beside his beloved Garrard and sing along with the record, conducting the music, encouraging us to sing along too. What pleasure those hours had brought to his careworn life. I promised myself that one day I would copy all his old shellac pressings onto audio cassettes and bring them to Toronto—in an act of homage, I told myself, clutching at a source of comfort, trying to assuage a sense of loss.

But there was something else I remembered: years ago, just before the age of vinyl had dawned in our home, my father had suddenly lost interest in his gramophone. The ritual had been abandoned. And it had saddened me, like the time when he had decided he would no longer accompany us on Sunday mornings to play cricket. I also remembered how much I had missed the joy and optimism which my father, with his music, could spread through the flat, with his confidence that everything would be all right in the end. And I remembered a thousand other things.

But remembering brings with it a benediction; it brings understanding. My father, I now felt, had made his peace with the hand that life had dealt him. Gradually, he had freed himself from the false burdens foisted on him by history. The place of refuge that he had created, he needed no longer. And his abandoned shelter would be useless to anyone who tried to take it over or to replicate it.

One could not go home again—that much I knew. But all those memories of youth and childhood, running endlessly through my mind, now taught me the corollary, that one could never leave home either. So the question persisted: how to make sense of the contradiction in these two?

But remembering is a benediction: in time, the answer began to crystallize. In the space between the two, where the paradox resides, the idea of home could be built, anew, with memory and imagination, scaffolded by language. The LP did not matter.

Sometimes, a delinquent loan is a blessing realized.

Norman, Oklahoma
September 28, 2012

MIA COUTO
THE 2014 LAUREATE

Mia Couto was born in 1955 in Beira, Sofala Province, Mozambique. He lived in Beira until he was seventeen, when he went to Lourenço Marques to study medicine. He interrupted his medical studies to start a journalistic career. On his own initiative, he returned to the university to study biology, and he currently works as a biologist in Mozambique. He has published more than thirty books that have been translated and edited in thirty different countries. His books cover many genres, ranging from romance to poetry, from short stories to children's books. He has received dozens of awards in his career, including (twice) the National Prize for Literature and the Camões Prize. In 2016 he was a finalist for one of the most prestigious international awards, the Man Booker Prize. His novel *Terra Sonâmbula* was considered by an international jury meeting in Zimbabwe as one of the ten best African books of the twentieth century. He is a member of the

Brazilian Academy of Letters. With his wife, Patrícia Silva, he has three children, all of whom live and work in Maputo.

In that very familiar and domestic moment, the very essence of what is literature was present: a chance to migrate from ourselves, a chance to become others inside ourselves, a chance to re-enchant the world.

—Mia Couto

Giving Birth to a New Land
Gabriella Ghermandi

When I was invited to be part of this most distinguished panel, the first thought that came to mind was that I would nominate an African woman writer. But then my heart spoke up and posed a question: What does being a writer mean to me? A writer is not simply a person who knows how to shape and mold words to tell a story, but who, in doing so, helps us view its limits and dream of a way of going beyond them, to where the dream takes on the power of the vision. Someone who is able to communicate not only with his/her "local" world but also with the "global" one, and who can express all this in words, in stories, in narratives. This being the case, there was only one possible candidate for me. Only him. Mia Couto, a writer from Mozambique, the author of *Sleepwalking Land*.

Condensing Mia Couto's work into a few pages is very difficult. I will therefore try to give you a short overview, hoping that I will be able to expand on it in person when we meet. In order to talk to you about Mia Couto and about his fascinating use of the written language, I must first say something about Mozambican history that is at the heart of Couto's construction of the self and, therefore, of his artistry, of the way he uses words. This history of Mozambique I am referring to is linked to five hundred years of Portuguese colonization. A colonization that, like all forced relationships and governments, coerced the country into a forced relationship between the center and the periphery. In this case, the center was the power—white, Portuguese—of the written language, and the periphery was black submission and oral culture. A fixed and hegemonic relationship.

In 1975, after the 1974 fall of the dictatorship in Portugal, the Frelimo Party (the Mozambique Liberation Front) gained independence from Portugal. Unfortunately, though, the belief system shaped by five hundred years of colonization did not disappear along with the colonizers. It remained in people's minds. After liberation, within the ruling Frelimo Party, certain centrifugal forces arose in opposition to the leadership. Frelimo was not able to change pace. It did not know how to accommodate the dissenting voices within the party. Finding itself in difficulty, it decided to resort to the familiar: it reestablished a fixed relationship between center and periphery, basically identical to the one enforced during colonial times.

The same thing happened within Renamo, the opposition party. This party was initially illegal because of its ties to Ian Smith's Rhodesia and to the belief system of South African Apartheid. When, many years later, it became legal and assumed the role of opposition party, it could not divest itself of the center-periphery model. Even if it put forward values that were different from the hegemonic model, it could not avoid duplicating its structure.

Therefore, it continued to produce identities that were absolutist, monochromatic, at odds with the richly diverse and multilayered society.

Even the cultural aspects were still based on colonial models. There was a certain stasis in the idea that writing equates with emancipation and should, in a short period of time, completely supplant the oral culture of the peoples of Mozambique: yet another aspect of the fixed relationship between center and periphery. A relationship that, once more, signified exclusion by creating a stereotype of emancipation as a static idea outside the country's cultural context.

These were the years that gave birth to Mia Couto's writing, a writing born expressly as a form of struggle against the center-periphery duality. A struggle that aims at breaking down the stereotypical idea of emancipation seen as the progressive increase in alphabetization and the gradual fading out of oral culture. This is the first target of his writing. Language, reports the writer, is one of the first traps in forced relationships. Language paints the landscape for our minds, it values and devalues, excludes and includes. Bearing in mind that Portuguese in Mozambique was the language of exclusion, it was therefore necessary to turn it upside down, forcing it to open up a dialogue with the excluded part that needed to be awarded equal importance.

In order to direct his writing and, as a result, his readers, towards this consideration, Mia Couto redesigns the Portuguese language. With the precise intent to confuse the reader and force him to abandon the by-now-automatic frames of reading and therefore of thought, Couto invents a "different" Portuguese language (*what follows is an attempt to give you an approximate taste in English of what Couto does with the Portuguese language*).

He adds prefixes where they don't exist: "redie"; he substitutes similar prefixes: "unashamed" for "disashamed"; he creates new words to produce new semantic and aesthetic meanings: "groanentia" ("groan" + dementia); he makes new words spring from onomatopoeic words of the oral culture ("my heart boomboomed"), or from Bantu meanings attributed to Portuguese words ("mammas"—used for many women in the family, not just the mother); he changes idiomatic expressions: "my word, my business" to "his/her word, our business." A recolonialized Portuguese language, capable of allowing room for the oral culture of the Mozambique peoples, pluralistic, symbolic, tied to its prelinguistic identity and to its prelinguistic form of communication.

A recolonization that springs from his deep knowledge of Portuguese—so deep a knowledge that it allows him to manipulate the language at will—and from his profound knowledge of the cultures of Mozambique. All of Mia Couto's writing is steeped in images from the oral culture of the peoples of Mozambique that intersect with written Portuguese. The result is a "frontier" language, in which "frontiers" refer to a marginalized territory that has an unmarked, indefinable border. This new language-tongue, in constant flux, is the message from the writer to the peoples of Mozambique: the various groups, the different parties must be involved in a dialogue in order to find a fluid identity, a shifting balance.

This is what is indispensable for Mozambique in order to have a possible future.

Sleepwalking Land is situated at the center of this message. The novel begins with two figures that appear in a Mozambique devastated by a long civil war. They are an old man and a child: Tuahir and Muidinga. They have escaped from one of the many refugee camps. They are fleeing from the war the only way they can: on foot. They are only looking for a quiet haven. A burned-out bus full of corpses, once cleansed of the death that had transformed it into a metal coffin, will do. So the *machimbombo* (the bus) becomes their lair: "If the bandits come, we'll act like we are dead. Pretend we died along with the bus."

Near the wreck there is a bag and inside, among other things, some notebooks, the pages filled with writing. The child knows how to read, and he begins to give voice to the letters in Kindzu's notebooks. And so the narrative begins, alternating between the present, that is the story of Tuahir, and Muidinga and the past, that is Kindzu's diary. Two furrows in the same hell.

Old Tuahir had met and saved Muidinga from certain death by taking responsibility for him. The child had completely lost his memory and Tuahir decided to call him Muidinga. The little one often asks him to tell him the story of how they met, truly a second birth for him, as when the old man renamed him after he had decided to "adopt" him. The child demands to hear the story of what are now his origins with the same obstinacy of one who demands his childhood, denied to him by history. His determined fight to fulfill this need has the force of a primeval instinct, of a survival instinct: "Conte, tio. Se é uma estória me conte, nem importa se é verdade" (Tell me, Uncle. If it is a story, it doesn't matter whether it is true or not).

It is a caring relationship between the two of them, a mutual caregiving, their roles sometimes reversing. Not only does the adult take care of the child, restoring to him a past and therefore a future, but the opposite also happens: the child, the only one who can read and write, reads him the stories in Kindu's notebooks, found near a burned corpse inside a bus, on a country road.

The child is the symbol of the new Mozambique, born of independence, the Mozambique that looks to the future, the Mozambique of the written world. A lost child who does not know his origins nor where he was born, who does not even remember his name. He knows he has a family somewhere and wants to find them, and he asks Tuahir to accompany him. Tuahir, symbol of the old Mozambique, who cannot read or write but knows how to tell stories following an ancient tradition. Stories capable of healing, of helping the child to remain rooted in life, in the land, in order to reach his goal.

Conversely, the old man is nourished by Kindzu's written diary through Muidinga's readings. A diary that ends at the conclusion of their journey. The pages they were leafing through turn into leaves when they return to the earth.

A final message built on the ambiguous Portuguese word *folha* that means both a sheet of paper and the leaf of a tree. Therefore the return to the earth as birthplace, as a last dwelling place, but also forging transformation for new growth.

Some critics have called Mia Couto "the smuggler writer," a sort of Robin Hood of words who steals meanings to make them available in every tongue, forcing apparently separate worlds to communicate. If, on one hand, Mia Couto's work is a message to his native land, for a complete decolonization that cannot ignore language, and consequently the mind and its tendency to stasis, on the other hand, he addresses the whole world seeking to resonate with each and every individual.

Constantly breaking the static nature of the written language and of linguistic codes, and, as a result, of a fixed identity (so as to become open to other cultures that exist in today's world) is a way of freeing oneself from the idea that growth takes place only when one of our identities is chosen as the superior one. Knowing how to pair the linearity of written language with the plurality of oral culture (that also has origins in the prelinguistic world, in the invisible, in symbology), keeping one's mind open to the languages of the soul, of nature, of the oral tradition and making these languages available to the rational self, allows man to follow the path of a particular bilingualism that puts into communication two worlds usually separate or subordinate. Mia Couto defines such a capacity as a "bilingualism," capable of giving birth to a new man, the nation-man who lives in an "unbalanced" balance in endless movement, dancing with its times, with its local and global context. A man who looks to the future while leaning on the past. A past that is so deep as to be timeless.

Bologna, Italy

Gabriella Ghermandi *is an Ethiopian-Italian performer, novelist, and short-story writer. Her stories have been published in several collections and journals, and her first novel,* Queen of Flowers and Pearls, *was published in 2007.*

Re-enchanting the World
Mia Couto

Dear friends,

It is a great honor to receive this award. I am saying this not just as a simple formality. It is a deeper feeling. The importance of this award goes far beyond the work of a particular writer. What we are celebrating here, in Oklahoma, year after year, is more than literature. With the Neustadt Prize we all praise the cultural diversity of our world and the cultural diversity of each one of us. That is crucial in a moment where personal and national identities are constructed like fortresses, as protection against the threats of those who are presented to us as aliens.

This prize is important for the relations between our worlds, which seem to be situated not only on different continents but on different planets. Despite all diplomatic and political efforts, a considerable reciprocal ignorance still prevails between Mozambique and the United States of America. We tend to assume this remoteness as natural, given the physical location of our countries. However, we must nowadays question what is presented as "normal" and "natural." There are, indeed, other reasons that lead to our mutual lack of knowledge. And those reasons have nothing to do with geography.

We have a common struggle for freedom, democracy, and independence. We share a past and a present of resistance against injustice and discrimination. But in the quest to affirm the uniqueness of our nations we have created, without knowing, a reductive and simplistic vision of the other, and of ourselves. We suffer from a narrow and stereotyped vision of a multicolor reality. We are only able to recognize one cultural dimension of reality. We have fallen into the temptation of the "Single Story" against which the Nigerian writer Chimamanda Adichie so eloquently warned us.

The Neustadt Prize has the merit of promoting dialogue between cultures and creating bridges where there is distance and, worse than that, mere indifference.

It's good to know that literature can help build neighborhoods in a world which imagines that the proximity between cultures is totally resolved by technological solutions.

Dear friends,

I am the second son of a Portuguese couple forced to emigrate, trying to escape from the fascist regime in Portugal. Each night, my mother and my father told me stories. They thought they were getting us to sleep. In fact, they were producing a second and eternal birth.

What fascinated me was not exactly the content of those tales. As a matter of fact, I can't remember a single one of those stories. What I remember, first of all, is having my parents just for me, next to my bed, next to my dreams. More than anything I remember the passion that they found in the invention of those stories. That intense pleasure had a reason: using words, they could travel and visit their missing homeland. They could erase time and distance.

In that very familiar and domestic moment, the very essence of what is literature was present: a chance to migrate from ourselves, a chance to become others inside ourselves, a chance to re-enchant the world. Literature is not only a way to affirm our existence. It is a permission to disappear and to allow the presence of those who seem to be absent.

We Africans come from a long and painful narrative to affirm our nations and our singular identity. I am afraid that, although historically necessary, part of the nationalist discourse has become a burden that prevents us from being plural, available to be others and to travel inside other lives. That availability is the essence of literature. And the essence of our humanity.

I come from a nation that is regarded as one of the poorest in the world. I don't know how poverty is measured, but many of the African languages spoken in my country do not have specific words for saying "poor." To designate a poor person, one uses the term *chissiwana*. This word means "orphan." A poor person is someone who lives without family and without friends. He is someone who has lost the ties of solidarity.

This other poverty, born of solitude, is more widespread than one might think. Never before has our world been so small, so simultaneous, so instantaneous. But this speed has not solved our solitude. Never before have there been so many roads. And never before have we made so few visits. What could bind us together would be the desire to tell and to listen to stories.

There are many hidden dimensions of the art of writing. A few years ago I experienced an episode that showed me a different meaning of what I do as writer.

It happened in 2008, in northern Mozambique in a coastal village called Palma. It's a remote region, without water, without electricity, in the middle of the savannah. I had finished my day's work as a biologist, and I was in the shadow of my tent, when a peasant came and called me. *Come here*, he said. *Come and see a man who's been killed.* I went into the darkness, and I followed the old man along a path in the middle of the bush. *How did he die?* I asked. And the man replied: *He was killed by a lion. That lion is still nearby. And he's going to come back to fetch the rest of the body.* I returned hastily to the tent, with no wish to see whatever he had to show me.

I closed the zipper of the tent, knowing how inadequate this gesture was as protection. A short distance from me lay a corpse ripped up by a lion, and a wild beast roamed nearby like a murderous shadow. During my professional life, I have worked for many years in regions where there are still dangerous animals. But I didn't know how to deal with a situation like that. I remember that the first thing I did was to switch on my small flashlight and begin writing in my notebook. I was not describing what was going on, because I didn't know, nor did I want to know what was happening. The truth is that until daybreak, I was busy writing in order not to be overcome with fear.

That fear was a primitive feeling, a memory of another time, in which our fragility was more evident. I am an urban man, born and raised in modernity. I had no defense against a fear that was more ancient than humanity itself. I gradually realized that the wild creatures were not lions but the monsters that have dwelt within us for centuries.

Only later did I understand; I wasn't really taking shelter in the tent.

I was taking shelter in fiction. I was creating a story like someone making a house not just to live in but to erase reality. Without knowing it, I was beginning to write a novel called *Confession of the Lioness.*

But another one of my novels served as the basis for the choice of this prize, the novel *Terra sonâmbula (Sleepwalking Land)*. This book speaks of a dramatic moment in the history of Mozambique. For sixteen years we suffered a civil war, which killed the economy and crippled the country.

Those sixteen years of conflict left a million dead out of a population of eighteen million. In its intention, violence is opposed to the art of telling stories: that intention is to dehumanize us, a dehumanization achieved in various ways. We were living in a kind of absolute solitude: isolated from hope, incapable of turning the present into a treasure trove of stories. We were all alone, the dead and the living. Without a past, without a future, without stories. The present was only worthwhile insofar as it was born to be forgotten.

Terra sonâmbula was the only book I found painful to write, because it was written during the war, at a time when I was also besieged by despair. For months I spent sleepless nights visited by friends and colleagues who had been killed during the conflict. It was as if they came knocking on the door of my insomnia, asking to live in stories, even if they were lies, or just a way for me to fall asleep.

I remember that once, after one of these sleepless nights, I came out of the building of the biology station where I was working and sat on the beach. And I realized that there, very close to the breaking waves, was a whale which had decided to come and die on the beach. Then I saw people arriving hastily at the beach. In an instant they rushed together at the dying animal to hack chunks from it, ripped to pieces with the greed of a hunger of centuries. It had not yet died, and its bones were already shining in the sun. Little by little, I came to think of my country as one of those whales coming to die in agony on the beach. Death had not yet come, and yet the knives were already stealing chunks of it, each person trying to take as much as possible for himself. As if that were the last animal, the final opportunity to grab a meal. I went back to my room weighed down by an incurable sadness. On that early morning I wrote the final chapter of my novel. Two months later, when I was delivering the text to my publisher, the news arrived of the peace agreement.

When the peace agreement was signed in 1992, we thought that revenge and the settling of scores would be inevitable. But it didn't happen like that. People decided on a kind of collective amnesia. The reminders of violence were cast into a pit of oblivion. We know that this oblivion was false. A war is impossible to forget. But we wanted the war to forget us.

Mozambique's experience showed how literature can play an active role in the construction of peace. Fiction and poetry do not cause the guns to fall silent. But they can reconcile us with the past, no matter how painful it might be. Fiction and poetry can help reconquer our inner tranquility and promote reconciliation with others. By means of stories, these others were freed from the condition of demons. I can say with pride that poets and writers have helped to rehumanize my country.

Unfortunately, it is not so much stories that unite humanity. What unites us today, in all countries, on all continents, is above all fear. The same feeling of abandonment and insecurity brings us together everywhere. There are no great or small powers that are safe from fear. We live the same anguish faced with the other transformed into an enemy. We all live in a small tent surrounded by the threat, real or imaginary, of a beast in the dark wanting to devour us.

The fear that rules us is, in large measure, nourished by the profound ignorance we have of one another. Literature can be a response against the invitation to fabricate fear and mistrust. Literature and storytelling confirm us as relatives and neighbors in our infinite diversity.

Dear friends,

It is very gratifying to know that the next laureate is an African as well. We know that the Neustadt Prize is not limited by the author's geographical origin; the only issue is the quality of his or her work. This means that Africans are imposing themselves on the international scene without recourse to any paternalistic criteria. In truth, for some years now, we African writers are freeing ourselves from a literature dominated by a desire to affirm our identity. Formerly, we felt a historic and psychological need to demonstrate that we were as able as others. This period of affirmation made sense after centuries of cultural and historical denial. But today we are more free to act without fulfilling our function as the Other.

A new generation of Africans is more and more free to act as universal writers. They feel free to write about any subject, in the language they choose. Our new literature is now less afraid of the accusation of not being faithful to genuineness, or not respecting the so-called "tradition." We are producing a literature that is free from having to show its Africanness as a kind of passport to be accepted.

Many of our young writers are using literature to denounce the arrogance, corruption, and nepotism of some current political leaders. But more than that, they are busy producing good literature. And they know that there are as many Africas as there are writers, and all of them are reinventing continents that lie inside their very selves. This is not a quest that is exclusively ours, as Africans. There isn't a writer in the world who doesn't have to seek out his or her own identity among multiple and elusive identities. In every continent, each person is a nation made up of different nations.

Dear friends,

The Neustadt Prize is announced as follows (and I quote): "This is the first international literary award of its scope to originate in the United States and is one of the very few international prizes for which poets, novelists, and playwrights are equally eligible."

I would like to thank the Neustadt family, the University of Oklahoma, and *World Literature Today* for the open and all-embracing conception of this initiative. The format of this celebration reveals a concern not to reduce the event to an award ceremony alone. In this way, justice is done to the principle that what is important are books and not so much their authors.

One of the merits of this prize is that it is guided by criteria devoted exclusively to literary quality. I present myself to you not as a representative of a place, of an ideology, of a religion. But I will never forget those who give meaning to my writing, the anonymous people of my country. Some of those

Mozambicans—who are, together with me, author of my books—do not know how to write. Many don't even speak Portuguese. But they are guardians, in their everyday lives, of a magical, poetical dimension to the world that illuminates my writing and gives delight to my existence.

It would be an injustice not to mention here the people who have given my presence here their support: The first of these people is Gabriella Ghermandi, the member of the panel that proposed me as a candidate. Without her, I would not be here. I would not be here if it weren't for my longtime translator, David Brookshaw. A translator is a co-author and should appear on the covers of books, and his presence in this ceremony is totally justified. Accompanying me is my wife, Patricia, who is my primary inspiration and my first reader. Present with us is my daughter, Luciana, and she represents here my other children, Madyo and Rita. No prize can prove stronger than the delight we have in seeing ourselves born in our own children. To them I owe this feeling of lived eternity.

I shall end by reading a poem I wrote some years ago. I remembered these verses when I discovered that the emblem for this prize was an eagle's feather. This symbolic representation is a metaphor for writing that seeks to have the lightness of wings. I shall ask David Brookshaw to read this poem, in his own translation.

In Some Other Life I Was a Bird

I preserve the memory
of landscapes spread wide
and escarpments skimmed in flight.
A cloud and its careless trace of white
connect me to the soil.
I live with the heartbeat
of a bird's wing
and plunge like lightning
hungering for earth.

I preserve the plume
that remains in my heart
as a man preserves his name
over the span of time.
In some other life I was a bird
in some other bird I was life.

Norman, Oklahoma
October 24, 2014

Translation from the Portuguese by Paul Fauvet

DUBRAVKA UGREŠIĆ
THE 2016 LAUREATE

Over the past three decades, **Dubravka Ugrešić** (b. 1949) has established herself as one of Europe's most distinctive novelists and essayists. From her early postmodernist excursions, to her elegiac reckonings in fiction and the essay with the disintegration of her Yugoslav homeland and the fall of the Berlin Wall, to her more recent writings on popular and literary culture, Ugrešić's work is marked by a rare combination of irony, polemic, and compassion. Following degrees in comparative and Russian literature, Ugrešić worked for many years at the University of Zagreb's Institute for Theory of Literature, successfully pursuing parallel careers as both a writer and as a scholar. In 1991, when war broke out in the former Yugoslavia, Ugrešić took a firm antiwar stance and became a target for nationalist journalists, politicians, and fellow writers. Subjected to ostracism and persistent media harassment, she left Croatia in 1993. Her books have been translated into over twenty languages. She has taught at a number of American and European universities and is the winner of several major literary prizes. Her recent books include the novel *Fox* and the book of essays *American Fictionary*, both published in 2018. Her latest book, *The Age of Skin,* appeared in autumn 2019. She lives in Amsterdam.

We should invest all our energies in supporting people who are prepared to invest in literature, not in literature as a way to sustain literacy but as a vital, essential creative activity, people who will preserve the intellectual, the artistic, the spiritual capital.

—Dubravka Ugrešić

Along a Path to Transnational Literature
Alison Anderson

In 1997 I was offered a job to teach English to adults in Croatia. Of course I had been following the events that had torn Yugoslavia apart between 1991 and 1995; and just as I was learning what I could about the newly independent country of Croatia, Dubravka had already left it behind, in 1993, to go into exile first in Berlin and then Amsterdam. The irony is that I ordered two of Dubravka's early books, to learn more about a country that, in fact, no longer existed, and where she no longer lived nor could feel at home. But these two books were a good introduction nevertheless: *Steffie Speck in the Jaws of Life* and *Fording the Stream of Consciousness* are both works of fiction and belong to a tradition of playful satire and black humor that was prevalent all through eastern Europe during the communist era. As a student of Russian I had read both the classics and the Soviet-era satirical work that followed, so there was something that felt wonderfully familiar about her fiction and new at the same time. Were it not for the accident of history, so to speak, Dubravka might have gone on writing novels in this satirical vein, poking fun at her fellow writers, or lovesick women, or life in the little republic of Croatia when it was part of the Socialist Federal Republic of Yugoslavia.

It is significant that the breakup of the country drove her into exile only four years after the fall of the Berlin Wall; it is also significant that the once-"dissident" writers of the Soviet bloc suddenly found themselves in a literary context that was utterly changed—they had freedom of expression at last, yes, but not necessarily the freedom to publish or be read; market forces suddenly determined everything that was published throughout the former Eastern bloc. The breakup of Yugoslavia meant not only the transition to a capitalist culture but also a severing of ties among the former republics that at times bordered on the absurd, as new dictionaries were created for each republic's "language"—no longer known as Serbo-Croatian but as Bosnian-Croatian-Serbian (and sometimes Montenegrin).

Now Dubravka found herself living in western Europe but writing in Croatian, living in, as she calls it, a literary out-of-nation zone. Who would read her? Who was her audience? Whom was she writing for? Back then, perhaps only a few dissenting Croats or fellow exiles, unhappy with the nationalistic regime of the 1990s; her Yugoslav audience had virtually vanished. Would the Germans, the Dutch read her in translation? Could she find a place as a European writer? These were some of the questions I asked myself as I began to learn both about Dubravka's biography and about life in Croatia in the late 1990s.

After the year I spent in Zagreb, I returned to the US and was heartened to see that Dubravka's books were appearing regularly in English: *Have a Nice Day, The Culture of Lies, The Museum of Unconditional Surrender, Thank You for Not Reading, Ministry of Pain, Nobody's Home*, etc. I realized too that she had found a new voice—the voice of exile, one might call it—and that the bubbly, sardonic novels of her youth had given way, for the most part, to incisive, often heartfelt and angry, but always ironic and cautionary essays about life in post-Yugoslavia, in Europe, and in the wider world. Her works appeared not only in English but in many countries, in translation, and she has, so fortunately for us, found her place, at latest count, in twenty-seven languages.

I would like to focus briefly on her novel from 1997, *The Museum of Unconditional Surrender*, because it is the pivotal work written from her first exile in Berlin, and it is also a work that echoes and reflects the events of the late 1980s and '90s in Europe. Before 1989 Berlin was a divided city, the very heart of the tension between western and eastern Europe; then, after the fall of the Wall it became the home not only to many refugees from the war in the Balkans but also to a host of economic migrants from eastern Europe in search of a better life. Russians, Poles, Hungarians, Romanians, and let's not forget East Germans all came in search of a new life in the open city of Berlin. Dubravka's novel brings that transitional, transitioning city to life with its migrants, refugees, lost souls, artists, exiles—there are Bosnians and Russians but also Brits and Indians; we also meet Americans and Portuguese as the narrator travels for her work. There are chapter headings in German, notably *Wo bin ich?*—"Where am I?"—and this refers not only to the narrator's or an immigrant's bewilderment in the situation of exile and a new language but also leads to the question *Wer bin ich?*—"Who am I?"—the question of identity totally turned on its ear, particularly for the former Yugoslavs, but even for the other ordinary migrants. Could a Russian now say he was German, or European? Was he still Russian? What is identity? How much of it is necessarily bound up in geographical location or place of birth; how much of it will be influenced by politics?

For that period of time in Berlin, Dubravka witnessed the distress of these immigrants and chronicled it, offsetting the passages set in Berlin with memories of her childhood, her mother and grandmother, and the dual loss of youth and home. *The Museum of Unconditional Surrender* is a novel that is deeply rooted in European history but has become uprooted from its "Croatian" context or tradition—other than the fact that it was written in Croatian—to move into, I would say, a category of its own. If one must categorize a book, the way clueless booksellers sometimes do, we could say this book belongs to the literature of exile. But there are no shelves in bookstores for "exile"; you will find Nabokov under American literature, Brodsky under Russian, Joseph Conrad among the classics, etc.

Unlike many other works of European literature, Dubravka's oeuvre is pan-European, in the sense that it deals with many different countries, and people from many different backgrounds and nationalities. Let me explain by providing a contrast. To name two of the most salient examples of contemporary European literature currently enjoying both critical and popular success in the US, there is, first of all, Karl Ove Knausgaard's *My Struggle*, then Elena Ferrante's Neapolitan Quartet. The first is very clearly set primarily in Norway, and its hero is very typically Norwegian in many respects, albeit his wife is Swedish and they live in Sweden; Ferrante's novels are even more bound to their location and its inhabitants—you could even say that Naples is a character throughout the novels. Granted, these are works of "fiction," so to speak, whereas Dubravka is now writing principally nonfiction, but all her books feature a rich variety of characters and places, usually quite specifically described, but with an intent to reveal the universal nature of the dilemma or situation in which these passing protagonists find themselves.

I have been thinking, since I was first invited to speak on this panel, of how I would situate Dubravka "in the context of contemporary European literature," and my conclusion is, to be honest, that I cannot. If I think of the novels I have translated from French over the last decade, most of them are very ethnocentric, very much part of a French tradition, or certainly taking for granted that they belong to the realm of "French literature," often catering to a French readership or, in any case, assuming that the primary readership will be French. There is no such easy assumption available for Dubravka's work; in fact, she said herself in a recent interview: "I have passionately propagated the notion of transnational literature . . . a literary territory for those writers who refuse to belong to their national literatures" (*Music & Literature*). Again, if we turn to her biography, her geographical history, it becomes very clear why this is. Very early on in the conflict, Dubravka was expected to take sides and could not, would not. She chronicled her outrage and disgust at her countrymen in *The Culture of Lies;* she continues to target Croatia—now a member of the European Union—for its lack of transparency, its corruption, its multiple shortcomings. She has seen through the tawdry nationalism of flag-waving; she is appalled by the population's fairly recent protests against the International Criminal Tribunal for the Former Yugoslavia regarding the war crimes trials of men whom Croatians refer to as "heroes." She has been a direct victim of that particular nationalism, but nationalism, as we hardly need reminding, is on the rise everywhere.

The work of Dubravka Ugrešić stands apart from any specific European literature precisely because she comes from a European literary tradition that gave her the tools to gaze coldly on the dangers of classifying and codifying, of pinning labels, the dangers of conformity and submission to a nation or an ideology. Nor is globalization the answer, as a reaction to nationalism; she illustrates this in *Karaoke Culture*, which describes a universal culture of dumbing down, conformity, and laziness. Dubravka's work belongs, rather, to its own "transnational" category, a literature that defies and crosses borders wherever there are readers who are open to the outside world, who are not afraid of the other, the foreigner, readers who do not want to go through life building walls to remain in a comfortable, blinkered, nationalistic homeland. She writes for those who, like herself, defend supranational values—freedom of speech, empathy, justice, and integrity.

Buchillon, Switzerland

Alison Anderson *is a novelist and translator. Her most recent novel,* The Summer Guest, *based on an episode in the life of Anton Chekhov, was published in 2016. She lives in Switzerland.*

A Girl in Litland
Dubravka Ugrešić

The first two books I wrote were for children. When I published my first book I was twenty-one. I soon gave up on writing children's literature when I realized that I didn't have the very particular god-given talent that only the exceptional writers for children possess. I still believe that the career of the children's author—with the gift of a Lewis Carroll—is the most joyous career a writer could wish for, and it is, at the same time, a "natural" choice: writing for children means living in an extended childhood. I say this because adults work at jobs that are useful, while children work at tasks that have no practical application. Literature, too, is a nonuseful task. It has no price tag, there can be no compensation for it—just as a child's drawing has no price tag—nor can it be manipulated, though many people are hard at work at precisely that, "manipulating" literature. Even writers, after all, do not hesitate to manipulate.

At a historical turning point for the cultural community it was decided that literature, this useless task, should be granted a more serious standing. The status of modern literature began at the moment when it became a subject of study at universities, and this happened only several hundred years ago. Any standing is vulnerable to change. In other words, a vast amount of time is needed to build a pyramid, even more to maintain it, but only a few short moments to tear it down. In this sense literature, as a system of knowledge devised and built by hardworking people over the centuries, is a fragile creation. Those who work at literature should keep this in mind. Perhaps it would be apt here to think back to Ray Bradbury's cult novel *Fahrenheit 451* as well as to the many postapocalyptic science-fiction movies. There are no books to be seen in the latter. At least I haven't seen one. And besides, when the time comes for everybody to start writing books—and that moment, thanks to technology, is upon us—there will no longer be literature. This is because literature is a system that requires arbitration. The arbiters used to be "people of good literary taste": theoreticians, critics, literature professors, translators, editors, and, don't forget, the attendant mediocrities: the censors, the salespeople, the "Salieris," the ideologues of various stripes—from religious to political. Today the market has anointed itself as arbiter, as have the readers. The market is allied with the "majority reader." Authors are no freer as a result—along with politicians and entrepreneurs, today authors are expected to *please* the consumer, to *lobby, blog, vlog, post, tweet,* to be *liked,* to spread with diligence to their digital fan base who will support them and buy their books.

I was born into a world in which the first technological wonder was the radio. I remember waking up at night and turning the big dial to move the red line across to the stations inscribed on the display while I listened to languages I didn't understand. Our radio was called a Nikola Tesla, and it had a green eye that glowed in the dark. I was born a few years after the close of the Second World War in a small country, poor and ravaged by war, where there was a pressing need to manufacture goods that were more utilitarian than those from a toy factory. That's why I got my first "real" doll when I was already too big to play with dolls. In my early childhood, what I found sensational had nothing to do with toys but with books, the radio, and Hollywood movies for grown-ups: the text, sound, and image gave me the illusion of flight from my provincial little town into the grand, thrilling world. I envisioned the world with the help of books, and the role played by interactivity—to use contemporary jargon—was huge. The field of the imagination is more circumscribed today; the cultural industry has satisfied every need we could only have dreamt of before. Here are our "prechewed" products (*Anna Karenina for Beginners*), or streamlined, readapted, and commercialized versions of original works (*Anna Karenina and the Zombies*), or experiments such as the use of hologram books. The new media today are filling the space of the imagination to its last inch: they are taking the soul, time, and money of their "consumers" and leaving nothing behind.

In my childhood and even in my student days, publishing was not yet referred to as an *industry*, nor was there a literary marketplace, and the borders between children's literature and writing for adults were not so sharply drawn. There were no psychologists hovering over the process of consumption; with passion we read whatever we could get our hands on. Thanks to the media and the marketplace, our taste today is standardized. The powerful industry nourishes every consumer capillary of the world. In the very poorest quarters of Kolkata where people inhabit space the size of a matchbox, they may be impoverished, but miniature screens (television and otherwise) glow day and night from their makeshift abodes.

In the bygone days of Yugoslav publishing there used to be an unpopular penalty known as *the pulp tax*. Those who chose to satisfy the more "pedestrian" tastes of the readership had to pay a special tax for the pulp fiction they published. If the tax for pulp were to be levied at a global level, this would amass a vast store of money, which could be used for publishing both high-quality and inexpensive books for a free and fine education, for teachers, for artists, for the creative folk. All this can be imagined, of course, but the only thing that defies the imagination is the decision of who would evaluate what fiction is pulp and what isn't. And it bears mentioning that the terms *pulp fiction* and *kitsch* have faded from the parlance. Some thirty years ago kitsch was still a subject for discussion and a focus of research among theoreticians of art and literature. Then the powerful global market elbowed the concept of *kitsch* out of its vocabulary. Anything that separates the "wheat from the chaff" is undesirable in a global marketplace that works to sell everything, and sell as much of it as possible.

There are key tags to be found in the vocabulary of the brilliant sociologist Zygmunt Bauman that have relevance not only for our age but for the culture industry, including that of literature right now. One of them is *waste*. Our industrially hyperactive civilization generates, among other things, waste. With the most popular commands of *copy and paste* there appears the need for a command to *save*. Our digital age is shaping the mind-set and physicality of the digital human. Our fingers are growing thinner, longer, and more adept, but we're keeping ophthalmologists busy as we constantly adjust the lenses in our eyeglasses. Our language, too, is changing. Now, not just children but adults rely on abbreviations and emoticons. Our emotions, too, have changed, as have our sensors for reception, our codes, our ways of communicating, and, foremost, our sense of time. We feel we're immersed in an all-accessible, domineering NOW. In this sense a feeling of cultural discontinuity has crept into older specimens of the human race, such as myself, despite the all-accessible search engines that can connect us, in seconds, to bygone times. In parallel to the emancipating and powerful sense of control through digital devices such as the smartphone, a *liquid fear*, as Baumann would put it, has come to dwell in people, a neurosis of insecurity (perhaps this being our need to leave millions of selfies in cyberspace to confirm that we lived).

The story "Who Am I?" was born out of a sense not only of security but of literary plenty thirty-three years ago, at a time when I was as happy as a mouse nesting in a wheel of cheese. My wheel of cheese was the library, a university job, the certainty that literature was autonomous and that the only thing worth dedicating myself to was literature. The short story that has been staged by the students from the OU Helmerich School of Drama, directed by Judith Pender, came about out of a powerful feeling of literary well-being, of continuity. I was intrigued by the idea of a defamiliarized reading within a profound familiarization with world literature.

Internet literature, the fan fiction I explored while writing my essay

"Karaoke Culture," is today guided by a similar principle, but the canon is different. These are not classic works of the literary canon but belong to a new, contemporary canon of millions of readers and viewers: *Harry Potter, Twilight Saga, Hunger Games,* and others like them.

Because of all this, and perhaps because of my unjustified feeling that the system of literature as we know it is on the way out—what with digital civilization taking over Gutenberg civilization—we should invest all our energies in supporting people who are prepared to invest in literature, not in literature as a way to sustain literacy but as a vital, essential creative activity, people who will preserve the intellectual, the artistic, the spiritual capital. I couldn't have dreamed that one day a student theater in Norman, Oklahoma, would be putting on the first-ever staging of my story, written thirty-three years ago. Literary continuity, therefore, does exist, and the fact that it describes an unexpected geographical trajectory only heightens the excitement.

The literary landscape that has greeted me in Norman has touched me so deeply that I, briefly, forgot the ruling political constellations. I forgot the processes underway in all the nooks and crannies of Europe, I forgot the people who are stubbornly taking us back to some distant century, the people who ban books or burn them, the moral and intellectual censors, the brutal rewriters of history, the latter-day inquisitors; I forgot for a moment the landscapes in which the infamous swastika has been cropping up with increasing frequency—as it does in the opening scenes of Bob Fosse's classic film *Cabaret*—and the rivers of refugees whose number, they say, is even greater than that of the Second World War.

A continuity of literary evaluation does, nevertheless, exist. The knowledge of what is good literature has not been lost for good. This is a moment to recall Vladimir Nabokov and his words, which belong to the realm of sorely needed literary evaluation:

There are three points of view from which a writer can be considered: he may be considered as a storyteller, as a teacher, and as an enchanter. A major writer combines all three—storyteller, teacher, enchanter—but it is the enchanter in him that predominates and

makes him a major writer. . . . To the storyteller we turn for enter-
tainment, for mental excitement of the simplest kind, for emotional
participation, for the pleasure of traveling in some remote region
in space or time. A slightly different though not necessarily higher
mind looks for the teacher in the writer. Propagandist, moralist,
prophet—this is the rising sequence. We may go to the teacher not
only for moral education but also for direct knowledge, for simple facts. . . . Finally, and above all, a great writer is always a great
enchanter, and it is here that we come to the really exciting part
when we try to grasp the individual magic of his genius and to study
the style, the imagery, the pattern of his novels or poems.

We are met here at the Neustadt Festival, a literary festival for celebrating
the enchanter, whoever he or she may be. We have gathered to celebrate all
those who have been, who are, and who will be our past, present, and future—
enchanters . . .

Norman, Oklahoma
October 28, 2016

Translation from the Croatian by Ellen Elias-Bursać

EDWIDGE DANTICAT
THE 2018 LAUREATE

Edwidge Danticat is the author of several books, including *Breath, Eyes, Memory*, an Oprah Book Club selection; *Krik? Krak!*, a National Book Award finalist; *The Farming of Bones*, an American Book Award winner; and the novels-in-stories *The Dew Breaker* and *Claire of the Sea Light;* as well as *The Art of Death*, a National Books Critics Circle finalist. She is also the editor of *The Butterfly's Way: Voices from the Haitian Dyaspora in the United States, The Beacon Best of 2000, Haiti Noir, Haiti Noir 2,* and *Best American Essays 2011*. She has written seven books for young adults and children—*Anacaona Golden Flower, Behind the Mountains, Eight Days, The Last Mapou, Mama's Nightingale, Untwine,* and *My Mommy Medicine*—as well as a travel narrative, *After the Dance: A Walk through Carnival in Jacmel,* and two collections of essays, *Create Dangerously* and *The Art of Death*. Her memoir, *Brother, I'm Dying*, was a 2007 finalist for the National Book Award and a 2008 winner of the National Book Critics

Circle Award for autobiography. She is a 2009 MacArthur Fellow. Her most recent book, *Everything Inside,* a collection of stories, was published in 2019.

Writing that story had reinforced for me the idea that the page— my writing home—has to also be free from death because creating anything, be it words, images, song, and dance, means that we believe in immortality.

—Edwidge Danticat

Bearing the Unforgivable
Achy Obejas

Thank you to the Neustadt Prize committee, Neustadt sisters and family, the University of Oklahoma, the incredible writers who served with me on the jury last year.

It is my great honor to introduce Edwidge Danticat. As you've no doubt experienced by now, Edwidge is a woman of exceptional poise and elegance, uncommon intelligence, and unusual wisdom.

You can see in her eyes—those very deep, endless pools—that there is inside her an immeasurable reservoir of kindness and an extensive capacity for forgiveness. This last quality, I think, is what singularly marks her work: a fierce forgiveness, a forgiveness that comes not from a fear of the hereafter or acceptance of any inevitability but rather from a kind of recognition, an acknowledgment of our capacity to fall into the temptations of violence, of selfishness, of irrationality, and still, somehow, also be able to nourish and love.

Sometimes we do terrible things for very good reasons; sometimes we do beautiful things for terrible reasons. But that we may be able to do these terrible things does not necessarily make us so terrible as to be exempt from redemption.

The worlds Edwidge writes about are complicated, and their inhabitants operate with complicated intentions and ethics, complicated moralities and spiritual paths. But they are also common, as common as you and me, as common as the daily tragedies of children separated from their mothers, and as common as the petty corruptions we've come to accept in our politicians.

And yet—Edwidge's work does not ask us to forgive. It isn't righteous; it does not make that argument. It does something much more profound: it asks us to consider our own capacity for the unforgivable, our ability to bear the unforgivable, and the measure of our own powers of forgiveness. Because that's how forgiveness is so often framed in her stories: as a kind of power. A very unsentimental, very divested power.

Forgiveness, not as forgetting, but as an awakening.

Forgiveness as foresight.

Forgiveness as essential, as essential as the air we breathe, and as essential as love.

There are many things I love about Edwidge and about her work—its tight discipline, the sheer beauty of her words, the sublime architecture of her sentences, the way it disturbs us and makes us question our day-to-day lives, the way it makes us wonder about the unknown burdens our neighbor may be carrying, the secret lives around us we may never fully know—but to me this powerful force for forgiveness is what brings me back to her over and over: we are imperfect, we are unfathomable, and without recognition and forgiveness, how could we possibly go on?

I've been reading Edwidge since her first book, almost twenty-five years ago, *Breath Eyes Memory*. I read her latest, *The Art of Dying*, as if it was a prayer, and this much I know: with each book, Edwidge's work gets stronger, more confident, more sage. With each new book, her already very personal and independent path grows longer and wider and makes room not just for more of her stories but also for those of so many others, for so many of us who are women, women of color, women of the Caribbean, island people, mothers and daughters, immigrants, wanderers, exiles. With each new book, her voice is ever clearer, ever more a clarion call. Each new story, each new word, brings a different kind of awe.

I feel an enormous sense of gratitude to Edwidge Danticat.

I'm honored to be here introducing her.

Norman, Oklahoma
October 11, 2018

Achy Obejas *is the author of the critically acclaimed* Tower of the Antilles *and a noted translator of works by Rita Indiana, Junot Díaz, Wendy Guerra, Megan Maxwell, and many others. A native of Havana, she is currently based in the San Francisco Bay area.*

All Geography Is Within Me:
Writing Beginnings, Life, Death, Freedom, and Salt
Edwidge Danticat

1

This past June I was in Haiti in part for the opening of a library in a southern town called Fond-des-Blancs. Fond-des-Blancs, which literally means "The Fountain of the Whites," is mostly known for being home to a large number of people of Polish lineage, the descendants of soldiers from a Polish regiment that switched alliances from the French armies they were fighting alongside in nineteenth-century Haiti to join the Haitians in their battle for independence from France in 1804. The mutinous Polish soldiers who ended up settling in Fond-des-Blancs were the only whites and foreigners who were granted Haitian citizenship after Haiti became the first black republic in the Western hemisphere in 1804.

The library we were there to celebrate had been started by a nonprofit called Haiti Projects, which was run by an acquaintance of mine whose mother is American and whose father is Haitian. The opening-week program included writing workshops and conversations with writers. I took part in a conversation and writing workshop with the Haitian novelist and short-story writer Kettly Mars. Our moderator, a Haiti-based educator named Jean-Marie Théodat, asked each of us to read both the beginning and the end of one of our short stories, then explain to the group of twenty-five or so eager teenagers why we had chosen to begin and end that story the way we had.

If you have ever spoken to a group of teenagers, you know how intimidating it already is to explain anything to them, but this was a bit extra-intimidating for me. It is much easier to explain or elaborate on an ending than a beginning. For endings, you can always say that it ended *this* way because it had begun *that* way. Or it ended that way because something popped up in the middle that led me there. Beginnings have a much bigger burden and are often less clear.

In the beginning was the Word, the Good Book tells us. And perhaps the Word—or the Words—was, were . . .

Once Upon a Time,

Il était une fois or

Te gèn yon fwa or

Krik? Krak!

I feel the same dilemma right now while trying to trace the geography, or cartography, both internal and external, that has brought me from my own beginnings to this moment.

Once upon a time, a little girl was born in Haiti during the middle part of a dynastic thirty-year dictatorship. Her parents were poor, though maybe not as poor as others. My parents didn't get very far in school because their parents could not afford it. My mother was a seamstress. My father, a shoe salesman and a tailor.

When I was two years old, my father left Haiti and moved to the United States to look for work. Two years later, my mother joined him and left me and my younger brother, Bob, in the care of my aunt and uncle in Port-au-Prince.

One of my earliest childhood memories is of being torn away from my mother. On the day my mother left, I wrapped my arms around her legs before she headed for the plane. She leaned down and tearfully unballed my fists so that my uncle could peel me off her. As my brother dropped to the floor, bawling, my mother hurried away, her tear-soaked face buried in her hands. She couldn't bear to look back.

If my life were the short story I was asked to explain the beginning of in that writing workshop with the teenagers in Fond-des-Blancs, this might have been my chosen beginning, the most dramatic one I can remember. After all, as the French-Algerian writer Albert Camus wrote, a person's art is "nothing but this slow trek to rediscover, through the detours of art, those two or three great and simple images in whose presence his heart first opened."

Since I was too young to remember my father leaving Haiti for the

United States, my mother's departure was one of the first images in whose presence both my heart and my art first opened, an art and a heart that suddenly expanded beyond geographical confines and also made me realize that one can love from both near and far.

In Haitian Creole when someone is said to be *"lòt bò dlo,"* on the other side of the water, it can either mean that they've traveled abroad or that they have died. My parents were already *lòt bò dlo*, on the other side of the waters from me, before I fully even knew what that meant. My desire to make sense of this separation, this *lòt bò dlo*-ness, is one of the things that brought me to the internal geography of words and how they can bridge distances.

One way I used to communicate with my parents was through letters. We spoke on the phone once a week while sitting in a telephone booth, where we had a standing appointment every Sunday afternoon, but we also communicated through cassettes that we sent back and forth with people who were traveling between New York and Port-au-Prince. We wrote letters too. Every month my father would send us a half-page letter composed in stilted French to offer news of his and my mother's health as well as details on how to spend the money he and my mother wired for my and my brother's food, lodging, and school expenses.

When my parents' letters and cassettes found their way to me from Brooklyn to Port-au-Prince, I again realized how words—both written and spoken—can transcend geography and time. My mother could tell me stories—once upon a time—in my mind. And I knew, because she later told me this, that she was imagining every day of my life, then whatever indispensable thing I needed to know, only she could tell me. The way she imagined my life in her absence was sometimes better and sometimes worse than what was actually happening to me at ages four, five, six, seven, eight, nine, ten, eleven and twelve, but we were constantly alive in each other's imagination. And because my mother did not write letters and because I did not ever want to forget the things I wished my mother were telling me, the stories I wish she were telling me, I tried to write them down in a small notebook I made from folded sheets of paper bound together by thread. In that notebook, I also sketched a series of stick figures, which were so closely drawn that they almost bumped each other off the page. But mostly I wrote stories, which I later found myself elaborating on. Stories like one of the first prose poems I would write years later and call "Legends."

"Legends" is about a desire, a hunger, I had developed both in my parents' absence and, much later, to tell stories. "Legends" is about a little girl who is dreaming of telling her immigrant mother a story. It's also about a mother who works in a sweatshop in the United States while dreaming of telling stories to her daughter back home in Haiti.

> Once, upon an endless night,
> I dreamed of telling you a story,
> Of pleating you a tale out of my breath
> And carving it into your flesh with my hair.

I imagined that my parents wanted to tell me stories because they were worried that I would forget not just them but the geographies within both me and them. I imagined they wanted to tell me what in Creole we call *lejann*, stories about night women, women with wings of flames who want to draw you out of your bed. Stories about three-legged horses rising at full speed to either snatch or rescue children who had lost their way.

I also imagined that they wanted to tell me what it was like to work in a sweatshop where they might or might not pay you at the end of the week because you're undocumented. Or how the immigration police might come and raid your workplace at anytime and take you to a detention center to await your deportation. I imagined that they wanted me to know even before I stepped foot in the United States that the streets were not littered with gold.

> Once, while cradling someone else's child in my arms,
> Standing at a kitchen stove,
> Stirring a soup for the child's hunger,
> I dreamed of telling you a story.
> A story that rains with salt.

I am telling you to open your mouth,
And catch as much of the salt as you can.
The salt sizzles on your tongue.
And suddenly you understand
That this story is all I know,
And that this story is all I have.

I often tell people about this salt by way of a question I am asked quite often. *Who taught you to write?* I always say that my best writing teachers were the storytellers of my childhood, who were not readers at all—and some not even literate—but who carried stories like treasures inside of them. In my mother's absence, my aunts and grandmothers told me stories. They told me stories in the evenings in the countryside, or when the lights went out in the city, or while they were doing my hair, or while I was doing their hair. This too is another possible beginning. These stories that were told to me in such intimacy by women like the ones the great writer Paule Marshall called kitchen poets. The kitchen poets in my life are also the *poto mitan*, the middle pillars of my beginning as a writer, because they taught me that no story is mine alone, that a story lives and breathes and grows only when it is shared.

2

I moved to the United States in 1981 at age twelve to join my parents soon after cases of acquired immunodeficiency syndrome (AIDS) were first discovered in the United States. The Centers for Disease Control named four groups at "high risk" for the disease: intravenous drug users, homosexuals, hemophiliacs, and Haitians. Haitians were the only ones solely identified by nationality, in part because of twenty or so Haitian patients who'd shown up at Jackson Memorial Hospital in Miami. Suddenly, every Haitian was suspected of having AIDS. At the public junior high school where my parents enrolled me, some of the non-Haitian students would regularly shove and hit me and the other Haitian kids, telling us that we had dirty blood. My English as a Second Language class was excluded from a school trip to the Statue of Liberty out of fear that our sharing a school bus with the other kids might prove dangerous to them.

But I also had a wonderful teacher at this junior high school, a Haitian exile named Raymond Dusseck. Mr. Dusseck was part of my beginning in the United States. Mr. Dusseck built science, math, and ESL lessons around games and songs to help us begin speaking in our new tongue. He taught us English songs that were full of stories, starting with the African American national anthem. I remember being enchanted by James Weldon Johnson's beautiful lyrics:

> Lift every voice and sing,
> Till earth and heaven ring,
> Ring with the harmonies of Liberty . . .
> Let us march on till victory is won.

I was eventually mainstreamed from ESL to a regular English class, where my English teacher, an African American woman named Mrs. Wright, asked me to write an essay about my first Thanksgiving. I wrote that I was looking forward to eating the "golden" turkey, which I thought was rather original. Later I would be horrified by my cliché, but she told me I had a great writing voice. Lift every voice, indeed.

In high school, I had a history teacher named Mr. Casey who taught an elective black history class during our lunch period. I wrote an essay for that class about wanting to be a writer, and Mr. Casey loaned me a book called *Black Women Writers (1950–1980): A Critical Evaluation*, which was edited by the African American poet, writer, and dramatist Mari Evans. It was in that book that I discovered, among others, Paule Marshall, Alice Walker, Audre Lorde, June Jordan, Gayle Jones, Sonia Sanchez, Gloria Naylor, Nikki Giovanni, Toni Morrison, and Zora Neale Hurston, who would become some of the great literary loves of my life.

They were not only part of my new beginning as a writer, but they, along with the great Haitian writers I began reading in New York, writers like Marie Vieux Chauvet, Jacques Roumain, Jacques Stephen Alexis, J. J. Dominique, Ida Faubert, and Dany Laferrière, gave me a place to stand.

"Give me a place to stand," the Greek mathematician Archimedes is believed to have said, "and I will move the earth." But how can we move the earth when all seems to be against it? I asked myself then and ask myself that now. Can words, language change some of the worst conditions we face, especially in situations that seem insurmountable?

The day that Donald Trump was sworn in as president of the United States, I went to hear the Alabama-based poet Ashley M. Jones read from her book *Magic City Gospel* at my local bookstore in Miami, a city that is home to one of the largest foreign-born populations in the United States. In his inaugural speech, Trump had repeatedly invoked "the people" and said, "And this, the United States of America, is your country," but it was hard to believe that he meant to include my black and brown neighbors, friends, and family, many of whom came to America as immigrants. Trump's speech was dark, rancorous. Political language, like poetry, is rarely uttered without intention. Afterward, I wanted to fall into a poet's carefully crafted, insightful, and at times elegiac words.

At the bookstore, I listened as Ashley M. Jones read a poem called "In the beginning there was sound":

After I was born,
I cried for three months straight . . .
Alive, I said.
Pain, I said.

Later that same week, some writer friends and I, along with dozens of others, rallied in front of Miami International Airport to protest Trump's executive order barring all refugees, particularly those from seven predominantly Muslim countries. At the airport rally, we carried signs, like mine, that said "No Human Being Is Illegal." A woman held one that read "Immigrants Are America's Ghostwriters." Another woman had simply scribbled on a piece of cardboard the word "No."

Throughout the rally, my thoughts kept returning to the late Gwendolyn Brooks and some lines from her ode to the singer, actor, and activist Paul Robeson:

> we are each other's
> harvest:
> we are each other's
> business:
> we are each other's
> magnitude and bond.

Once again, I was seeking a new beginning in words.

How far do we have to go through to provoke new beginnings? Does it take the image of children in cages, cell-phone videos of policemen and women shooting black men, women, and children in the back?

What does the artist do to move the world? I want to say we can begin by bearing witness. Not everyone is comfortable with the term *witness*. But no matter what term we use, it means, to me, being as Henry James said, "one of those on whom nothing is lost."

In a 1984 *New York Times* interview, James Baldwin had the following exchange with the writer Julius Lester:

> "Witness is a word I've heard you use often to describe yourself. What are you witness to?" Lester asked.
>
> Baldwin answering in the simplest terms said, "Witness to whence I came, where I am. Witness to what I've seen and the possibilities that I think I see."

Witness is not just where I began but also where I want to end up as a writer. This is the kind of writer I would like to be. Sometimes we cannot fully move the world, but it can move us with its vastness, its expanse, its limitless-ness, its geography or geographies, its beginnings and endings, its injustices, and *lòt bò dlo*-ness.

A few weeks ago, a friend I was talking to about this week told me that I should talk about love. I started considering all the things I could possibly have to say about love, but then I realized that, without sounding too lofty here, that every word I put down on paper is in some way an act of love. And I'm sure that I am not the only writer for whom this is true.

I also started thinking about what James Baldwin wrote about love in *The Fire Next Time.* In that essay, he talks to us about the geography of love that is potentially within us all. "Love takes off the masks that we fear we can-not live without and know we cannot live within," Baldwin wrote. "I use the word 'love' here not merely in the personal sense but as a state of being, or a state of grace—not in the infantile American sense of being made happy but in the tough and universal sense of quest and daring and growth." Yes, that kind of love is also part of my beginning.

So along with this particular kind of love, I decided instead to also talk about the geographies within me, starting with my beginnings.

3

After Zora Neale Hurston's mother, Lucy, died and she was forced to leave her home and travel to places previously unknown to her, she wrote in her autobiography, *Dust Tracks on a Road,* that she realized that she was suddenly forced into "the beginning of things" and that "all that geography was within me. It only needed time to reveal it."

All that geography was within me. It only needed time to reveal it. I love this line so much that sometimes I misquote it as "All geography is within me. It only needs to reveal itself."

When, after graduating from high school in Brooklyn, I had yet another beginning and became a student at Zora Neale Hurston's alma mater, Barnard College, I felt as though her ghost was shadowing me. This new and unex-pected geography—Barnard and Zora—was now within me too, along with all the others from my past and the possibility of other geographies in the future. Like reading and writing, this type of geography can take you away and bring you back, internally and spiritually, back to the source, back to the ground from which you had been wrestled away.

Zora's ghost was also shadowing me in the car in March 2014 after my mother had been told by her doctor that she had terminal ovarian cancer. At a red light, where I stopped for too long, my mother spoke up for the first time since we'd heard the news and warned, "Don't suddenly become a zombie." My mother was telling me not to lose my good sense, to keep my head on my shoulders, but it popped up in my mind that a motherless Zora had gone to Haiti to study zombies.

When we got home from the doctor's that day, my mother made us each a small cup of coffee that she sprinkled with salt. According to Haitian folklore, one way zombies can be liberated from their living death is by eating salt. People who suddenly receive terrible news are also given salt, in coffee for example, to help ward off the *sezisman*, the shock, so that we are able to pick ourselves up and keep moving.

This salt is for me the source of all forceful beginnings and the source of all freedom. We are here because in some way we were given the salt. For some of us that salt is *words*. For others, it is *paint*. For others, it is *music*. For others, it is God. For some it is simply the ability to survive.

When I first came to this country, I remember being shocked that salt was powdery white. In my household in Haiti, we would often buy rock salt in the market, and it often looked like little crystals or small pebbles, which were unevenly shaped and had dark streaks either on the surface or inside. You always had to wash the crystals before putting them in food, and even after you washed them they looked more gray than white. This is the salt I imagined those seeking their liberation wanting to be fed.

This type of salt shows up in another part of "Legends":

And what was that Sleeping Beauty,
If not a zombie?
And what was it that gave her freedom

From the sleeping sickness,

If not the taste of salt on the prince's lips?

Let no one tell you that it was the man's breath itself.

Everyone knows—or Manman knows—that it was the salt.

It is always the salt that wakes the dead.

And brings the children home.

This home for me is first and foremost the page. And the page is both full of death and free of it. Full of death because a trail of bodies from the Middle Passage lies behind me in the sea that made the first kind of salt I ever knew.

"The sea is salt," Zora Neale Hurston wrote.

"The sea is History," Derek Walcott wrote.

The sea has been part of both our beginnings and our endings.

The story whose beginning I chose to explain to the teenagers at the library in Fond-des-Blancs is from my 1995 short-story collection *Krik? Krak!* and is called "Children of the Sea." It is about a group of Haitian refugees who are trying to reach the United States by boat, like so many refugees and migrants have been trying to reach so many shores, lately including European shores.

I began the story the way I did, I told them, with lines borrowed from a Haitian proverb: "Dèyè mòn gen mòn." Behind the mountains are more mountains. The story begins with "They say behind the mountains are more mountains. Now I know it's true." I began it this way because that story had reminded me that some people's potential new beginnings can also lead to their end. Writing that story had reinforced for me the idea that the page—my writing home—has to also be free from death because creating anything, be it words, images, song, and dance, means that we believe in immortality, that we believe we can survive, even on the other side of the waters, even *lòt bò dlo*.

You never know a person until you've eaten salt together, Toni Cade Bambara writes in *The Salt Eaters*. And this week we have all had the privilege of eating salt together, by yes, breaking bread together, but also with the words we have spoken, the songs we have sung, the ways that we have moved our bodies through these dances that have come to us, both ancestral memory and more recently acquired knowledge. And for this I do not have enough words to say thank you. So, I will offer my gratitude in the voices of those who came before me, with all my honor and respect (Onè, Respè).

Mèsi anpil, anpil.

Thank you.

Norman, Oklahoma
October 11, 2018

Acknowledgments

As the editor of this anthology, I am indebted, first and foremost, to the Neustadt family. Serving as the editor in chief of *World Literature Today* is in itself an honor, and helping facilitate the visits of writers from around the world to the University of Oklahoma is one of the great pleasures of the work we are entrusted to carry out. Since I arrived on campus in 2000, I've always looked forward to the annual Neustadt Festival as one of the highlights of the fall social calendar, especially the culminating banquets that are replete with august traditions and a sense of literary history in the making. Until he passed away in 2010, it was always Walter Neustadt Jr. who, with great charm and modesty, presided over the family's role in presenting the Neustadt Prize to that year's laureate, with his wife, Dolores, at his side. Since then, their daughters—Nancy, Susan, and Kathy—have lifted the torch of the family's philanthropic ideals even higher. Their counsel and friendship have made us all more faithful stewards of the mission we are privileged to sustain.

My thanks as well to my predecessors as editors, in particular Roy Temple House (fellow Nebraskan), Robert Vlach, Bernice Duncan, Ivar Ivask, and William Riggan, who each brought editorial acumen and erudition to the "misery and splendor" of running a literary journal. We're fortunate, indeed, that Ms. Duncan was finally able to persuade Dr. Ivask to pick up stakes and move to the Southern Plains, with the result that what many perceived to be a literary backwater became a cosmopolis of culture.

Special thanks to Dr. Riggan, whose deep institutional knowledge proved invaluable as I delved into the early history of the Neustadt Prize, as did the many photocopies of articles and rare correspondence that he provided.

To my current colleagues at *WLT*—RC Davis-Undiano, Jen Blair, Kay Blunck, Michelle Johnson, Terri Stubblefield, and Rob Vollmar—the pleasure of working together to help make Norman, Oklahoma, "one of the undeclared capitals" of literary modernity will forever be one of the highlights of my professional career as well as a true personal privilege. Dr. Davis-Undiano, in particular, gave me the support and encouragement to undertake this book project, with enthusiasm and wise counsel along the way.

Without the editorial assistance of Adrienne Crezo, Patrick Ortez, and Grey Simon, it would have been impossible to finish my work on this project in timely fashion.

During my tenure at *WLT*, President David L. Boren, President Joseph Harroz Jr., Provost Nancy L. Mergler, and Provost Kyle Harper have given *WLT* unflagging support as we approach the milestone of one hundred years of continuous publication.

To our colleagues in Monnet Hall—the curator and staff of OU's renowned Western History Collections—I'm indebted for having been given unrestricted access to the *Books Abroad* and *World Literature Today* archives. Librarian Jacquelyn Slater Reese, in particular, helped facilitate my research in OU's rich institutional archives.

Thanks as well to Lynette Lobban, director of publications for the OU Foundation, for providing a copy of Boyd Gunning's September 25, 1969, letter to Doris Westheimer Neustadt, which helped me connect the dots between the early history of the Neustadt family's legendary generosity to the university with Walter Neustadt Jr.'s 1972 decision to endow the Neustadt Prize in perpetuity. She also graciously offered feedback on the penultimate draft of my introduction, as did Dr. Riggan.

My thanks to all the living laureates who granted permission to reprint their acceptance speeches, and I owe a debt to many of the past jurors as well.

I'm also grateful to the following literary agents for their kind assistance in helping secure reprint rights: Andrew Nurnberg Associates, literary agent for Assia Djebar; Nicole Aragi, literary agent for Nuruddin Farah and Edwidge Danticat; and Jane Novak, literary agent for David Malouf.

Yinan Wang's illustrations of all the past laureates—a continuation of work she first undertook while a student intern at *WLT*—provided an elegant aesthetic touch to the anthology, as did Jen Blair's guiding art direction and cover design.

I'm also grateful to David Shook for immediately offering to publish this volume when I first approached him about it in December 2018. While it's been a privilege to witness his meteoric rise from all-star *WLT* intern to international cultural impresario, David has also been an inspiration as a fellow poet, translator, and editor.

To Will Evans, executive director and publisher of Deep Vellum, whose infectious enthusiasm for publishing an elegant hardcover trade edition inspired me to imagine an audience for the book beyond the circle of those who already knew about the prize.

Finally, my eternal thanks goes to my wife, Alba, and to our three daughters for their support and wings of love that lift me up and inspire me more than any book will ever do.

—Daniel Simon

The 1969 Charter

Announcement of the Establishment of the *Books Abroad*
International Prize for Literature

PREAMBLE

Since its inception, *Books Abroad* has manifested a lively concern for the annual choices made by the Swedish Academy for that most respected of writing awards, the Nobel Prize for Literature. Under the original editorial aegis of Roy Temple House, we find in the quarterly such critical symposia as "Prodding the Nobel Prize Committee" (1932), "Nominations for the Nobel Prize for Literature" (1935), and *"Books Abroad's* Super-Nobel Election" (1940). The second editor, Ernst Erich Noth, sponsored an exchange of ideas entitled "What's Wrong with the Nobel Prize?" (1951), and the late Robert Vlach convened the most comprehensive discussion of all, the "Nobel Prize Symposium" of 1967. As guest editor of the last named issue, Professor Herbert Howarth (University of Pennsylvania) even sketched some possible guidelines for the Swedish Academy to consider, such as ". . . not to the *best-wishing* maker but to the best maker-even if the best maker appears to wish ill." He recommended that poets and dramatists be considered on a par with novelists; that the Prize should not necessarily crown a life's work, but should upon occasion direct attention to an important life work *in progress;* finally, that authors from the less-known literatures should not be regarded as the least eligible.

In spite of such critical scrutiny, in *Books Abroad* as in other journals throughout the world, no other important international literary prize has been established. To date, there is no competition to the criteria set up by the Swedish Academy, with its attendant perquisites of professional status and monetary compensation. We propose therefore that *Books Abroad,* as the oldest international literary review in the English language, sponsor the establishment of a new award to be known as the *Books Abroad* International Prize for Literature.

I

In the beginning, the Prize is to be awarded in alternate years, later perhaps annually. The choice will be announced in February-fittingly, it is felt, since *Books Abroad* began publication with the Winter issue of 1927. The first award is to be made in 1970, the amount to be $10,000 or more, contingent upon support from certain foundations and private donors who will be approached. The award will be presented at the University of Oklahoma in Norman approximately thirty days after the announcement of the choice.

II

Candidates for the Prize will be reviewed by an international Board of Selection which will meet for a three-day weekend conference in February of the year in which the Prize is to be offered. The Board will meet at the University of Oklahoma in Norman, which sponsors the publication of *Books Abroad*. In addition to the Editor of the quarterly, who will be the only permanent member, the Board is to include eleven members to be chosen by the Editor in consultation with the Editorial Board of *Books Abroad*. With the exception of the Editor, the Board of Selection will be composed of new members for each year that the Prize is to be offered. The following Board is suggested for the Prize of 1970:

1. *J. P. Clark* (Nigeria)
2. *Heinrich Böll* (Germany)
3. *Frank Kermode* (England)
4. *Richard Wilbur* (USA)
5. *Gaëtan Picon* (France)
6. *Jan Kott* (Poland)
7. *Piero Bigongiari* (Italy)
8. *Mario Vargas Llosa* (Peru)
9. *A. K. Ramanujan* (India/USA)

10. Andrei Voznesensky (USSR)
11. René Wellek (USA)

III

Eligibility. Each Board member is invited to present to the jury a maximum of three names to be considered for the Prize. The final choice shall be made by balloting, the winner to be decided by a majority vote (seven votes or more). No writer shall be eligible whose work is not currently available or cannot be presented to the Board in a major Western language.

Candidates may also be suggested by the public at large to the Editor of *Books Abroad,* but without any guarantee that they will necessarily be presented to the Board for consideration.

IV

In years in which the Prize is awarded, *Books Abroad* will devote one of its issues to a critical symposium on the work of the recipient. The University of Oklahoma Press will also consider the publication of a book by or on the laureate chosen for the International Prize.

V

Since *Books Abroad* is only the international forum charged with administering the Prize, the University of Oklahoma will seek contributions from foundations, publishers, and individuals in order to make the award financially worthwhile and representative of American concern for genuine achievement in world literature.

PEN International Congress
Menton, France
September 15, 1969

Books Abroad 43, no. 4 (Autumn 1969): 483–84

About the Neustadt Family

The Neustadt family's major support of the University of Oklahoma has been crucial to the institution's development. From the gift to the university of land for Max Westheimer Airpark to the addition of the Neustadt Wing of the Bizzell Memorial Library, sponsorship of the Neustadt International Prize for Literature, and establishment of the Neustadt Professorship in Comparative Literature, through three generations of active, visionary leadership, the Neustadt family has promoted excellence in higher education.

The Neustadt family endowed what was then known as the Books Abroad International Prize for Literature in 1972. **Walter Neustadt Jr.** (1919–2010) had received his master's degree from OU in 1941 and was a member of the Board of Regents and a trustee of the OU Foundation when President Paul F. Sharp announced the $200,000 gift on May 17, 1972. The award received its present name, the Neustadt International Prize for Literature, in 1976. In 1992 Walter received the Oklahoma Governor's Arts Award for his support of literature and the arts in the state and an honorary Doctor of Humane Letters degree from OU in 2005.

With the NSK Neustadt Prize for Children's Literature, a new generation of the Neustadt family has dedicated itself to advancing the cause of literary excellence at the University of Oklahoma. The letters "NSK" stand for Nancy, Susan, and Kathy, the children of Walter and Dolores Neustadt and the benefactors of the prize. The three sisters decided to encourage the improvement of writing for children by honoring an accomplished contemporary writer or illustrator of children's literature every other year. All three were honored with Regents' Alumni Awards in 2011 for their dedication and service to the university.

Nancy Barcelo lives in Watertown, Massachusetts, with her husband, Scott. She is a retired hospice volunteer director and was involved in all aspects of hospice for twenty-five years. She has always loved books and received a BA in English from Skidmore College. She received a master's degree as a reading specialist from Lesley College in Cambridge, Massachusetts. Nancy's husband, Scott, is a lifelong scholar of Eastern religion and philosophy and received a master of divinity degree from Harvard University. Sam Barcelo received his MBA degree at Boston University with an emphasis on the nonprofit sector, and Emma Barcelo graduated from Colorado College and has developed political digital media aimed for millennials.

Susan Neustadt Schwartz cofounded Equest, a therapeutic horseback-riding program, in 1981 and continues to serve on its board of directors. She also helped start a therapeutic horseback riding program in a women's prison in Canada in 2010. She served on the Shelton School and Evaluation Center's board of directors from 2006 to 2014 and the Fairhill School board of directors from 1982 to 1986. She graduated from the University of Oklahoma with a BFA and went on to receive her master's degree in education from Southern Methodist University. Before starting Equest, she taught at Fairhill School for twelve years and tutored children at Shelton and Saint Philip's School. Her awards include the volunteer of the year award from the international organization PATH, the Professional Association for Therapeutic Horsemanship, and the Woman of Distinction Award from Lake Forest Academy in Chicago. She has two daughters, Elizabeth and Kate, and fostered two boys, Aaron and Elijah, whose parents died when they were very young.

Kathy Neustadt lives in Denver and is a freelance field producer for ABC News. Before television, she worked in radio broadcasting in the mountains of Colorado for five years before going to work at KCNC-TV in Denver as a news writer. Kathy works extensively in not-for-profits in the Denver area. She is on the board of trustees at the Rose Community Foundation in Denver, current board chair of the Mizel Arts and Culture Center, and the former chair and longtime board member of the Staenberg-Loup Jewish Community

Center. In 2012 Kathy endowed what is now the Neustadt JAAMM Festival, which features Jewish authors, speakers, music, and film at the JCC every fall. She attended the University of Oklahoma and graduated from the University of Denver with a degree in mass communications. She loves to ski and hike in the Rockies and has two children, Tess and Josh Hankin.

After the announcement of the endowment of the Books Abroad Prize by the Neustadt family at the University of Oklahoma, May 17, 1972. *Seated from left:* Doris Westheimer Neustadt, Walter Neustadt Jr., and Nancy Davies, president of the OU Board of Regents. *Standing from left:* University of Oklahoma president Paul F. Sharp, Dolores Neustadt, Marilyn Neustadt, and Allan Neustadt.

The Neustadt Silver Eagle Feather
Mike Dirham

Like the laurel leaf from the sacred tree of Apollo, woven into a garland to crown the poet, the hero, the laureate, so the eagle feather signified success for the original Americans. In many cultures the eagle has been associated with the life of the spirit, with the transcendent experience, and among North American Plains tribes the eagle symbolized the Great Powers themselves.

Catching the eagle for its feathers was a holy task accompanied by prayer and fasting, and when the eagle came, it was received as a gift from those Powers it represented. It was accepted as a reward for human effort both physical and spiritual. The feather of the eagle was worn with great reverence and humility and respect.

Two traditions come together here. Two traditions—the eagle feather of the American Indian and the quill of the poet—are united in this prize. It is an appropriate fusion of meanings for an award to honor the highest achievements in the literature of the world.

Books Abroad 47, no. 3 (Summer 1973): 443

Mike Dirham *(1941–2018), former art director of* Books Abroad / World Literature Today, *designed the Neustadt silver feather.*

Laureates by Country and Their Nominating Jurors
1970–2018

A complete list of past jurors and their respective nominees can be found on the Neustadt Prize website (neustadtprize.org).

Year	Laureate	Country	Juror(s)
1970	Giuseppe Ungaretti	Italy	Piero Bigongiari (Italy)
1972	Gabriel García Márquez	Colombia	Thor Vilhjálmsson (Iceland)
1974	Francis Ponge	France	Michel Butor (France)
1976	Elizabeth Bishop	United States	John Ashbery (US) and Marie-Claire Blais (Canada)
1978	Czesław Miłosz	Poland / United States	Joseph Brodsky (USSR/US)
1980	Josef Škvorecký	Czechoslovakia / Canada	Arnošt Lustig (Czechoslovakia/US)
1982	Octavio Paz	Mexico	Manuel Durán (Spain/US)
1984	Paavo Haavikko	Finland	Bo Carpelan (Finland)
1986	Max Frisch	Switzerland	Adolf Muschg (Switzerland)
1988	Raja Rao	India	Edwin Thumboo (Singapore)
1990	Tomas Tranströmer	Sweden	Jaan Kaplinski (Estonia)
1992	João Cabral de Melo Neto	Brazil	Silviano Santiago (Brazil)
1994	Kamau Brathwaite	Barbados	Kofi Awoonor (Ghana)
1996	Assia Djebar	Algeria	Barbara Frischmuth (Austria)
1998	Nuruddin Farah	Somalia	Ngũgĩ wa Thiong'o (Kenya/US)
2000	David Malouf	Australia	Ihab Hassan (Egypt/US)
2002	Álvaro Mutis	Colombia	Juan Gustavo Cobo Borda (Colombia)
2004	Adam Zagajewski	Poland	Bogdana Carpenter (Poland/US)
2006	Claribel Alegría	Nicaragua / El Salvador	Daisy Zamora (Nicaragua/US)
2008	Patricia Grace	New Zealand	Joy Harjo (US)
2010	Duo Duo	China	Mai Mang (China/US)
2012	Rohinton Mistry	India / Canada	Samrat Upadhyay (Nepal/US)
2014	Mia Couto	Mozambique	Gabriella Ghermandi (Ethiopia/Italy)
2016	Dubravka Ugrešić	Croatia / The Netherlands	Alison Anderson (US/Switzerland)
2018	Edwidge Danticat	Haiti / United States	Achy Obejas (Cuba/US)

Recommended Reading

Historic correspondence about past Neustadt juries, press releases, and the like can be found in the World Literature Today / Books Abroad *archives in the Western History Collections at the University of Oklahoma, Norman.*

LAUREATES' ACCEPTANCE SPEECHES / LECTURES

Claribel Alegría, "The Sword of Poetry," trans. David Draper Clark, *World Literature Today* 81, no. 3 (May 2007): 30-32.

Elizabeth Bishop, "Laureate's Words of Acceptance," *World Literature Today* 51, no. 1 (Winter 1977): 12.

Kamau Brathwaite, "Newstead to Neustadt," *World Literature Today* 68, no. 4 (Autumn 1994): 653-60.

João Cabral de Melo Neto, "Laureate's Acceptance Speech," trans. Djelal Kadir, *World Literature Today* 66, no. 4 (Autumn 1992): 603-6.

Mia Couto, "Re-enchanting the World: The 2014 Neustadt Prize Lecture," trans. Paul Fauvet, *World Literature Today* 89, no. 1 (January 2015): 50-53.

Edwidge Danticat, "All Geography Is Within Me: Writing Beginnings, Life, Death, Freedom, and Salt," *World Literature Today* 93, no. 1 (Winter 2019): 59-65.

Assia Djebar, "Neustadt Prize Acceptance Speech," trans. Pamela A. Genova, *World Literature Today* 70, no. 4 (Autumn 1996): 783-84.

Duo Duo, "This Is the Reason We Persevere: The 2010 Neustadt Prize Lecture," trans. Mai Mang, *World Literature Today* 85, no. 2 (March 2011): 46-47.

Nuruddin Farah, "Celebrating Differences: The 1998 Neustadt Lecture," *World Literature Today* 72, no. 4 (Autumn 1998): 709-12. Reprinted by permission of Nuruddin Farah and Aragi, Inc.

Max Frisch, "Neustadt Prize Acceptance Speech," *World Literature Today* 62, no. 1 (Winter 1988): 11-13.

Gabriel García Márquez. *See* Ivar Ivask, "Allegro Barbaro."

Patricia Grace, "The World Is Where You Are: The 2008 Neustadt Lecture," *World Literature Today* 83, no. 3 (May 2009): 28-31.

Paavo Haavikko, "Laureate's Acceptance," trans. Philip Binham, *World Literature Today* 58, no. 4 (Autumn 1984): 500–501.

Ivar Ivask, "Allegro Barbaro, or Gabriel García Márquez in Oklahoma," *Books Abroad* 47, no. 3 (Summer 1973): 439–40.

——, "Homage to Giuseppe Ungaretti: The Old Captain's Last Voyage," *Books Abroad* 44, no. 4 (Autumn 1970): 543–51.

——, "Notes toward a 'Francis Ponge in Norman,'" *Books Abroad* 48, no. 4 (Autumn 1974): 647–51.

David Malouf, "A Writing Life: The 2000 Neustadt Lecture," *World Literature Today* 74, no. 4 (Autumn 2000): 701–5.

Czesław Miłosz, "Laureate's Words of Acceptance," *World Literature Today* 52, no. 3 (Summer 1978): 368–71.

Rohinton Mistry, "'The Road from There to Here': The 2012 Neustadt Prize Lecture," *World Literature Today* 87, no. 1 (January 2013): 44–50.

Álvaro Mutis, "Álvaro Mutis on Himself," trans. David Draper Clark, *World Literature Today* 77, no. 2 (July 2003): 9–11.

Octavio Paz, "Laureate's Words of Acceptance," *World Literature Today* 56, no. 4 (Autumn 1982): 595–96.

——, "The Turning House" [poem], trans. Ivar Ivask, *World Literature Today* 57, no. 3 (Summer 1983): 386.

Francis Ponge. *See* Ivar Ivask, "Notes toward a 'Francis Ponge in Norman.'"

Raja Rao, "Laureate's Words of Acceptance," *World Literature Today* 62, no. 4 (Autumn 1988): 534–35.

Josef Škvorecký, "Laureate's Words of Acceptance," *World Literature Today* 54, no. 4 (Autumn 1980): 501–4.

Tomas Tranströmer, "Laureate's Words of Acceptance," *World Literature Today* 64, no. 4 (Autumn 1990): 552–53.

——, "Oklahoma" [poem], *World Literature Today* 64, no. 3 (Summer 1990), 436.

Dubravka Ugrešić, "A Girl in Litland: The 2016 Neustadt Prize Lecture," trans. Ellen Elias-Bursać, *World Literature Today* 91, no. 1 (January 2017): 58–60.

Giuseppe Ungaretti. *See* Ivar Ivask, "Homage to Giuseppe Ungaretti."

Adam Zagajewski, "Poetry for Beginners: The 2004 Neustadt Lecture," trans. Clare Cavanagh, *World Literature Today* 79, no. 2 (May 2005): 10–13.

JURORS' ENCOMIA / NOMINATING STATEMENTS

N.B. *No formal nominating statement from Piero Bigongiari appears in the archives, only his letters to Ivar Ivask presenting the names of his two nominees: Giuseppe Ungaretti and René Char.*

Alison Anderson, "Dubravka Ugrešić and Contemporary European Literature: Along a Path to Transnational Literature," *World Literature Today* 91, no. 1 (January 2017): 61–63.

Kwame Anthony Appiah, "For Nuruddin Farah," *World Literature Today* 72, no. 4 (Autumn 1998): 703–5.

John Ashbery, "Second Presentation of Elizabeth Bishop," *World Literature Today* 51, no. 1 (Winter 1977): 8–11.

Kofi N. Awoonor, letter to Djelal Kadir nominating Kamau Brathwaite for the 1994 Neustadt Prize, September 9, 1993, *World Literature Today* archives, box 125, Western History Collections, University of Oklahoma, Norman.

Marie-Claire Blais, "Presentation of Elizabeth Bishop to the Jury," *World Literature Today* 51, no. 1 (Winter 1977): 7.

Joseph Brodsky, "Presentation of Czesław Miłosz to the Jury," *World Literature Today* 52, no. 3 (Summer 1978): 364.

Michel Butor, "Francis Ponge: Presentation to the Jury," trans. Ivar Ivask, *Books Abroad* 48, no. 4 (Autumn 1974): 658.

Bo Carpelan, "Presentation of Paavo Haavikko to the Jury," *World Literature Today* 58, no. 4 (Autumn 1984): 497–98.

Bogdana Carpenter, "A Tribute to Adam Zagajewski," *World Literature Today* 79, no. 2 (May 2005): 14–15.

Juan Gustavo Cobo Borda, "Nominating Statement for Álvaro Mutis," trans. David Draper Clark, *World Literature Today* 77, no. 2 (July 2003): 6–8.

Manuel Durán, "Octavio Paz: The Poet as Philosopher," *World Literature Today* 56, no. 4 (Autumn 1982): 591–94.

Barbara Frischmuth, "A Letter to Assia Djebar," trans. William Riggan, *World Literature Today* 70, no. 4 (Autumn 1996): 778–80.

Gabriella Ghermandi, "Nominating Statement for Mia Couto" [2014], previously unpublished.

Joy Harjo, "In Honor of Patricia Grace," *World Literature Today* 83, no. 3 (May 2009): 34–36.

Ihab Hassan, "Encomium: David Malouf," *World Literature Today* 74, no. 4 (Autumn 2000): 710–12.

Djelal Kadir, "The Rigors of Necessity: Encomium for João Cabral De Melo Neto," *World Literature Today* 66, no. 4 (Autumn 1992): 599–602. [for Silviano Santiago]

Jaan Kaplinski, "Presentation to the Jury," *World Literature Today* 64, no. 4 (Autumn 1990): 552.

Arnošt Lustig, "Encomium for Josef Škvorecký," *World Literature Today* 54, no. 4 (Autumn 1980): 505–8.

Mai Mang, "Duo Duo: Master of Wishful Thinking," *World Literature Today* 85, no. 2 (March 2011): 48–50.

Adolf Muschg, "Presentation of Max Frisch to the 1986 Neustadt Prize Jury," *World Literature Today* 60, no. 4 (Autumn 1986): 543–47.

Ngũgĩ wa Thiong'o, "Kamau Brathwaite: The Voice of African Presence," *World Literature Today* 68, no. 4 (Autumn 1994): 677–82.

———, "Nuruddin Farah: A Statement of Nomination to the 1998 Neustadt Jury," *World Literature Today* 72, no. 4 (Autumn 1998): 716.

Achy Obejas, "Bearing the Unforgivable: A Tribute to Edwidge Danticat," *World Literature Today* 93, no. 1 (Winter 2019): 66–67.

Luciano Rebay, "Encomium for Giuseppe Ungaretti," *Books Abroad* 44, no. 4 (Autumn 1970): 551–56.

Silviano Santiago, "João Cabral de Melo Neto" [1992 Neustadt Prize nominating statement], trans. Djelal Kadir, *World Literature Today* archives, box 126, Western History Collections, University of Oklahoma, Norman.

Edwin Thumboo, "Encomium for Raja Rao," *World Literature Today* 62, no. 4 (Autumn 1988): 530–33.

Samrat Upadhyay, "Rohinton Mistry's Omniscient Gaze," *World Literature Today* 87, no. 1 (January 2013): 51–52.

Thor Vilhjálmsson, "Presentation of Gabriel García Márquez," *Books Abroad* 47, no. 1 (Winter 1973): 10–11.

Daisy Zamora, "Knowing Claribel Alegría," *World Literature Today* 81, no. 3 (May 2007): 44–45.

ABOUT THE HISTORY OF THE PRIZE

Mike Dirham, "The Neustadt Silver Eagle Feather," *Books Abroad* 47, no. 3 (Summer 1973): 443.

David Draper Clark, "*Books Abroad / World Literature Today:* Past, Present and Future," *Publishing Research Quarterly* 18, no. 1 (Spring 2002): 38–45.

Ivar Ivask, "Announcement of the Establishment of the *Books Abroad* International Prize for Literature," *Books Abroad* 43, no. 4 (Autumn 1969): 483–84.

———, "The *Books Abroad* / Neustadt International Prize for Literature 1972: A Progress Report," *Books Abroad* 46, no. 3 (Summer 1972): 426.

———, "Giuseppe Ungaretti: Laureate of Our First International Prize for Literature," *Books Abroad* 44, no. 2 (1970): 191–94.

———, "Revised Charter of the *Books Abroad* International Prize for Literature," *Books Abroad* 46, no. 2 (Spring 1972): 253–54.

———, "World Literature Today, or Books Abroad II and Geography III," *World Literature Today* 51, no. 1 (Winter 1977): 4–6.

Walter Neustadt Jr., "Address at the Banquet Honoring the 1972 Jury of the *Books Abroad* / Neustadt International Prize for Literature," *Books Abroad* 47, no. 3 (Summer 1973): 441–42.

William Riggan, "A Conversation between William Riggan and Janette Turner Hospital," in *Dictionary of Literary Biography Yearbook: 2002*, edited by Matthew J. Bruccoli and George Garrett (Gale, 2003), 171–84.

———, "The Nobel Connection," *Sooner Magazine*, Spring 1981, 16–20.

———, "The Nobel Prize in Literature: History and Overview," in *The Nobel Prize Winners: Literature, 1901–1926*, ed. Frank N. Magill (Englewood Cliffs, NJ: Salem Press, 1987), 1–26.

———, "The Swedish Academy and the Nobel Prize in Literature: History and Procedure," *World Literature Today* 55, no. 3 (Summer 1981): 399–405.

WHAT OTHERS HAVE SAID ABOUT THE NEUSTADT (AND THE NOBEL)

Patrick Healy, "Oklahoma's Coveted Literature Prize," *Chronicle of Higher Education*, January 10, 1997, B8–9.

Herbert Howarth, "A Petition to the Swedish Academy," *Books Abroad* 41, no. 1 (Winter 1967): 4–7.

Ivar Ivask, "Greek Poet Odysseus Elytis, Nobel 1979, and Czech Novelist Josef Škvorecký, Neustadt 1980," *World Literature Today* 54, no. 2 (Spring 1980): 189–95.

Olof Lagercrantz, "A Literary Prize in Oklahoma," *Books Abroad* 48, no. 3 (Summer 1974): 445–46.

William Marling, "The Neustadt Prize and the Framing Effect," *World Literature Today* 90, nos. 3–4 (May 2016): 42–45.

Edwin McDowell, "The Oklahoma 'Nobel,'" *New York Times*, February 26, 1982.

"Nobel Prize Symposium," *Books Abroad* 41, no. 1 (Winter 1967).

"Nobel Prize Symposium II: Choices and Omissions, 1967–1987," *World Literature Today* 62, no. 2 (Spring 1988), 197–241.

Barbara Palmer, "Oklahoma's Nobel: OU's Neustadt Prize for Literature Shines in the Shadow of the Nobel," *Oklahoma Today*, January–February 1999, 40–43.

Chad W. Post, "The American Nobel: Oklahoma's Neustadt Prize," *World Literature Today* 91, no. 1 (January 2017): 64–65.

Maarten Van Delden, "Claribel Alegría, the Neustadt Prize, and the World Republic of Letters," *World Literature Today* 81, no. 3 (May 2007): 45–48.

Lawrence Van Gelder, "Footlights," *New York Times*, February 26, 1998.

MORE ABOUT *WORLD LITERATURE TODAY*

Genova, Pamela Antonia, ed. *Twayne Companion to Contemporary World Literature: From the Editors of* World Literature Today. New York: Twayne, 2003.

www.worldlit.org

Contributors' Index